D1731011

Political Power and Tribalism in Kenya

Westen K. Shilaho

Political Power and Tribalism in Kenya

palgrave
macmillan

Westen K. Shilaho
University of Johannesburg
Johannesburg, South Africa

ISBN 978-3-319-65294-8   ISBN 978-3-319-65295-5   (eBook)
https://doi.org/10.1007/978-3-319-65295-5

Library of Congress Control Number: 2017950390

Cover illustration: © John Rawsterne/patternhead.com

Printed on acid-free paper

This Palgrave Macmillan imprint is published by Springer Nature
The registered company is Springer International Publishing AG
The registered company address is: Gewerbestrasse 11, 6330 Cham, Switzerland

For my mother, Sophia Ayuma

ACKNOWLEDGEMENTS

I would like to thank Prof. Chris Landsberg for the mentorship and promotion of epistemic contestation. Your constant reminder that scholarship has no place for mini-mes was inspirational. I am grateful to Prof. Gilbert Khadiagala for the incisive guidance through the corpus of literature on Kenyan politics, and insightful comments. Prof. Adekeye Adebajo deserves a 'thank you' for his encouragement and giving impetus to the idea of writing this book. I am grateful to Dr David Monyae for encouraging free expression of ideas. Thanks to Prof Mzukisi Qobo for asking about the book. It inspired me to complete it. I wish to thank Prof. Sheila Meintjes, my teacher and mentor, for her invaluable guidance, patience and incisive critique. I am grateful to my teachers: Profs James Ogude, Isabel Hofmeyr, CJ Odhiambo, Joyce Nyairo, Bhekiziziwe Peterson, Dan Ojwang', Prof (Fr) Joseph K Kahiga, Phillip Frankel, Tom Mboya, Busolo Wegesa, Tirop Simatei, Basil Okong'o, Peter Amuka, Rok Ajulu, Abdul Rahman Lamin, Pamela Abuya and Tobias Otieno. I am grateful to the two anonymous reviewers. Great appreciation to Anca Pusca, Ben Bailey and Alina Yurova, and Hari Swaminathan of Palgrave Macmillan for their unstinting assistance and patience.

I am indebted to Fr. Peter, an exemplary human being and priest. Rest with the angels, Fr! Bishop Maurice Makumba Muhatia, my teacher and a dedicated priest and Fr. Kizito Sabatia, a shepherd. I extend my appreciation to my research assistants, Julius Odemba, JM Kariuki, Patrick Machanja, Sheila Bosire and Kennedy Onzere, for helping me locate the respondents. I wish to thank my interviewees from various parts of Kenya for their cooperation and frank expression of their views. However, few respondents' views are reflected in this book owing to brevity. I thank the staff at the Kenya National Archives for their kindness and assistance. I am grateful to the National Research Foundation in South Africa. My many teachers, friends, and colleagues, that I have interacted with in the course of my scholastic pursuits have contributed in one way or another to the realisation of this book. I could not mention all of you. Thank you all. My appreciation to all the members of the South African Research Chair (SARChI) in African Diplomacy and Foreign Policy, University of Johannesburg.

It would be remiss of me not to mention my parents, Charles and Sophia Kwatemba. I couldn't thank you well enough! Boniface and James, I am highly indebted to you. Timothy and Consolata, I cherish your incalculable contribution. Rest with the angels! Hillary, Wilkister, and, Violet, Thank you so much. To Dr Emma Lubaale, sincere appreciation, dear!

CONTENTS

ABBREVIATIONS

ACJHR	African Court of Justice and Human Rights
ASP	Assembly of States Parties
AU	African Union
ACK	Anglican Church of Kenya
BBC	British Broadcasting Corporation
CICC	Coalition for the International Criminal Court
CIPEV	Commission of Inquiry into Post-Election Violence
COTU	Central Organisation of Trade Unions
DP	Democratic Party of Kenya
DRC	Democratic Republic of the Congo
EA	Electoral Authoritarian
ECOWAS	Economic Community of West Africa States
ECK	Electoral Commission of Kenya
EISA	Electoral Institute for Sustainable Democracy in Africa
EACC	Ethics and Anti-Corruption Commission
EU	European Union
EU EOM	European Union Election Observation Mission
FM	Frequency Modulation
FORD	Forum for the Restoration of Democracy
FORD-A	Forum for the Restoration of Democracy—*Asili (Original)*
FORD-K	Forum for the Restoration of Democracy—Kenya
FORD-P	Forum for the Restoration of Democracy—People
FPTP	First-Past-The-Post
GEMA	Gikuyu, Meru, and Embu Association
GNU	Government of National Unity
GSU	General Service Unit

HRW	Human Rights Watch
ICC	International Criminal Court
ICG	International Crisis Group
ICTR	International Criminal Tribunal for Rwanda
ICTY	International Criminal Tribunal for Yugoslavia
IEBC	Independent Electoral and Boundaries Commission
IMF	International Monetary Fund
IREC	Independent Review Commission
KADU	Kenya African Democratic Union
KACC	Kenya Anti-Corruption Commission
KAMATUSA	Kalenjin, Maasai, Turkana, and Samburu
KANU	Kenya African National Union
KBC	Kenya Broadcasting Corporation
KENDA	Kenya National Democratic Alliance
KHRC	Kenya Human Rights Commission
KLA	Kenya Land Alliance
KNCHR	Kenya National Commission on Human Rights
KPU	Kenya People's Union
LDP	Liberal Democratic Party
Legco	Legislative Council
LRA	Lord's Resistance Army
LSK	Law Society of Kenya
MCA	Member of County Assembly
MoU	Memorandum of Understanding
MP	Member of Parliament
MRC	Mombasa Republican Council
NAK	National Alliance Party of Kenya
NARC	National Rainbow Coalition
NASA	National Super Alliance
NDP	National Development Party of Kenya
ODM	Orange Democratic Movement
ODM-K	Orange Democratic Movement- Kenya
OMCT	World Organisation Against Torture
PNU	Party of National Unity
PSC	Public Service Commission
SAPs	Structural Adjustment Programmes
SDP	Social Democratic Party
SID	Society for International Development
TJRC	Truth, Justice, and Reconciliation Commission
UNSC	United Nations Security Council

UPDF	Uganda People's Defence Force
US	United States
USSR	Union of Soviet Socialist Republics
VoK	Voice of Kenya
YK '92	Youth for KANU '92

List of Tables

CHAPTER 1

Introduction: Ethnicity and Politics in Kenya

Abstract The chapter nuances the nexus of ethnic nationalism, competition for state control and fragmented tribal alliances in Kenya. It highlights the link between politics devoid of principles, ethnic-based political parties and state fragility in Kenya. The chapter traces the instrumentalisation of tribalism by Kenya's successive governments to the stratagem of divide and rule by the British colonialists. However, it argues that Kenyan post-colonial politicians rationally mobilised along ethnicity for personal gain owing to their retention of the discriminatory and alienating colonial state. Kenya's ethnic politics was not predetermined. The centralised state, the lack of a regulated political party system and the absence political will to enforce the rule of law and the persistence of exclusive politics, made the appeal to ethnicity almost inevitable. However, the masses are not simply victims of false consciousness devoid of agency in this combustible identity politics.

Keywords Tribalism · Colonialism · Post-colonial
Ethnic nationalism

Ethnicity acquires enormous power to mobilise people when it becomes a predominant identity and means more than just a particular ethnic origin; it comes to define people as speakers of a certain language, belonging to a particular religion, being able to pursue some careers but not others, being able to preserve and express their cultural heritage, having access to

© The Author(s) 2018
W.K. Shilaho, *Political Power and Tribalism in Kenya*,
https://doi.org/10.1007/978-3-319-65295-5_1

positions of power and wealth or not. In short, when ethnicity becomes politically relevant and determines the life prospects of people belonging to distinct ethnic groups, it is possible to mobilise group members to change a situation of apparently perpetual discrimination and disadvantage or in defence of a valued status quo (Wolff 2006: 31).

The excerpt shows that once ethnicity becomes more than an expression of cultural identity and gets connected to social status, it determines people's fortunes in life and becomes politicised. It makes it possible for those who feel aggrieved as a result of discrimination and those in power who want to protect their privileges to invoke ethnicity. In Kenya's political context, ethnicity is a factor in political competition and in the allocation of national resources hence its salience. It is for this reason that the Constitution promulgated in 2010, sought to streamline political parties. It contains a framework for political parties principally meant to rid the country of ethnicity-driven political parties. The Constitution also spells out the devolution of power and resources between the national and 47 county governments, the second tier of government, and stipulates that the face of the civil service must reflect Kenya's ethnic diversity (Republic of Kenya 2010). Since independence in 1963, members of the President's tribe had disproportionately dominated the civil service. First, it was the Kikuyu from 1963 until 1978, then the Kalenjin until 2002 (Ajulu 2002). The Kikuyu were resurgent after 2002 to date. Significantly, ethnicity was a determining factor in party loyalty during multiparty elections. Political leaders across the political divide formed political parties and campaigned on the strength of ethnicity. The upshot was ethnic bloc voting. However, Kenya's politics seemed to transcend ethnicity at during the formative stage of Kenya's state, immediately after independence in 1963. Chege shows that in 1961, the electorate in the then Nairobi East constituency overlooked ethnic differences and voted for Tom Mboya. Mboya, a Luo, defeated Dr. Munyua Waiyaki, a Kikuyu, despite the electorate being 64% Kikuyu (Chege 1981: 76). The electorate in this particular constituency evaluated the two candidates on the basis of leadership qualities. In the 1950s, Oginga Odinga, a Luo, had led a campaign calling for the release of Jomo Kenyatta, a Kikuyu and others from detention (Karimi and Ochieng' 1980: 16; Morton 1998: 88–89). However, Morton linked this call to a power struggle within the Kenya African National Union (KANU) in which the Odinga faction tried to use it to neutralise a rival one (Morton 1998: 102). This nationalist approach to politics had been replaced by ethnic solidarity in which politicians tended to campaign on the basis of tribalism and stood by errant fellow tribesmen and women at the expense of Kenya's interest. Under multiparty Kenya, a candidate almost stood no chance in a constituency in which his tribe was the minority unless he was part of a crosscutting ethnic alliance. It was almost impossible for a presidential candidate from one of the so called small tribes to be elected President because formidable presidential candidates were tribal Big Men from the populous tribes.

Although referring to Africa generally, Meredith offered insight into Kenya's shift from a sense of national identity into subnational loyalty. He observed that in the first elections before independence, African politicians conducted politics around national identity, thus candidates were voted for regardless of ethnic belonging. However, the issue of access to state largesse in the form of scarce resources heightened the political stakes. The result was that some politicians abandoned policy-oriented politics and resorted to canvassing for electoral support along ethnic lines (Meredith 2006: 156). Meredith argued that politics took an ethnic form because of lack of class identity among African societies (Meredith 2006: 156). I argue that ethnicity is the most significant variable under Kenya's multiparty democracy because politicians compete for power and the attendant state resources in a polity in which there was a fusion between the rural and the urban. Thus the society impinged on the state rendering the latter susceptible to tribal politics. has made it hard for politicians to devise alternative bases for political organisation such as class. Hyden acknowledged this point when he argued that the influence of "community-centred networks" in African politics was due to the inability of class-based identity to dislodge kinship ties (Hyden 2006: 55).

Ethnic divisions among the first generation of Kenyan politicians over the control of the state had two significant outcomes. It led to the assassination of Tom Mboya and the political marginalisation of Oginga Odinga, both politicians from the Luo community. Mboya, an astute politician, had been a key player in the political neutralisation of Odinga by Kenyatta's allies. The two politicians battled for political supremacy within the Luo community (Maloba 1996: 18). Kenyatta's allies perceived Odinga as a threat to their hold on power. He had the capacity to mobilise political support and create an alternative political powerbase, was opposed to the politics of wealth accumulation and remained among a tiny group of Kenyan politicians inclined towards ideological politics. Kenyatta and close allies including Mboya frustrated Odinga out of the government. Odinga resigned in 1966 as both the country's and the KANU Vice President and formed the Kenya People's Union (KPU) (Morton 1998: 125).

However, Mboya's ability to garner support among Kenyans of diverse ethnicities in the 1960s posed a political threat to Kenyatta and his inner court, predominantly from his Kikuyu ethnic group, as he was a front-runner in the Kenyatta succession. Mboya had political acumen, and financial backing from America (Ochieng' 1996: 101). This elevated him to another a centre of power among Luo thus rivalling Odinga. With Odinga successfully eased out of the mainstream politics, Mboya was assassinated in 1969, allegedly at the behest of some influential individuals in the Kenyatta government (Muigai 2004: 213). The Luo who had split their loyalty between Mboya and Odinga closed ranks and rallied behind Odinga (Karimi and Ochieng' 1980: 18). Mboya's assassination threw a wedge between the Kikuyu and Luo communities and contributed to the politics of resentment in Kenya that publicly erupted through a confrontation between Odinga's Luo supporters and Kenyatta when the latter visited Kisumu in 1969 (Owuor and Rutten 2009: 313). The sidelining of Odinga and his allies and the assassination of Mboya was meant to create room for the exclusive access to power and the attendant economic advantages for the Kikuyu elite. Since then, Kenya's polity had become so ethnically polarised that ethnicity took precedence over policy-based politics. Ethnicity became the ideology[1] that informed political choices.

Kenyatta was widely considered as the founding father of Kenya, yet I argue that he contributed to sowing the seeds of Kenya's post-colonial instability. The challenges bedevilling the country such as exclusionary politics based on tribalism, regional inequalities because of skewed allocation of national resources in favour of the President's region, corruption and lack of national identity required to harness Kenyans' energies and talent for the attainment of economic progress were reinforced under the Kenyatta régime (The Final Report of the TJRC of Kenya 2013). Disregard for the rule of law and manipulation of the Constitution to serve the interests of the ruling elite[2] was part of Kenyatta's legacy too. The Kenyatta régime arbitrarily amended the Constitution to achieve the political and economic ends of himself and his allies (Ochieng' 1996: 104). The legitimacy of Kenyatta's leadership, as the case was across Africa, was alien in that it appeared Kenyatta was opposed to colonial personnel during the anti-colonial struggle but was an apologist of colonial principles such as divide-and-rule and use of repression against dissent (Ekeh 1975: 101). This false start had undermined efforts towards transforming the Kenyan state to rid it of repression, and divisiveness, attributes that survived the colonial state. The legacy of colonialism in the form of a politics of ethno-regionalism remained intact. Under Kenyatta, the ethnic dominance of one group, the Kikuyu, over others occurred and led to a kind of tribal exclusion that prevented an overall national vision from developing to resolve the problems of development. Ethnic politics dominated the post-colonial period and blocked the process of developing an equitable politics that might have produced a society that met the needs of Kenyans irrespective of tribal affiliation. The patronage politics that emerged was based on ethnic alliances that precluded some and thus benefitting certain regions over others.

In the 1970s, the "Change the Constitution group" made up of Kikuyu and other tribes under the Gikuyu, Embu, Meru Association (GEMA) tribal grouping, tried to block the then Vice President, Daniel arap Moi, and any other politician from outside the GEMA grouping from ascending to the presidency. These politicians attempted to amend the Constitution to remove the provision that allowed the Vice President to automatically succeed the President (Karimi and Ochieng' 1980; Ochieng' 1996: 104–105). The motive was tribal politics and the intention was to safeguard the interests of this group in the absence of Kenyatta. This group had infused into the country's body politic a culture of impunity due to disregard for the Constitution and tribal mobilisation. Therefore, Kenya's post-colonial upheavals were compounded by the development of an exclusionary politics based on tribalism that was reinforced under the Kenyatta régime, despite his rhetoric to the contrary.

Through speech Kenyatta tried to portray himself as a nationalist who abhorred tribalism. He spoke in favour of ethnic inclusiveness. However, the Kenyatta régime was biased towards the Kikuyu and to some extent the other closely related Meru and Embu tribes. This belied his nationalist rhetoric. Two years into independence, Kenyatta appeared to confront tribalism:

> Tribalism is the ready-made weapon in the hands of the enemy of our Nation. This is why I will never be able to compromise with the tribalists. It is true that each of us belongs to a tribe and that we cannot change our tribes, but we must suspect the motives of those who masquerade as leaders; but yet appeal to tribal emotions. We must condemn those who seek to exploit such emotions for personal support and prestige. We must disown those who try to put one tribe against another, either by pretending to defend the interests of their own tribe or by generating hate and dislike of one tribe or group of tribes. These are the actions which the colonialists and their Agents used when they fought against African Nationalism. I am telling you today that no one can be both a true nationalist and a tribal politician at the same time. (Speech by Mzee Jomo Kenyatta during Kenyatta Day celebrations in 1965: 361)

The speech portrays Kenyatta as a politician who strove for an ethnically cohesive Kenya in which ethnicity was subsumed under national identity. Kenyatta favourably contrasted himself with his opponents, whom he accused of spreading tribalism. However, Kenyatta's legacy built on colonial ethnic balkanisation and exposed a lacuna between political pronouncements and corresponding action. Muigai suggests that Kenyatta "entrenched ethnicity as the most dominant basis of political mobilisation" (Muigai 2004: 215). Karimi and Ochieng' writing more than 20 years earlier, showed how the Kenyatta régime had exploited ethnicity to survive (Karimi and Ochieng' 1980: 15–23). In 2017, 54 years since independence, the Kenyan state was still undermined by this deleterious legacy.

Kikuyu politicians particularly from Kenyatta's home district of Kiambu dominated the state during his period in power. Politicians belonging to this inner court earned the sobriquet, the "Kiambu mafia" (Leys 1975: 246). The moniker connoted the ruthlessness with which they pursued their political and economic ends. It entailed physically eliminating perceived opponents and politically neutralising others through detention without trial. Kenyatta's inner circle was composed of both political and economic allies and family members. His close political allies came from Kiambu district and other parts of Mount Kenya region whom Karimi and Ochieng' referred to as "the Family" (with a capital "F") because they were united by financial and political interests. This group was distinguished from "the family", Kenyatta's immediate relations by blood and marriage (Karimi and Ochieng' 1980: 15). The exclusionary exercise of state power by these groups elicited resistance from excluded politicians some of whom were Kikuyu (Ajulu 2002: 261; Muigai 2004: 211). Karimi and Ochieng' argued that the Kikuyu tribe at the time was not homogeneous, as it were, since there had been internal rivalry along regional lines between those from Kiambu and Kikuyu from other districts and between the colonial collaborators and "freedom fighters" (Karimi and Ochieng' 1980: 41–43). The colonial collaborators, derisively referred to as the homeguards, upstaged the 'freedom fighters' in succeeding the British colonialists, a situation that accounted for the non-transformation of the Kenya state. The British colonialists banned Mau Mau or the self-styled The Land and Freedom Army 'freedom fighters' in 1950, and the organisation remained proscribed until 2003 when the ban was lifted (BBC News, 31 August 2003).

Omolo observed that the Kenyatta régime was biased towards Kikuyu with access to the state largesse, capital for private business and public appointments (Omolo 2002: 221). He cited two appointments in the academy and one in the provincial administration to support his claim.

He mentioned Kenyatta's appointment of Dr. Josephat Karanja as the Vice Chancellor of the University of Nairobi at the expense of several senior academics from other tribes and the appointment of another Kikuyu, Koinange, who had a certificate in education, as the college principal of Kenyatta University, Kenya's second institution of higher learning that opened in 1972. Kenyatta appointed yet another Kikuyu, also a Koinange, who had no formal education as the Provincial Commissioner (Omolo 2002: 221). Critics of the régime derisively referred to Kenyatta's rule as the "Kikuyunisation" of the Kenyan state (Omolo 2002: 221; Murunga 2004: 187–188). At this nascent period of Kenya's period of state formation, these appointments were indicative of a régime oblivious of ethnic sensibilities and inclusiveness. This discriminatory exercise of power validated Horowitz's cynical claim that "ethnicity entailed not the collective will to exist but the existing will to collect" (Horowitz 1985: 104).

During the Kenyatta régime, ethnicity waxed and waned depending on the opportunities and threats that the régime encountered. Although "the Family" and "Kiambu mafia" Mafia benefited almost exclusively from the extractive politics, whenever the régime faced a backlash from other tribes, it whipped up ethnic sentiment among the Kikuyu. When the régime was suspected of involvement in the assassination of Tom Mboya, Kikuyu politicians responded to the near countrywide anger by organising oath-taking rituals to bind the community so that they could defend "their presidency" (Nyong'o 1989: 245, 247). Atieno-Odhiambo argued that although the Kiambu politicians mobilised the Kikuyu to swear not to allow the presidency to leave the community, the oath was meant to ensure that the presidency remained within a certain clan from the Kiambu district (Atieno-Odhiambo 1996: 42–43). Those who were ferried to Gatundu, Kenyatta's home, took the oath and swore that "the flag of Kenya shall not leave the house of Mumbi", i.e. Kikuyuland (Ochieng' 1996: 102). These politicians exploited ethnic sentiment for economic and political capital. They were driven by self-interest so much that they defined ethnic belonging to the exclusion of not only other Kenyan tribes but also Kikuyu who did not belong to Kenyatta's clan.

POLITICAL PARTY FORMATION: THE BACKGROUND

The formation of political parties along tribal lines had been part of Kenya's political system since before independence. On the threshold of independence, ethnicity became the basis of political organisation as Kenyan politicians differed over whether the country should adopt a unitary or *majimbo* (federalist) Constitution (Morton 1998: 108). The issue was access to resources particularly land and the question of ethnicity, twin challenges that have afflicted Kenya's politics since then. Ajulu, on the basis of his evidence, argued that at the threshold of independence Kenya's political parties were based upon ethno-regional politics as the departing colonialists pitted the "big tribes" against the "small ones" (Ajulu 2002: 257). The then so-called small tribes such as the Kalenjin coalesced under the Kenya African Democratic Union (KADU) and insisted on a federalist (*majimbo*) Constitution for fear that under a unitary state the populous tribes would not only dominate them but also access their land.

However, the KANU dominated by the Kikuyu and Luo favoured a unitary state and opposed the devolution of power through *majimbo*. The KANU argued that regional governments were cumbersome and promoted tribalism (Morton 1998: 108). The Coastal and Rift Valley tribes particularly the Kalenjin that supported the KADU preferred a *majimbo* system because they believed it would safeguard their land against encroachment by the so-called big tribes, especially the Kikuyu (Morton 1998: 111–118). Kenya attained independence in 1963 under a federalist Constitution that recognised multiparty politics. But the KANU and KADU merged a year later making the country a de facto single-party state (Wanyande 2003: 137–138). Kenyatta capitalised on the KANU monopoly in parliament to abolish the post of Prime Minister and replace it with a powerful and autocratic President stifling nascent multiparty politics. Kenyatta was then able to wield imperial Presidential powers.

According to Barkan, KADU members claimed that they had defected to KANU "in the interest of national unity" (Barkan 1992: 171). However, Ajulu suggested that the KADU politicians crossed over to KANU in pursuit of patronage opportunities (Ajulu 2002: 259). Morton suggested that KADU disintegrated because the government starved the Rift Valley and Coast regions of resources and directed them to government supportive regions (Morton 1998: 118). The two regions were homes to the so-called small tribes that supported federalism and devolution. The dissolution of KADU bore testimony to the capacity of the powerful presidency to stymie multiparty politics a tactic that KANU resorted to once again when Kenya returned to multiparty politics in 1991. KANU became de facto the only political party in the country until 1966 when Oginga Odinga resigned from it and formed the KPU owing to a power struggle in KANU.

Odinga and his supporters were compelled to seek re-election under KPU following a Constitutional amendment to that effect (Karimi and Ochieng'

1980: 17). Kenyatta exploited the immense powers at his disposal to thwart attempts by KPU to find a foothold outside the Nyanza region predominantly inhabited by Luo. Muigai pointed out that Kenyatta marshalled the state's resources and invoked ethnic animosity to ensure that KPU was reduced to a Luo party during "the little general election"[3] held in 1966 (Muigai 2004: 213). Kenya's experiment with multiparty politics was short-lived since Kenyatta proscribed KPU in 1969 following a confrontation between him and Odinga in Kisumu, the latter's political stronghold.

The 1969 confrontation between Kenyatta and Odinga witnessed the Luo protest against Mboya's assassination. In the ensuing violence, Kenyatta's security personnel shot people dead (Leys 1975: 237). Kenyatta then detained Odinga and some KPU activists (Morton 1998: 141). Kenya became once again a *de facto* single-party state. Nyong'o argued that at this point the Kenyatta inner circle began to consolidate power in the presidency since the challenge posed by Oginga from the opposition and Mboya from within had been contained and alternative political parties proscribed (Nyong'o 1989: 245). The Kenyatta régime alienated the rest of the country from the state as the other communities accused it of exploiting state control for his benefit and that of the Kikuyu elite.

Moi succeeded Kenyatta in 1978 at a time when the world was defined by the Cold War politics that reinforced single party and military dictatorships in Africa. Moi did not reform the state, but instead further consolidated power in the presidency. Kenya's single party rule ended in 1991 when the country reverted to multiparty politics following a synergy of local and international pressure accelerated by the collapse of the bipolar world in 1989. One of the features of Kenya's multiparty politics since then had been the high turnover of political parties, as politicians sought political office at all costs. These politicians viewed political parties as avenues to power but not anchors of democracy. Consequently, political parties emerged and collapsed regardless of their electoral performance. First, electoral victory, especially for the presidency, was sought at the expense of devoting energies and resources to popularising and strengthening political parties distinguished by ideological orientations other than that of tribalism. Second, these were essentially tribalism inspired political parties prone to internal ethnic wrangles that often disintegrated them. These political parties lacked attributes such as discipline, membership, and a philosophy. They were fundamentally fiefs of ethno-regional Big Men that heavily depended on them or rent seekers for funding. Party loyalty and membership were not based on a conviction but tribalism.

Until the enactment of the Political Parties Act of 2007 that had been amended several times since, there was no law to regulate political parties in Kenya. Opportunistic defections and internal party quarrels were common. It was normative for politicians to profess allegiance to multiple political parties at the same time. It gave rise to a situation that once in parliament, some politicians actively supported a different political party from the one that had sponsored them. The Act created the office of the Registrar of Political Parties in order to regulate the formation of political parties, streamline funding, and provided a mechanism through which internal disputes within these parties could be resolved (Republic of Kenya 2009). The Act provided for government funding to political parties in proportion to their parliamentary representation and outlawed multiple party membership. Following the enactment of the 2010 Constitution, the Act was amended to align with it. The Act barred government officers such as cabinet members from holding offices in political parties in an attempt to depoliticise the bureaucracy. It also outlawed the formation of political parties along sectarian, gender, regional and ethnic interest (Republic of Kenya 2011).

The 2011 Political Parties Act spelled out procedures for the formation of mergers and coalitions with the intention of curbing opportunistic actions aimed at either winning elections or retaining power. An attempt to outlaw pre-election coalitions was thwarted by a parliamentary majority in the lead up to the 2013 elections. The formation of expedient and ephemeral winning ethnic alliances had been the easiest way to power in Kenya's polity in which policy-based politics had little chance to emerge. Politicians with the intention of forming such alliances in the run up to the 2013 elections mobilised MPs to pass the Act with a clause that recognised pre-election coalitions. The press reported that some politicians observed that the inclusion of this clause had drastically whittled down the Political Parties Act to the extent that its originally envisaged aim had been defeated (The Standard August 16, 2011). Kenya's politicians largely disregarded the Act without attracting sanction either from the parties that sponsored them to parliament or the Registrar of Political Parties.

Yet Kenya's politicians rebelled against the sponsoring parties and publicly campaigned and promoted different ones. Even after the enactment of the Act, cabinet members doubled as party leaders and refused to relinquish either of the posts. After the 2013 elections, some cabinet ministers, renamed cabinet secretaries, still openly engaged in partisan politics to the advantage of the ruling party. The legacy of weak and partisan institutions made it difficult for the office of the Registrar of Political Parties to enforce the law. The holder of the office, Lucy Ndung'u,

seemed to act at the behest of the government. In 2017, she was still acting in the post since 2011 when her mandate expired. In the wake of
the 2007 elections, she had acted at the behest Party of National Unity
(PNU) faction of the grand coalition government composed of previous
political adversaries. This government was characterised by divided loyalty
whereby politicians and bureaucrats were either aligned to Raila Odinga
or Mwai Kibaki, the protagonists during the violently disputed presidential elections in 2007. The Political Parties Act covered the funding
for political parties to address the influence of wealthy politicians upon
political parties. Previously political parties solely relied on party leaders and other individuals with vested interests for financial support. This
contributed to lack of internal party democracy and hamstrung Kenya's
democratisation process. Although this regulatory framework looks
elaborate, the challenges to Kenya's political parties remained ethnic
factionalism, a lack of a morally binding fidelity to the law among politicians, funding from dubious sources, and a compromised Registrar of
Political parties. Shadowy political party sponsors recouped their money
through corruption riddled mega tendering processes and other heists
once the sponsored presidential candidate and political party assumed
power. Thus, the Goldenberg Scandal defined the Moi regime, the Anglo
Leasing Scandal marred the Kabaki regime while the Eurobond Scandal
characterised the Uhuru Kenyatta regime. These were major corruption
scandals in which Kenyan tax-payers lost astronomical amounts money.

The Weak Political Party System

While Kenya had a high turnover of political parties this occurred without a commensurate turnover among the ruling elite. What did this lack
of change of leadership in Kenya's political parties imply for democracy?
Was it an indication of a fundamental weakness in the emerging democracy
in Kenya? I argue that one of the greatest hindrances to the nurturance of
democracy in Kenya is a failure to recognise political parties as an indispensable component to multiparty democracy. This is exemplified in the somewhat cavalier manner in which political leaders treated their own parties.
Instead of trying to build a solid party organisation based upon the support
of voters for a manifesto presenting its fundamental principles and policies
for the nation, political leadership since the advent of multiparty democracy
was based upon individual and regional interest or ethnic appeal (Mueller
2008: 199). Cheeseman suggests that Big Man politics continued to dominate despite the emergence of party politics (Cheeseman 2008: 172).

Wealthy ethno-regional politicians exploited communal and patronage ties to mobilise support even in the absence of institutionalised political parties (Cheeseman 2008: 172). Before the promulgation of the 2010 Constitution, political parties were registered under the Societies Act, the same Act from which associations such as clubs, welfare groups and women's groups derived their legal existence (Kadima and Owuor 2006: 198). Unlike these organisations, political parties are distinct in the sense that they are formed with the sole aim of attaining power and forming a government (Wanyama 2010: 63). The location of political parties under the Societies Act was a drawback to institutionalisation of the political party system because opposition political parties in particular were then at the mercy of government manipulation. For example, at the behest of Moi, the Registrar of Societies easily registered splinter opposition parties to exacerbate divisions among the opposition politicians as was the case with the Forum for the Restoration of Democracy (FORD) before the 1992 elections. In other instances, there was delay in registering parties perceived to be a threat to the ruling elite. The founders of "Safina" (Noah's Ark) were refused registration until just days before the 1997 elections. The party had no impact in that year's elections for among other reasons, lack of time to organise and mobilise for support. The Kibaki régime was quick to register the Orange Democratic Movement (ODM) under the names of individuals who had not been party to the successful campaign against the 2005 Constitutional referendum. The word "Orange" had been the buzzword in mobilising against the proposed draft Constitution. The intention was to scuttle momentum among the opposition politicians towards the 2007 elections.

Although Kenya's political parties have Constitutions that stipulate rules and regulations to guide their operations, these rules and regulations are often ignored. As a result, these parties do not practise internal democracy. Kenya's political parties are known for the undemocratic manner in which they conduct primaries (nominations) largely owing to the non-institutionalisation of these political parties. A particular issue is that Kenya's political parties have no registered party membership to identify supporters. Party leaders take it for granted that members of their ethnic groups would support the parties they form. The association between party support and ethnicity seems to be axiomatic. Although in principle, the dispute following the 2007 general elections pitted ODM against PNU, militias targeted people on the basis of ethnicity (Republic of Kenya 2008b). Disputed presidential elections in 2007, 2013 and 2017, saw the security forces respond with lethal force against protesting opposition supporters targeted on account of ethnic and therefore political affiliation as had been the case throughout the country's multi-party politics and before.

In most cases, the election of national party officials and special delegates' conferences are choreographed events. Wanyama observed that in 2007 there was a dispute with regard to the KANU delegates' list used to assemble members that endorsed the party's cooperation with PNU. Politicians in support of the cooperation allegedly hired delegates and locked out the "bona fide delegates" and had a resolution endorsing the cooperation passed (Wanyama 2010: 73–74). In 2002, KANU held a delegates' conference that rubber-stamped Moi's choice of Uhuru Kenyatta as his successor against the wishes of some party members as shown in Chap. 5. Evidence from elsewhere also shows, for instance, that primaries are consistently characterised by bribery, rigging, and worse, violence (Wanyama 2010: 76–85; Republic of Kenya 2008a: 56–57; 2008b: 62, 74). Moreover, losers in primaries get nomination certificates to stand for general elections thanks to their connections with party leaders. These anomalies were preponderant in Luo Nyanza, the bastion of ODM, because victory in primaries almost guaranteed one of a victory in parliamentary elections and other seats in contention, that is, governor, women representative, Member of County Assembly (MCA) and senator due to ethnic bloc voting. James Orengo, a received a nomination certificate despite losing in primaries in Ugenya constituency in 2007 (Wanyama 2010: 82). Despite Orengo's impeccable track record as a gallant lawyer, a steadfast anti-establishment politician and a prominent figure in Kenya's democratisation struggle, this was an infraction of democracy. A national identity card and a voter's card were sufficient requirements for one to participate in these primaries. This made it possible for people to influence outcomes in political parties they did not support. Previously, political parties had deliberately held nominations on separate days with some hoping to cash in on last minute defectors. However, the amended Political Parties Act outlawed party hopping-losers in primaries could not defect to other political parties. Such politicians were, however, eligible to run as independent candidates as long as they resigned from their respective political parties. Furthermore, parties had no way of vetting aspirants and so individuals of questionable character such as those implicated in corruption, incitement to ethnic violence, forged academic qualifications and even egregious crimes against humanity, were elected.

A high number of aspirants for political office were related to the economic benefits that came with political office. During the 2017 elections, there were 33 Member of County Assembly (MCA) candidates vying for

Chitago Borabu ward in Kisii county. There was a record 42 candidates vying for the ODM ticket in Chepalungu constituency of the Rift Valley region during the 2007 elections (Wanyama 2010: 78–79). The European Union Election Observation Mission (EU EOM) report suggested that high salaries for MPs motivated the high number of candidates during the 2007 elections (EU EOM 2008: 19). The International Crisis Group in its report showed that unpopular politicians, some of whom held national positions in their parties, were issued "direct nomination" thus being exempted from the primaries (International Crisis Group 2008: 5–6). The three leading parties during the 2007 elections, ODM, PNU and ODM-K, conducted a disorganised, if not shambolic, process of nominations that was a precursor to the irregularities that the EU EOM revealed in its 2008 report. The EU EOM report showed that the elections were riddled with irregularities that in some respects explain the chaos of the 2007 general elections themselves and the subsequent post-election violence (EU EOM 2008: 2). These challenges marred the 2013 primaries as well an indication that they were systemic (Shilaho 2014). The 2017 primaries were not qualitatively better either. As the Independent Review Commission (IREC) suggested the void created by the absence of a regulated political party system encouraged the tribalism that propelled politics and that encouraged the preponderance of "briefcase" political parties engaged in "political mercantilism" (Republic of Kenya 2008a: 57–58). Party hopping had been common because political party formation remained fluid. Sometimes politicians in Kenya changed parties in a comical fashion.[4]

EXPLAINING THE SALIENCE OF ETHNICITY IN KENYA'S MULTIPARTY POLITICS

Kenya's centralised state enhanced the salience of ethnicity in the polity. Since independence until the passage of the 2010 Constitution, the President and the ruling politicians related to the state instrumentally. It was a veritable gatekeeper state as Cooper would describe it that politicians took charge of and enriched themselves by exploiting its resources derived from the export–import trade and other local revenue generating activities (Cooper 2002: 156–159). Thus, control of the state had to be exploited for the political and economic gain of the power holders. The President enjoyed overwhelming powers and had the prerogative to make virtually all the appointments within the bureaucracy, top administrators in public universities, diplomatic postings, military and security forces. He prorogued, summoned, dissolved parliament and even determined the date of elections before the current Constitutional dispensation (Amutabi 2011). Moi exploited the latter prerogative to enjoy the upper hand during the 1992 elections. He called for elections at a time when the opposition parties were in a state of disarray. Although vetting of would be bureaucrats and public officers before appointment was an innovation of the 2010 Constitution, the president's nominees hardly got rejected on the basis of lack of integrity since ethno-regional considerations, especially in the parliament and senate, overrode integrity, probity and the national interest.

The core functions of the state were centralised in Nairobi and the provincial administration had been the enforcer of the Presidential edicts. Cohen identified the provincial administration as an integral part of Kenya's centralised state (Cohen 1995: 8). At the top of this relic of the colonial system was the President while at the bottom was the non-salaried, village headman. Although Kenyans asked that the provincial administration be scrapped through submissions to various commissions on reform, the draconian system remained in place. Patronage, and more crucially, corruption[5] had thrived in Kenya's centralised state because of the revenue and other opportunities at the disposal of the President and his allies. The state remained the biggest employer even after the enforcement of the Structural Adjustment Programmes (SAPs) in the early 1990s had called for a reduction in the government wage bill through redundancies and the privatisation of non-performing state corporations.

Allocation of resources such as award of government contracts, procurement processes, sinecures and the ability to skew development projects such as asphalt roads, electricity, potable water, hospitals and educational institutions in favour of the President's region, encouraged competition for power along ethnic lines. John Cohen's analysis pointed to the influence of ethnicity in the allocation of development projects, corruption and economic mismanagement during the Kenyatta and Moi régimes (Cohen 1995). There was the widespread logic in Kenya that a community could only benefit from state resources if its member was elected President. It stemmed from an ethnically influenced allocation of state resources throughout the country's independence period. Intelligence and security procurement processes were not subject to oversight ostensibly because of state security reasons. This enabled corruption for the financial benefit of top ranking military officers and the ruling political elite, as documented by a former military officer implicated in the attempted overthrow of the Moi régime in 1982 (Diang'a 2002). The press also exposed similar irregularities between high-ranking military officers and politicians under the Kibaki régime (The Standard October 31, 2010). Entanglement of top military officers and other heads of security forces into patronage networks compromised legitimate instruments of coercion. It rendered them loyal to the incumbent and government but not the state thus the involvement of security forces in partisan politics through violent suppression of opposition leaders and their supporters during protests, abuse of the intelligence in partisan politics and extrajudicial executions. Therefore winning the presidency came with economic gains for the incumbent and his supporters. Despite devolution of some powers and 15% of state revenue to the second tier of government composed of 47 counties, contestation for the presidency remained intense and ethnically polarising because the national government retained the bulk of state revenue and so the most lucrative prize on Kenya's political totem pole.

Kenya's politics has operated in a zero sum political framework in which elections produce winners and losers, if not permanent winners and permanent losers in the sense that among Kenya's four presidents since independence to date, three were Kikuyu while the other was Kalenjin. In a country in which ethnicity was, in large measure, the wind that propelled political sails, this seemingly tribal hegemony evoked resentment from the alienated politicians and their respective tribes. It accented the sense of marginalisation among those excluded from the state on account or tribalism. Since there had not been checks and balances against presidential powers for most of Kenya's post-colonial period, it was almost impossible for the incumbent to lose an election since 1992 when the presidency was up for contestation for the first time. Kenya's régimes had not experienced "incumbency vulnerability" defined as "the possibility for an incumbent government to be ousted and replaced...." Bogaards observed that the catchword is "possibility" in that "vulnerability" applied only in a case where a government operated with the realisation that its continued existence depended on how it conducted itself (Bogaards 2000: 176). On occasions when the incumbent felt at risk of losing elections, he had resorted to unorthodox means to retain power such as the use of state violence to displace and disenfranchise opposition supporters and engagement in electoral fraud.

The controversy around the 2013 and 2017 elections in which Raila Odinga accused Uhuru Kenyatta and the electoral body of electoral fraud, showed that the 2010 Constitution had not rendered the incumbent susceptible to electoral defeat and that devolution, expected to mitigate zero-sum politics, was yet to find traction. The yet again divisive elections reignited a discourse about secession by the tribes that had supported Raila Odinga. The secession discourse had persisted in Kenya. Since the late 1990s, the Mombasa Republican Council (MRC), a group based at the Coastal region, had advocated secession on account of sustained marginalisation by successive governments. In 1998, Mwai Kibaki, then an opposition politician, led Mount Kenya MPs affiliated to DP in calling for secession by GEMA tribes due to state sponsored killings at the Coastal region and other parts of the country during the 1997 elections (*Kenya Today*, 23 August 2017). These politicians accused the Moi regime of violently targeting Kikuyu. As such, sections of Kenyans, who felt discriminated against and brutalised by the state based on tribal and political affiliation, imagined that secession would alleviate their grievances (*Saturday Nation*, 26 March 2016). The endurance of the sense of alienation regardless of change of government, was illustrative of the flawed character of Kenyan state and politics bereft of principle.

The other factor that enhanced appeal to ethnicity by politicians is that administrative and tribal boundaries coincided. The corollary was that certain ethnic groups dominated most administrative units. The Luhya had been dominant in Western Province, the Luo in Nyanza and the Kikuyu in Central Province. The "County" replaced the "Province" as a unit of administration in the 2010 Constitution, but sections of the media, pundits, polling firms, and politicians continued to be obsessed with the "Province". Most of the 47 counties were dominated by the five most populous ethnic groups which constituted more than half of Kenya's total population (Kenya Census 2009). These were Kalenjin, Kamba, Luhya, Luo, and Kikuyu. Since the advent of multiparty politics, politicians had regarded the Province as a reservoir of ethnic votes because of what Bates referred to as the "politics of apportionment and delimitation" (Bates 1983: 161).

The centralised state under the one-party system suppressed alternative political views and so curbed the eruption of ethnic-based political organisations and mobilisation and the attendant violence. Once the country reverted to multiparty politics in 1991, it was possible for opposition and KANU politicians to canvass for support along ethnic lines. The Kenyatta-Moi one-party state had assumed the face of the tribe of the incumbent President. The emerging political parties in the 1990s propagated this political orientation that thrived on patronage, violence and the exclusionary definition of leadership through a tribal lens. The opposition politicians were unable to devise an alternative form of politics because almost all of them had been part of the KANU and occupied prominent positions in the Kenyatta and Moi regimes and so had stakes in the extant politico-economic status quo (Ndegwa 1998: 194).

Ethnicity influenced political competition in the multiparty period because Kenya's politicians defined citizenship in terms of ethnic belonging at the expense of national citizenship (Ndegwa 1997). This exclusionary politics was a continuation of the ethnic balkanization of Kenyan communities that had pertained under the colonial divide-and-rule strategy. Mamdani argued that the administrative and legal units of the state separated and discriminated between people in terms of the indigenous and non-indigenous. He further argued that the outcome of this distinction was that those defined as the indigenous enjoyed customary rights, the foremost being the right to land, while those defined as foreigners were denied those rights, no matter how long they had occupied the land (Mamdani 2004: 7). This autochthonous politics separated "sons and daughters of the soil" from "aliens". Ethnic belonging became the qualification for running for political office and promoted the politics of exclusion and discrimination pitting "aborigines" against "foreigners". The Moi régime resorted to violence to displace the non-indigenous people in the Rift Valley in order to gain demographic advantage during the 1992 and 1997 elections.

WHY THE ABSENCE OF CLASS-BASED POLITICS?

Kenya's democratisation process is also hampered by a lack of identification along class lines. Kenya's middle class could not act as the bastion and catalyst for the democratisation process because it was ethnically fragmented and defined by tribalism, material possessions and consummerism to the exclusion of shared norms, and values, that they could bring to bear on the country's political culture. It was not immune to tribal politics since its economic fortunes were affected either positively or otherwise by the government of the day (Cooper 2002: 176). The cyclic tribal violence under multiparty system testified to the fragility of Kenya's democracy and state. Richard identified two characteristics among Africa's middle class that held true about Kenya too. He observed that Africa's middle class could not assist in entrenching democracy because it was precariously hinged to the state bureaucracy and therefore lacked a self-sustaining entrepreneurial instinct (Joseph

1997: 363). The country's middle class promoted ethnic politics in the media, universities, and the bureaucracy because of competition for the opportunities of modernity.[6] Kenya's workers could not assert their influence to bear on the process of democracy in the country either.

To begin with, sections of the media had problems with conceptualising the phrase "working class" which they applied to mean "people who have a job" to the exclusion of the unemployed. This resulted in a limited understanding of the concept. In this regard, a lawyer, a bank manager, a university teacher, a journalist and even a doctor were referred to as members of the "working class" (The Standard September 25, 2011). The economic meaning of the concept "worker" that referred to those without the means of production and who were in wage labour was not popularly understood. Kenya's working class lacked mobilisation ability since it was caught in the ethnicisation of identity and of politics. Trade unionism had not recovered from the legacy of the monolithic single-party state. In the aftermath of the banning of Oginga Odinga's KPU party in 1969, Kenyatta consolidated power and even reserved for himself the power to appoint the boss for the umbrella workers' organisation the Central Organisation of Trade Unions (COTU) (Ochieng' 1996: 102). Since then the COTU leadership had tended to be closely associated with the government. The COTU seldom invoked industrial action in challenges facing the workers. Most strike action involved organisations whose membership included the middle class such as teachers, medical doctors, nurses and lecturers. The inability by the trade unions to influence the government, and even pose a threat to its stay in power, was underscored by numerous strike actions in the lead up to the 2017 elections over poor terms of service. The strike action by nurses persisted through the elections and thereafter. These industrial actions did not dent Uhuru Kenyatta's re-election prospects. Furthermore, crosscutting economic concerns such as the high cost of living, rampant corruption and lack of basic goods did not provide an adhesive for a crossethnic resentment and mobilisation against the regime. Uhuru Kenyatta's popularity among his supporters, workers inclusive, remained intact.

The lacuna created by the absence of independent oversight institutions, policy differences and ideology among politicians and political parties also accounted for the influence of ethnicity in politics in Kenya and elsewhere in Africa (Gyimah-Boadi 2007: 27). Kenya's electorate did not vote based on the manifestos of the competing political parties. Democracy in Kenya existed more in the rhetoric of what Wolff referred to as "political entrepreneurs" (Wolff 2006: 73) than in the practical conduct of politics according to the dictates of democracy. A government report on the disputed 2007 elections observed that successive elections since 1992 were marred by politicisation of ethnicity, rigging, cultural stereotypes, hate speech, intimidation of opponents and ethnic violence (Republic of Kenya 2008a). Democracy presupposes that the electorate votes for candidates and parties after evaluating their manifestos and that today's winners would be tomorrow's losers and vice versa. But Kenya's elections were uncertain because politics were conducted in an atmosphere without discernible rules and norms and by politicians who were reluctant to subject their conduct to the rule of law (The Standard on Sunday February 6, 2011). The process preceding the elections was often murky to guarantee a predetermined outcome.

THE BOOK STRUCTURE

This book is about Kenya's transition from authoritarianism to more democratic forms of politics and its impact on multiparty politics on Kenya's multi-ethnic society. It explains the perennial issues of political disorganization through state violence and ethnicisation of politics and the state in Kenya. In addition, the book considers the significance of the concept of justice in Kenya, a country characterised by inequalities, tribalism, impunity, violence, authoritarianism and patron-client type of politics. The book highlights the trajectories that Kenya's politics has taken since the autocratic single-party state into multiparty politics.

The book is divided into seven chapters. The Introduction chapter sets a background to the politicisation of ethnicity in post-colonial Kenya. In response to the question as to why ethnicity is so salient in Kenya's multiparty system, the chapter presents the thesis that tribalism in Kenya is a by-product of power politics and the attendant economic opportunities for which the political elite and the intelligentsia compete. Since independence in 1963, even before, Kenya's politicians have exploited ethnicity as an ideology for political and economic gain. Regional inequalities and poverty, a lack of ideologically anchored political parties, weak state institutions, and disregard for the rule of law had colluded to create an incendiary political milieu once the country reverted to multiparty politics in 1991. Kenya's challenge in its bid to democratise revolves around the need to address long-term disputes particularly related to land injustices, inclusive politics, equity, and establishment of the rule of law to ensure justice and trust within the body politic.

Chapter 2 highlights the theoretical perspectives regarding ethnicity that undergird the book. It argues that although ethnicity is a colonial construct, Kenya's post-colonial politicians had reified rather than demobilised it. The chapter conceptualizes tribal politics and shows that ethnicity is part of modernity and so is intrumentalised during contestation over power and attendant benefits. Ethnicity is not an anachronism that recedes as modernity advances. The chapter shows how the institutional single-party framework shaped the period of multiparty politics, created a zero sum political system and promoted the salience of ethnicity in Kenya's politics. Throughout the book, I use the words ethnicity/tribalism, tribe/ethnic group interchangeably. Kenyans talk about "tribe" and "tribalism" but not "ethnicity" to explain the impediments they encounter in their lives.

Chapter 3 examines the single-party autocracy and big man politics in Kenya. Personal rule had impeded issue-driven politics leaving tribe as the "agenda" in the country's elections in both single party and multiparty Kenya. The chapter highlights the deleterious effects of personal rule on the rule of law, and the absence of a sense of nationhood in Kenya. The tenure of Daniel arap Moi—Kenya's second president (1978–2002)—popularly known as the *Nyayo* or "footsteps" era was characterised by authoritarianism, deft manipulation of tribalism, personality cultism, impunity and corruption. Moi was a continuation of his predecessor, Jomo Kenyatta. The weakening of the judiciary and parliament and criminalisation of dissent resulted in the construction of a one-party autocracy. The chapter traces the loss of legitimate violence by the state to the Kenyatta and Moi regimes. This set in motion state violence euphemistically called ethnic clashes upon revert to multiparty party elections. These regimes exploited extrajudicial executions, tribal militias and other unorthodox means to crush dissent and retain power.

Chapter 4 focuses on Kenya's multiparty elections specifically, the founding ones in 1992. The chapter argues that since the founding multiparty elections in 1992, Kenya's politics did not change substantively and so there was no transformation in political organisation. The salience of ethnicity in multiparty politics degenerated into tribal violence. Neither the ruling party nor the opposition had a transcendental vision. They engaged in ethnic mobilisation that was indicative of the overarching influence of the single-party legacy. Moi and opposition leaders lacked clearly differentiated ideologies and a commitment to reform. Political expediency held sway reducing Kenyans to mere pawns on the politicians' chessboard. At each subsequent election, the incumbent and his rivals mobilised along tribal lines reducing elections to a mere ethnic census. A self-reproducing tribal plutocracy held onto state power.

Chapter 5 covers the period between the 2002 transitional election and the disputed one of 2007. The chapter argues that although the 2002 elections constituted a watershed in Kenya's political history, the leadership transition from Moi to Kibaki, did not inculcate transformative politics into the country's polity. It was significant that 2002 was the first credible presidential elections in Kenya. Significantly, the Kikuyu-Luo alliance that eluded the opposition in 1992 and 1997 materialised, ensuring the defeat of KANU. However, the National Rainbow Coalition (NARC) broke up owing to disagreements over a pre-election power-sharing pact. Kibaki presided over a resurgence of Kikuyu hegemony in Kenya's politics that elicited resistance from other tribal Big Men who had been instrumental to his victory in 2002. The elite fragmentation accounted for ethnic polarisation that manifested in the ethnically divisive 2005 referendum, and the 2007 elections and the post-election violence. The 2007–2008 post-election violence was a culmination of unresolved historical issues such as land disputes, inequitable resource distribution, weak institutions and impunity. The violence signalled the perilous trajectory the country had embarked on since independence and called for substantive reform to avert instability during subsequent elections.

Chapter 6 examines the International Criminal Court (ICC) and the quest for justice by the victims of atrocities committed during the 2007–2008 post-election. It focuses on the politics of the ICC in the run up to Kenya's 2013 elections. This chapter argues that the indictment of prominent Kenyans by the ICC for the 2007–2008 post-election atrocities was the first attempt in Kenya's post-colonial history to address impunity deeply entrenched in the country's body politic. Uhuru Kenyatta and William Ruto exploited cases against them to whip up ethnic sentiment, polarise the country and ascend to power despite facing crimes against humanity charges before the ICC. Crucially, the ICC precipitated uncertainty among Kenya's politicians, especially the ruling ones. Kenyatta's controversial victory in 2013 was both personal and oligarchic as it ensured continued dominance of Kenya's political and economic spheres by an enduring plutocracy. With control over state apparatus, Kenyatta and Ruto successfully fought back against the threat posed by the ICC and derailed justice for the victims of the 2007–2008 post-election atrocities. The chapter analyses ICC politics, impunity, and ethnic politics through the prism of crimes against humanity charges against Kenyans at the ICC.

Chapter 7 concludes and synthesises the arguments of the book as a whole and contains some recommendations on how to ensure Kenya managed ethnic diversity.

NOTES

1. Ekeh referred to ideologies as "conscious distortions or perversions of truth by intellectuals in advancing points of view that favour or benefit the interests of particular groups for which intellectuals act as spokesmen" (Ekeh 1975: 94).

2. I use the phrase "political elite" to refer to all Kenyan politicians not gate-keepers only. It underscored their privileged status sustained by the pursuit of their own political economic and social interests in disregard of the challenges besetting the *wananchi* (populace) whom they purported to represent. The gatekeepers within the government and in the opposition exhibited this behaviour.

3. The elections were held specifically to neutralise Oginga Odinga after he fell out with Jomo Kenyatta and formed his own party, Kenya People's Union (KPU). Kenyatta's allies amended the Constitution to require MPs sympathetic to the KPU to seek re-election since they were considered as having defected. Most of Odinga's supporters were fellow Luo and so the elections were confined to the Nyanza region predominantly inhabited by the Luo community. Odinga's Kikuyu allies such as Bildad Kaggia were virtually driven out of politics due to what Muigai called "ethnic pressure" (Muigai 2004: 213).

4. For instance George Nyanja, the FORD-Asili MP for Limuru constituency (1992–2002) set out in November 1997, a month away from the general elections, to find an alternative political party upon realising that Kenneth Matiba, would not be contesting the elections since, among other reasons, he had no voting card. Nyanja had poor relations with Martin Shikuku, the party leader. "Although he had been accepted by the DP, it quickly dawned on him that he might not be nominated by the party. Assuming that he could easily be embraced by Paul Muite and Richard Leakey of Safina party, he announced that he had shifted camp to the newly registered "Safina". However, the "Safina" leadership did not admit him into the party because of his past utterances in reference to Europeans

and Asians living in Kenya. "Safina" was trying to carve an image for itself as a party of principled individuals with a vision of a united nation, free from ethnic and racial bigotry. Nyanja quickly sought to join the SDP, but was not embraced by Charity Ngilu or Peter Anyang' Nyong'o. At this point he tried to rejoin the DP. When the DP shut the door in his face, Nyanja instantly and desperately turned to Raila Odinga and the NDP. As it turned out for the Limuru voters, it did not matter which party ticket Nyanja was going to run on so long as he did so on an opposition ticket. The legislator went on to become the only MP from central Kenya to win a seat on an NDP ticket. Nyanja's initial hesitation to seek NDP nomination had to do with ethnicity and the fear of rejection by his voters if he joined a Luo-led party" (Njogu 2001: 389–390).

5. Chabal and Daloz (1999: 95–109) demonstrate that the concept of corruption in Africa is nuanced because of communal influences such as kinship ties.

6. Kenyan university students organised, mobilised and voted along tribal lines during student elections thus induction into exclusionary ethnic politics among Kenya's middle class partly took place at the university.

References

Books & Book Chapters

Atieno-Odhiambo, E. 1996. The Formative Years 1945–1955. In *Decolonisation and Independence in Kenya*, ed. B.A. Ogot, and W.R. Ochieng'. Nairobi: East African Educational.

Barkan, J. 1992. The Rise and Fall of a Governance Realm in Kenya. In *Governance and Politics in Africa*, ed. G. Hyden, and M. Bratton. Boulder: Lynne Rienner.

Bates, R. 1983. Modernization Ethnic Competition and the Rationality of Politics in Contemporary Africa. In *State Versus Ethnic Claims: African Policy Dilemmas*, ed. D. Rothchild, and V. Olorunsola. Boulder, Colorado: Westview Press.

Chabal, P., and J. Daloz. 1999. *Africa Works Disorder as Political Instrument*. Oxford: James Currey.

Cooper, F. 2002. *Africa Since 1940*. Cambridge: Cambridge University Press.

Diang'a, J. 2002. *Kenya 1982 the Attempted Coup the Consequences of a Single Party Dictatorship*. London: Pen Press.

Gyimah-Boadi, E. 2007. Political Parties, Elections and Patronage: Random Thoughts on Neo-Patrimonialism and African Democratiztion. In *Votes, Money and Violence Political Parties and Elections in Sub-Saharan Africa*, ed.

M. Basedau, G. Erdmann, and A. Mehler. Scottsville: University of Kwazulu-Natal Press.

Horowitz, D. 1985. *Ethnic Groups in Conflict*. Berkeley: University of California Press.

Hyden, G. 2006. *African Politics in Comparative Perspective*. New York: Cambridge University Press.

Kadima, D., and F. Owuor. 2006. The National Rainbow Coalition Achievements and Challenges of Building and Sustaining Broad-Based Political Coalition in Kenya. In *The Politics of Party Coalitions in Africa*, ed. D. Kadima. EISA: Auckland Park.

Karimi, J., and P. Ochieng'. 1980. *The Kenyatta Succession*. Nairobi: Transafrica Press.

Leys, C. 1975. *Underdevelopment in Kenya: The Political Economy of Colonialism*. London: Heinemann.

Mamdani, M. 2004. Race and Ethnicity as Political Identities in the African Context. In *Keywords: Identity for a Different Kind of Globalization*, ed. N. Tazi. London: Alliance of Independent.

Meredith, M. 2006. *The State of Africa: A History of Fifty Years of Independence*. London: Free Press.

Morton, A. 1998. *Moi: The Making of an African Statesman*. London: Michael O'Mara Books Ltd.

Muigai, G. 2004. Jomo Kenyatta and the Rise of the Ethno-Nationalist State in Kenya. In *Ethnicity & Democracy in Africa*, ed. B. Berman, D. Eyoh, and W. Kymlicka. Oxford: James Currey.

Njogu, K. 2001. The Culture of Politics and Ethnic Nationalism in Central Province and Nairobi. In *Out for the Count: The 1997 General Elections and Prospects for Democracy in Kenya*, ed. M. Rutten, A. Mazrui, and F. Grignon. Kampala: Fountain Publishers Ltd.

Ochieng', W. 1996. Structural and Political Changes. In *State Versus Ethnic Claims: African Policy Dilemmas*, ed. B.A. Ogot, and W.R. Ochieng'. London: James Currey.

Wanyama, F. 2010. Voting Without Institutionalised Political Parties: Primaries, Manifestos, and the 2007 General Elections in Kenya. In *Tensions and Reversals in Democratic Transitions*, ed. K. Kanyinga, and D. Okello. Nairobi: Society for International Development and Institute for Development Studies-University of Nairobi.

Wanyande, P. 2003. The Politics of Alliance Building in Kenya: The Search for Opposition Unity. In *The Politics of Transition in Kenya: From KANU to NARC*, ed. W. Oyugi, P. Wanyande, and C. Odhiambo-Mbai. Heinrich Boll Foundation: Nairobi.

Wolff, S. 2006. *Ethnic Conflict: A Global Perspective*. Oxford: Oxford University Press.

Journals

Ajulu, R. 2002. Politicised Ethnicity, Competitive Politics and Conflict. *African Studies* 61 (1): 251–268.

Amutabi, N. 2011. Interrogating the Tumultuous Relationship Between Parliament and the Executive in Kenya Over the Past 45 Years: Retrospection. *Kenya Studies Review* 3 (3): 17–40. Online: http://kessa.org/yahoo_site_admin/assets/docs/p21_44_Maurice_N_Amutabi_Kenya_Studies_Review_KSR-december_2011-2.351102134.pdf. Accessed 6 July 2012.

Cheeseman, N. 2008. The Kenyan Elections of 2007: An Introduction. *Journal of Eastern African Studies* 2 (2): 166–184.

Chege, M. 1981. A Tale of Two Slums: Electoral Politics in Mathare and Dagoretti. *Review of African Political Economy* 20: 74–88.

Ekeh, P. 1975. Colonialism and the Two Publics in Africa: A Theoretical Statement. *Comparative Studies in Society and History* 17 (1): 91–112.

Joseph, R. 1997. Democratization in Africa After 1989: Comparative and Theoretical Perspectives. *Comparative Politics* 29 (3): 363–382.

Murunga, G. 2004. The State, Its Reform and the Question of Legitimacy in Kenya. *Identity, Culture and Politics* 5 (1&2): 179–206.

Mueller, S. 2008. The Political Economy of Kenya's Crisis. *Journal of Eastern African Studies* 2 (2): 185–210.

Ndegwa, S. 1998. The Incomplete Transition: The Constitutional and Electoral Context in Kenya. *Africa Today* 45 (2): 193–212.

Nyong'o, P.A. 1989. State and Society in Kenya: The Disintegration of the Nationalist Coalitions and the Rise of Presidential Authoritarianism. *African Affairs* 88 (351): 229–251.

Omolo, K. 2002. Political Ethnicity in the Democratisation Process in Kenya. *African Studies* 61 (1): 209–221.

Owuor, S., and M. Rutten. 2009. Weapons of Mass Destruction: Land, Ethnicity and the 2007 Elections in Kenya. *Journal of Contemporary African Studies* 27 (3): 305–327.

Shilaho, W. 2014. 'I Do Not Know Who Won the Elections': How Not to Conduct Elections and Kenya's Democratic Reversals. *Politeia* 33 (3): 44–67.

Reports

European Union Election Observation Mission (EU EOM). 2008. *Kenya Final Report General Elections*, December 27. Available Online: http://www.scribd.com/doc/3869389/EU-observer-mission-Final-Report-on-the-Kenyan-General-Election-2007. Accessed 3 Aug 2016.

International Crisis Group. 2008. *Kenya in Crisis*. Report No. 37, February 21. Online: http://www.crisisgroup.org/~/media/Files/africa/horn-of-africa/kenya/137_kenya_in_crisis_web.pdf. Accessed 12 Jan 2016.

Kenya Census. 2009. *2009 Population and Housing Census Results*. Online: http://www.scribd.com/doc/36670466/Kenyan-Population-and-Housing-Census-PDF. Accessed 12 Jan 2016.

Republic of Kenya. 2008a. *Report of the Independent Review Commission on the General Elections held on 27th December or 'the Kriegler Commission'*. Government Printer: Nairobi.

Republic of Kenya. 2008b. *Commission of Inquiry into Post-Election Violence (CIPEV) or 'the Waki Commission'*. Nairobi: Government Printer. Online: http://www.dialoguekenya.org/docs/PEV%20Report.pdf. Accessed 10 Nov 2011.

Republic of Kenya. 2009. *(2007) The Political Parties Act*. Online: http://www.kenyalaw.org/Downloads/Acts/Political%20Parties%20Act%20(Cap.%207A).pdf. Accessed 12 Jan 2012.

Republic of Kenya. 2010. *The Proposed Constitution of Kenya*. Nairobi: Government Printer.

Republic of Kenya. 2011. *The Political Parties Act*. Online: http://cickenya.org/sites/default/files/Acts/Political%20Parties%20Act%2C%202011_0.pdf. Accessed 12 Jan 2012.

Newspapers

The Standard. 2010. Kenya's 'New' Fighter Jets Cannot Take Off, October 31. Online: http://www.standardmedia.co.ke/InsidePage.php?id=2000021374&catid=4&a=1. Accessed 9 Oct 2015.

The Standard. 2011. Kenya's Filthy Working-Class, September 25. Online: http://www.standardmedia.co.ke/InsidePage.php?id=2000043467&cid=349. Accessed 5 Dec 2011.

The Standard. 2011. Parliament Endorses Pre-Election Coalitions, August 16. Online: http://www.standardmedia.co.ke/InsidePage.php?id=2000041006&cid=4&ttl=Parliament%20endorses%20pre-election%20coalitions. Accessed 13 Jan 2015.

The Standard on Sunday 2011. Sincerity and Goodwill by Politicians Must Complement Good Constitutions, February 6.

Presidential Speeches

BBC News 2003. Kenya lifts ban on Mau Mau. August 31. Online: http://news.
bbc.co.uk/1/hi/world/africa/3196245.stm. Accessed 28 August 2017.

Bogaards, M. 2000. Crafting competitive party systems: Electoral laws and the
opposition in Africa. *Democratisation*. 7 (4): 163–190. Online: http://www.
tandfonline.com/doi/pdf/10.1080/13510340008403688. Accessed 16 Jan
2017.

Cohen, J. 1995. Ethnicity, Foreign Aid and Economic Growth in Sub-Saharan:
The Case of Kenya. HIID Development Discussion Paper No. 520. Online:
http://www.cid.harvard.edu/hiid/520.pdf. Accessed 12 Jan 2017.

Kenya Today. 2017. In 1998 Opposition Leader Mwai Kibaki led Mt Kenya MPs
in Calling for Secession to Form 'Central Kenya Republic', Give Dr Ndii a
Break. August 23. Online: https://www.kenya-today.com/opinion/1998-
opposition-leader-mwai-kibaki-led-mt-kenya-mps-calling-secession-give-dr-
david-ndii-break. Accessed 25 August 2017.

Maloba, W. 1996. Decolonisation: A Theoretical Perspective. In *Decolonisation
and Independence in Kenya*, ed. B.A. Ogot and W.R. Ochieng'. Nairobi. East
African Educational publishers.

Ndegwa, S.N. 1997. Citizenship and Ethnicity: An Examination of Two
Transition Moments in Kenyan Politics. *American Political Science Review*.
91 (3): 599–616.

Saturday Nation 2016. Kenya is a cruel marriage: It is time we talk divorce.
March 26. Online: http://www.nation.co.ke/oped/Opinion/Kenya-is-a-
cruel-marriage--it-s-time-we-talk-divorce/440808-3134132-2i7ea3/index.
html. Accessed 25 August.

Speech by H.E. Mzee Jomo Kenyatta During Kenyatta Day Celebrations in
1965. In *Kenya Presidential Speeches 1963–1988 Kenyatta Day Speeches*. Kenya
National Library Archives Central Government Library.

CHAPTER 2

The Kenyan State and the Ethnicity Challenge

Abstract This chapter highlights theoretical perspectives that provide a prism through which Kenya's politics is subsequently discussed. It argues that although ethnicity is a colonial construct, Kenya's post-colonial politicians chose to reify rather than demobilise it. This chapter interrogates the interface between ethnicity and political party politics, and state power in Kenya. 'Tribalism', as ethnicity is commonly known in Kenya, is not anachronistic but is part of modernity. The elite and the populace voted along tribal lines in response to perceived fears and the opportunities of modernity at stake. Although policies featured in Kenya's politics, they hardly inspired the electorate across the ethnic divide reducing elections to ethnic censuses. This does not imply that voting patterns in Kenya were immutable. Crosscutting ethnic voting took place but was more informed by ephemeral ethnic alliances than the individual voter's decision based on competing visions for the country.

Keywords Ethnicity · Modernity · Tribalism · Electorate
Ethnic census · Colonial

INTRODUCTION

This chapter shows that the idea that an ethnic group is a social construct that is reflected in the lack of a concrete definition. Although the word 'tribalism' is no longer in common usage in social science, I use it in the book. It is the word that Kenyans apply in discussing 'ethnicity'

© The Author(s) 2018   29
W.K. Shilaho, *Political Power and Tribalism in Kenya*,
https://doi.org/10.1007/978-3-319-65295-5_2

and related challenges. The chapter demonstrates that ethnic politics is of relevance to Kenya's politicians who, together with the intelligentsia, instrumentalise ethnicity in contestation for political power and economic opportunities. In this context, ethnic politics has political and economic value in the sense that access to the benefits of modernity depends on ethnic affiliation as opposed to other considerations such as meritocracy, efficiency, probity and performance. This chapter repudiates the claim that tribal politics is a relic of a bygone era, and obtains only among the 'unsophisticated' masses alienated from the state and its benefits because of their socio-economic conditions. The chapter argues that a combination of patronage politics and inability to consolidate democracy following Kenya's transition into multiparty politics made it possible for politicians to exploit tribal politics in party formation and mobilisation. This stymied the emergence of class-based politics.

THE FLUIDITY OF ETHNICITY

The definition of the concept of ethnicity is controversial. Brown defines an ethnic group as that community which claims common ancestry and sees the proof of this in the fact that its members display distinctive attributes relating to language, religion, physiognomy or homeland origin (Brown 2000: 6). Although his work is relatively recent, Brown's definition is problematic because it suggests that one can identify members of a given ethnic group by physical appearance. This attribute is dangerous especially in the context of ethnic cleansing or genocide. Le Vine observes that of all the markers of ethnicity, language is universally recognised as the most significant (Le Vine 1997: 51). Wolff argues that ethnic markers make it possible to draw differences not only between individuals but also between groups (Wolff 2006: 34). Young and Turner argued that ethnicity is a relational concept in the sense that 'we' and 'they' are dichotomous concepts in the sense that, 'we' can only find relevance in 'they' and those who define themselves as 'we' ascribe to themselves positive attributes and reserve pejorative ones to the 'they' group (Young and Turner 1985: 139). In Kenya's context, some Kikuyu politicians exploited the circumcision ritual to mobilise against and dismiss their Luo counterparts as unfit to occupy the presidency since traditionally the Luo community did not practise circumcision. Ndegwa observed that the ritual had a status value among the Kikuyu (Ndegwa 1998: 202). Atieno Odhiambo put it succinctly when he quoted Freud, 'The narcissism of small differences' he said of Kenya's politics, 'the tendency to think of ourselves as superior to others because of some laughably superficial and non-essential feature' (Atieno-Odhiambo 2002: 243). Thus the cultural aspects of an individual's identity came to be used in the political discourse to attack the capability of politicians. Thus the onetime MP for Limuru, George Nyanja, dismissed Oginga Odinga in 1992 by saying 'Odinga cannot lead anybody because he is not circumcised' (Oyugi 1997: 51).

Kasfir writing in the 1970s argued that some of the attributes of ethnicity such as language, territory, and cultural practices were objective because both insiders and outsiders of a given ethnic community saw them as bases for political mobilisation (Kasfir 1976: 77). However, Young contested this understanding. He argued that the defining attributes of ethnicity were not constant because communities were in a state of flux. He explained that in a given political situation, these defining attributes may include language, territory, political unit, cultural values or symbols while in another some of these attributes may be absent which meant that ethnic attributes were fluid (Young 1976: 48). Bates's view of ethnicity was in consonance with Young's in the sense that he upheld that ethnic groups were not objective but dynamic and in some cases were invented (Bates 1983: 165). Yet other scholars like Naomi Chazan and her associates suggest that ethnicity was an issue of subjective perception with regard to common origins, historical memories, ties and aspirations (Chazan et al. 1999: 108). Ultimately, the concept of ethnicity is fluid and political. In the Kenyan state, competition for resources such as land and political power and discriminatory government policies, accounted for the emotionalism with which people related to ethnicity. It also explained the emergence of power-centred tribal alliances in the lead up to elections.

The Discourse of Tribalism

In this book, the word 'tribalism' and 'ethnicity' are used interchangeably. Kenyans themselves talk about 'tribe' and 'tribalism' while discussing the country's political and economic challenges. This is an aspect that a Kenyan scholar, Atieno-Odhiambo, acknowledged.[1] Archie Mafeje suggested that the 'ideology of tribalism' was significant to some intellectuals foreign to Africa and Africa's middle class for three reasons. First, he argued that the ideology of tribalism did not capture the dynamics of 'economic and power relations' among Africans and between Africa and the rest of the capitalist world. Second, he was of the view that the ideology sought to draw 'an invidious and highly suspect' divide between Africans and the rest of the world. Third, Mafeje referred to the ideology of tribalism as 'an anachronistic misnomer' that hampered analysis of cross-cultural issues (Mafeje 1971: 261). Berman observed that there was a ring of stigma around the word 'tribalism' to such an extent that Western social scientists denounced it as 'retrogressive and shameful, an unwelcome interruption of the pursuit of modernity' but he emphasised that African politicians reinforced ethnic differences because ethnicity propped up patronage networks from which their power sprang (Berman 1998: 306).

John Lonsdale coined the term 'political tribalism' to refer to the salience of ethnicity in politics that differed from what he referred to as 'ourselves-ing', which refers in his view, to moral ethnicity (Lonsdale 2004: 76). Berman observed that moral ethnicity referred to internal communal matters that involved negotiations between people and their authority over issues such as rights to land and property—the innocuous aspect of ethnicity that other scholars such as Mamdani mentioned as well. Political tribalism in contrast emerged from the different ways in which colonialism impacted on different African communities especially with regard to access to resources of modernity and economic advancement (Berman 1998: 324). Kenyan politicians exploited political tribalism to incite co-ethnics against other communities and canvass for support during electioneering. Mamdani argued that tribalism played two divergent roles in colonial Africa. It provided the basis for indirect rule adopted by the British whereby local chiefs acted as agents of colonialism at the grassroots level, and it was also through tribalism that resistance against colonialism happened. In Mamdani's view, Ethnicity had a dual role whereby it signified both 'the form of rule and the form of revolt against it. Whereas the former is oppressive, the latter *may be* (emphasis in source) emancipatory' (Mamdani 1996: 183). In Kenya, the British employed direct rule but still underscored the element of tribe through the creation of 'homogenous' tribal reserves in which communities were confined.

THE MODERN STATE, ETHNICITY AND POWER

Horowitz argued that ethnicity had often been analysed in the context of modernization (Horowitz 1985; 97). He was of the view that there were three ways of relating ethnic conflict to the modernisation process. First is to dismiss ethnicity as a mere relic of an outmoded traditionalism that could not stand the incursions of modernity. Second is to regard ethnic conflict as a traditional but unusually stubborn impediment to modernization. Third is to interpret ethnic conflict as an integral part—even a product—of the process of modernization itself (Horowitz 1985; 97). However, Horowitz argues that most modernisation theories are inadequate because they place emphasis on elites, the modern stratification system, and the modern sector of developing societies in general but do not sufficiently explain the conflict motives of nonelites, whose stake in the benefits being distributed is often tenuous at best (Horowitz 1985; 102). The modernization interpretation of ethnicity hinges on the argument that conflicts arise not because people are different but because they are essentially the same. Put differently, it is by making people 'more alike', in the sense of possessing the same wants that modernization tends to promote conflict (Horowitz 1985; 100).

Ethnicity is a phenomenon that post-colonial Kenyan politicians instrumentalised because of the fears and opportunities they encountered as they interacted with those whom they defined as the 'other'. Leys attributed the emergence of ethnic consciousness in Kenya at the point when people had to compete against one another due to a change in the mode of production from a system based on barter to one based on profit:

> The foundations of modern tribalism were laid when the various tribal modes and relations of production began to be displaced by a capitalist one, giving rise to new forms of insecurity, and obliging people to compete with each on a national plane for work, land and ultimately for education and other services...(Leys 1975: 199).

Like Leys slightly over two decades earlier, Berman illuminates the link between ethnicity and change in the mode of production and the resultant impact on post-colonial politics (Berman 1998: 311). Kenya's successive governments, since colonial times, had politicised and accented ethnic diversity because this form of politics sustained the political and economic ends of the country's politicians. Therefore, ethnic identity is a consequence of colonialism. Mafeje, writing four decades ago, argued that before the advent of colonialism, Africans identified themselves in terms of territory (Mafeje 1971: 254).

Ethnicity heightened and dissolved into violence with the advent of political pluralism in Kenya in 1991. Berman and other scholars suggest a link between ethnicity and the democratisation process in Africa but that the influence of ethnicity in Africa's politics began with the divide and rule strategy during the colonial period (Berman et al. 2004; Posner 2005: 23). Horowitz argued that Africa's ethnic groups are historical

constructs and the claim to ethnic distinctiveness began during the colonial period when most of them came into contact with one another for
the first time (Horowitz 1985: 98). Why did colonialists accent ethnic
identity? Mafeje contends that colonialists as well as anthropologists had
an essentialist view of Africa in the sense that they regarded African communities as basically tribal. The emerging African elite socialised through
the colonial education system reified tribal identity too (Mafeje 1971:
253). For Mafeje, then, the 'ideology of tribalism' explained the seemingly immutable view of Africa as tribally organised (Mafeje 1971: 253).

In Kenya, the reification of ethnicity led to ethnic profiling. Badejo[2],
Raila Odinga's biographer, traced tribal innuendoes and stereotyping prevalent in Kenya's politics to colonialism (Badejo 2006: 45–46).
Corola Lentz contended that 'cultural specialists' reified ethnic groups
through the creation of the 'we' groups with the attendant attributes
that distinguished them from the 'others' before the advent of colonialism. The author, however, observed that there was scant literature to
prove this (Lentz 1995: 319–20).

Kenya's independence in 1963 eliminated colonialism as the adhesive
that held various ethnic groups together. Yet Jomo Kenyatta and his close
allies perpetuated the divide-and-rule tactic by defining the contestation
for state power against rivals through the ethnic logic. Cooper explained
that rents accrued from control of the gatekeeper state heightened stakes
owing to the centralisation of power. The zero sum politics that characterised gate-keeping politics precipitated accusations of tribalism among the
competing groups of politicians (Cooper 2002: 159). This set in motion
the ethnic factionalism among politicians who invoked ethnicity in their
struggle to access or monopolise power. The Kenyatta régime tried to con-
vince the rest of the Kikuyu community to regard his régime as a Kikuyu
entity that they had to collectively defend against competing tribes.

Mafeje argued that ethnicity was false consciousness, because the poor
did not stand to benefit materially from tribalism and to that extent,
their acquiescence to this type of politics predisposed them to exploitation by the ethnic apologists who purported to represent their interests
(Mafeje 1971: 258–259). That is why the Jomo Kenyatta régime tapped
into the ideology of tribalism to entrench itself in power and dismiss
critics, politically ostracise and even assassinate opponents. Mafeje distinguished the cynical exploitation of the ideology of tribalism to maintain power from the people's noble intention to maintain 'the traditional
integrity and autonomy' of their community in relation to other communities (Mafeje 1971: 258). Therefore the politicisation of ethnicity had a

disorganising affect on politics in Kenya and elsewhere on the continent. In this way too, violence became an option in vanquishing opponents and their supporters. Even after the advent of multiparty politics, Kenya had to contend with this obstacle as it struggled to transition to a new political ethos characterised by accountability, national identity, the rule of law[3] and responsive governance.[4]

COLONIALISM AND ETHNICITY IN KENYA

The colonial penetration of Kenya and its uneven impact on different ethnic groups set the stage for the politicisation of ethnicity after independence. The Luhya, Luo and Kikuyu communities accessed education earlier than the nomadic and pastoral communities owing to contact with the missionaries (Ajulu 2002). It was therefore not coincidental that members of these communities featured prominently in Kenya's post-colonial politics and dominated the bureaucracy. The fact that these tribes were among the most populous in the country was significant too. Oyugi observed,

> A combination of colonial attitudes and strategies and the responses to them by the various ethnic groups were later to provide the setting for future competition and conflict... the "development" strategies devised tended inevitably to benefit some groups at the expense of others. "Open" areas with more missionary stations received early and relatively better education...Education was to prove crucial as a criterion of access to gainful employment and other economic activities...some groups adapted much earlier than the others...(Oyugi 1997: 43).

Colin Leys observed that the Kikuyu adapted to the capitalist mode of production earlier than the other ethnic groups in Kenya (Leys 1975: 200). Traditionally, the Kikuyu prized individual as opposed to communal ownership of property such as land (Morton 1998: 132). The Jomo Kenyatta, Mwai Kibaki and Uhuru Kenyatta régimes built on the dominance of members of the community in Kenya's economy in comparison to other tribes. The economic impact of colonialism on other communities was varied. The Luo experienced a process of underdevelopment after an initial positive response to colonial markets in the 1930s (Hay 1976). Ajulu observed that the Luo were therefore reduced to providers of wage labour in the urban areas and on plantations while competition over fertile land in some parts inhabited by the Luhya resulted in land fragmentation which forced its members to search for wage labour too (Ajulu 2002: 254). Tea and horticultural plantations were established in the Rift Valley region in which the Luo and Luhya had provided wage labour for years. This had rendered them vulnerable to cyclic state induced ethnic violence during the multiparty period and particularly the 2007–2008 post-election violence that afflicted workers in the horticultural farming in the Rift Valley sub-county of Naivasha.

The advent of colonialism in Kenya resulted in the 'invention' of certain ethnic groups (Lynch 2006: 237). Several culturally and linguistically related communities in the Rift Valley attained the name 'Kalenjin' during colonialism (Lynch 2006: 237). Ndegwa observed that other Kenyan communities such as the Luhya, Kikuyu, Giriama and Mijikenda were creations of colonialism as well (Ndegwa 1998: 601). The Luo had culturally and linguistically assimilated the Abasuba, a Bantu speaking tribe with close linguistic and cultural ties with the Baganda of Uganda, to the extent that the Abasuba had almost completely lost their identity as a distinct ethnic group (*Daily Nation*, 2010a, b). The invention of tribes was a phenomenon that took place across Africa. Berman suggested that pre-colonially, ethnic groups such as the Shona of Zimbabwe and Yoruba in Nigeria existed as cultural and linguistic entities, not necessarily as ethnically conscious groups (Berman 1998: 310). Berman observed that ethnic boundaries are fluid and people move back and forth in a contested and negotiated fashion (Berman 1998: 328). Le Vine averred that ethnic identity was so elastic that 'the contents, expressions and boundaries of ethnicity change' making it difficult to define ethnicity (Le Vine 1997: 53).

There was nothing inevitable about Kenya's colonial legacy of ethnic divisions. Ethnicity is not fixed, immutable and primordial (Le Vine 1997: 53). Other African countries are just as ethnically diverse and inherited a similar colonial legacy. The post-colonial African politicians had agency despite the colonial legacy of divide-and-rule. The evocation of ethnicity in political mobilisation was a rational choice that successive governments in Kenya made in pursuit of economic and political interests. Moreover, ethnicity became a means for advancing the politics of individual self-interests masked as patrimonialism and patronage. In contrast, Tanzania's Julius Nyerere while promoting a different collectivist ideology known as *Ujamaa* (Hyden 2006: 117) was among a rare breed of African leaders who avoided exploiting the state for personal enrichment (Hyden 2006: 102–103; Meredith 2006: 249). Perhaps his greatest legacy was a sense of national identity among Tanzanians drawn from over 120 ethnic groups (Meredith 2006: 157). Cheeseman seemed to attribute Tanzania's relative national cohesion to colonialism. He stated that colonialism did not politicise ethnic identities in Tanzania and so Nyerere did not have to deal with ethnically conscious communities once in power unlike in neighbouring Kenya (Cheeseman 2015: 206).

Cowen and Laakso suggested that the politicisation of religious, ethnic and regional identities in Africa enabled Africa's political elite to realise their political and economic interests (Cowen and Laakso 2002: 2). Smith similarly held this position and attributed politicised ethnicity to the advent of multiparty politics in Africa (Smith 2000: 25). The end of the Cold War brought forth the rubric of economic assistance from the International Monetary Fund (IMF) and World Bank based conditionally on the implementation of economic and political policies, Structural Adjustment Programmes (SAPs), that reduced public spending on education, health and general public services, but was also tied to the promotion of democratic practice and governance. Consequently, Africa's Big Men including Daniel arap Moi came under pressure to conform to these conditionalities. The 1992 founding multiparty elections afforded the opposition the opportunity to challenge Moi's uninterrupted hold on power since 1978 and as a countermeasure, the régime whipped up ethnic animosity as demonstrated in Chap. 4.

Although Mamdani argued that ethnicity existed in pre-colonial Africa, he distinguished 'ethnicity as a political entity from ethnicity as a cultural entity' (Mamdani 2004: 7). According to Mamdani, the latter entails a mutually agreed upon set of values and customs while the former depended on the legal and administrative functions of the state (Mamdani 2004: 7). The modern state, a creation of colonialism, exploited and reinforced ethnic differences through processes like the issuance of identity cards denoting one's ethnic background as happened in Rwanda under the Belgians or confining people in 'homogenous tribal reserves' (Ndegwa 1998: 607). The administrative demarcations that separated people into regions each, inhabited almost exclusively by members of a given ethnic community had contributed to the politicisation of ethnicity in the post-colonial Kenya. But, exclusionary politics, historical injustices, dysfunctional institutions, predatory politics, and impunity were some of the substantive causations of ethnic conflict in Kenya. There were no axiomatic and monocausal explanations of tribalism in Kenya's politics. Only a multi-dimensional approach illuminated the ideology of tribalism.

Berman advanced four reasons to argue that 'political tribalism' in Africa stemmed from imbalances in relations among different ethnic groups within the colonial establishment. First, the obvious power imbalance between European and African communities due to British rule and European claims to racial and cultural superiority. At independence, the template remained and the tribe that 'ascended' to power such as the Kikuyu under Jomo Kenyatta in Kenya, sought to occupy the status previously reserved for the colonialists. This elicited resentment from the other tribes whose members were excluded from the state. Second, the colonial régime fragmented the indigenous people according to economic activities. Thus we had 'martial groups, trading and administrative groups, cash crop farmers and migrant labourers' (Berman 1998: 328–329). Berman observed that this process was steeped in stereotypes and therefore created a recipe for ethnic tension and conflict in the post-colonial period. Third, he observed that the uneven development of the market economy and access to markets within and between regions and communities resulted in competition and differential benefits. Fourth, rural–urban movement led to the formation of ethnic enclaves and differentiated communities as such (Berman 1998: 328–329). People who moved from rural areas gravitated towards fellow tribesmen and women for cultural reasons as well as for a soft landing in the anonymity of the urban setting.

Young argued that the politicisation of ethnicity in Africa began on the eve of independence with the introduction of political parties and electoral competition. At this point, the question 'Who am I?' which was increasingly posed both bluntly and threateningly gained currency (Young 1976: 166). Elite fragmentation in Kenya happened before independence and ruptured the nascent state formation immediately after independence in 1963. It straddled the continued existence of 'tribal' structures within the new state. After the reintroduction of multiparty politics in 1991, Kenya plunged into destabilising ethnic politics in which overt ethnic mobilisation and stereotyping were normative.

The Intelligentsia and Ethnicity

Young argued that the politicisation of ethnicity was preceded by a process of reification of ethnic groups by the intelligentsia (Young 1976: 182). Despite linguistic, gender, class, regional and religious differences within an ethnic group, politicians and even some scholars promoted narratives that made members of a given tribe believe that they belonged to a concrete tribe bound by, among others, linguistic and cultural attributes that distinguished them from other tribes. Young indentified intellectuals as responsible for constructing ethnicity out of a sense of

shared identity through art and literary works and language standardisation (Young 1976: 181–182). Berman argued that standardisation of
languages and dialects by missionaries, as well as the work of anthropologists, contributed to the invention of tribes in Africa (Berman 1998:
322). Kenya's post-colonial leaders such as Jomo Kenyatta, Daniel arap
Moi, Mwai Kibaki and Uhuru Kenyatta were beneficiaries of missionary
education and perpetuated the belief in the notion of concrete ethnic
groups. Days to the 2017 elections, Uhuru Kenyatta 'created' the Indian
tribe as Kenya's 44th one through a government gazette yet the Indians'
presence in the country predates independence. The link between this
bizarre fiat and the elections, was patent. It was consistent with the
politicisation of ethnicity, albeit subtly. In January 2017, Kenyatta recognised the Makonde, originally from Mozambique, as Kenya's 43rd tribe.
From then henceforth, they were recognised as Kenyan citizens and
had a sense of belonging having been stigmatised as stateless people for
about 80 years. Analyses by scholars such as Young, Ekeh, Mamdani and
Berman illuminated the ways in which the ideology of ethnicity was perpetuated in Kenya's state institutions, universities, civil society, religious
groupings and the media.

Writing in the early 1980s, Bates observed that ethnicity tended to
collapse people into the same mould irrespective of social status, religion,
gender, lifestyle and even language (1983: 161). Since Kenya's founding multiparty 1992 elections, ethnic politics had displaced any other
form of political organisation, such as class or political ideology. Even
the 2002 elections that appeared exceptional still had ethnic undertones
as my analysis in Chap. 5 shows. In Kenya, it was common for Luo or
Kikuyu or Kalenjin resident in upmarket urban neighbourhoods and
their fellow tribesmen and women in either informal settlements or rural
areas to vote for the same Presidential candidate and party as if they had
the same economic concerns. This ethnic bloc voting applied to almost
all ethnic groups in the country too.[5] Ethnic loyalty had more influence
than national identity and class interest. Writing at a time when most
African countries had adopted multiparty politics, Greertz suggested that
people related to their ethnic groups from an emotional perspective and
that explained why it was easier for someone in what he called a 'traditional and modernising' society to owe loyalty to one's ethnic group as
opposed to the nation state (Geertz 1996: 41–42). The conflict in the
Balkans in the early 1990s demonstrated that the process of building a
sense of national identity was protracted and continuous. Scholars such

as Daley observed that most people in Kenya placed the tribe above the state as seen through recruitment in the civil service, ethnic divisions in civil society and religious fraternity and ethnic bloc voting patterns because it played a role in determining who ascended the socio-economic ladder and who did not (Daley 2006).

THE MODERN AND THE ANACHRONISTIC IN ETHNICITY

The Kenyatta-Moi-Kibaki régime instrumentalised ethnicity for the consolidation of power and accumulation of wealth for the President and their supporters. Instrumentalism conceptualises African politics as characterised by manipulation of ethnic identities and loyalties for political and economic ends (Wolff 2006: 33). Ethnicity is not an anachronism. Neither is it a relic of the past but 'part and parcel of the very process of becoming modern' (Horowitz 1985: 101). The modernisation approach to ethnicity accents the link between the role of elite ambitions and the differential impact of modernisation on ethnic groups (Horowitz 1985: 101). Horowitz observes that the modern middle class earlier thought to be detribalised were the ones who advanced their interests through the invocation of ethnic support. Kenya's elites competed for what Horowitz referred to as 'good jobs, urban amenities, access to schools, travel, prestige' (Horowitz 1985: 101). Kenya's rural dwellers participated in ethnic politics as a result of political mobilisation, grievances caused by asymmetrical allocation of state resources and dissemination of tribalism through the media-electronic media that broadcast in vernacular, established media, and social media. Kenya's rural areas tended to be inhabited by members of the same tribe and so the question of competition for resources that pitted members of different tribes against one another, could not easily arise, yet in 2007 and early 2008 the post-election violence occurred in both rural and urban areas. Clan-based politics, a variation of ethnic politics, influenced choice of candidates in rural areas especially during primaries.

Horowitz's argument in 1985 that there was need to understand the logic behind the intense passion that accompanies ethnic conflict thus becomes critical in explaining the violence in the aftermath of the 2007 elections. The mass hysteria that led to the destruction to property belonging to members of the rival tribes, hacking them to death, setting a church ablaze because members of the 'enemy' tribe were sheltering inside, could not be attributed to grievances related to extractive politics *per se*. Young, writing a decade later, observed that in this case primordialism illuminated instrumentalism in that it helps us make sense of 'the emotionality latent in ethnic conflict, its disposition to arouse deep-seated anxieties, fears, and insecurities, or to trigger a degree of aggressiveness not explicable in purely material interest terms' (Young 1993: 23). As Horowitz presciently noted, the ethnic group is not synonymous with a trade union whose solidarity depended on the tangible benefits that members pursued and sometimes achieved as a collective (Horowitz 1985: 104). For Horowitz, the participation of the peasantry and lumpenproletariat in ethnic politics appeared more nuanced than simply being labelled as a case of 'false consciousness' (Horowitz 1985: 105). The masses were not simply victims of herd mentality, had agency and were politically conscious but not mere pawns in political struggles. Ethnicity was constantly in a state of flux. There was no homogenous community in Kenya and ethnic groups tended to contract and expand depending on the threats and opportunities that they confronted (Brown 2000: 13). Whereas contestation for elective posts other that the presidency foregrounded clan and sub-tribal politics, presidential elections often forced tribes to collapse into monoliths regardless of internal fissures.

There is nothing anachronistic about the exploitation of tribalism for political and economic advantage. Chapter 1 and 2 show that although ethnic groups are colonial constructs, both Kenyatta and Moi, in conjunction with cohorts of allies from their ethnic groups, underscored and exploited ethnicity in order to rule. At this embryonic stage of Kenya's independence, ethnicity became the ideology that guided Kenya's politics. Ethnic mobilisation became the means of access to and retention of political power. Political power translated into economic gain for the President and his network of clients that in turn necessitated the instrumentalisation of ethnicity to guarantee continued and uninterrupted dominance of the state. The oathing campaigns by Kenyatta and his inner circle in the aftermath of the assassination of Tom Mboya fell under what Chabal and Daloz (1999: 46) guardedly referred to as the realm of the 'irrational'. Ancient as these rituals were, they were meant to mobilise the masses of the Kikuyu into safeguarding the privileges of Kenyatta and the cabal surrounding him in a modernising economy. The resort to the ancient 'Kalenjin warrior' tradition, (as shown in Chap. 4) to violently neutralise opposition against Moi in the Rift Valley region under Kenya's multiparty system, was a case of the exploitation of tradition by Moi and his allies in a struggle for power, privilege and other economic benefits.

The alleged oath taking ceremonies by Kalenjin politicians in the lead up to the disputed 2007 elections and mobilisation of youth from the community to commit atrocities against 'enemy' tribes during the subsequent post-election violence was yet another illustration of the fusion between the ancient ritual and the struggle for power and its benefits (ICC 2012b). This question of 're-traditionalising' that Chabal and Daloz grapple with as they strive to square the paradox of the resurgence of ethnicity, tribal politics and the resultant inter-tribal violence in modernising Africa arises (Chabal and Daloz 1999: 45–47). Ekeh, a Nigerian social scientist, in his seminal work written in (1975), talked about Africa's two publics and their influence on politics. One was the primordial public that included 'primordial groupings, sentiments, and activities' and the civic public identified with the colonial state and its appurtenances such as 'the military, the police, the civil service'. Unlike the former, Ekeh argued, the civic public has no moral connection with the private realm and so corruption and patronage prevailed. Ekeh observed that African politicians were able to concurrently operate within the two publics with ease, a distinguishing characteristic of African politics (Ekeh 1975: 92–93).

THE POLITICS OF PATRONAGE

In Kenya, ethnicity intersected with patronage politics to stifle political competition based on programmes of action. The overarching influence of personal rule that spanned the entire period of the single-party state provided the basis for a politics devoid of ideology and principle. Personal rule undermined multipartyism and manifested through impunity and whimsical politics under Jomo Kenyatta, Daniel arap Moi, Mwai Kibaki and Uhuru Kenyatta. Jackson and Rosberg defined personal rule as 'a distinctive type of political system in which the rivalries and struggles of powerful and wilful men, rather than impersonal institutions, ideologies, personal policies, or class interests, are fundamental in shaping political life' (Jackson and Rosberg 1984: 421). The promulgation of the 2010 Constitution[6] put in place a rule-based framework to rid Kenya of a personality centred politics. However, the Kenyatta-Moi-Kibaki oligarchy had obstructed its implementation. It was for this reason that since independence the Presidency had been a preserve of the incumbent and a tiny clique of supporters largely drawn from his tribe and surrogates from cooperative tribes. The single-party autocratic state ensured clientelist networks beginning from the office of the President cascading downwards to the village level through the provincial administration. Under the multiparty system, some opposition leaders established parallel patronage networks although access to the state provided unrivalled amounts of resources. Patronage stifled the emergence of internal party democracy since primaries and party elections defied democratic procedures as some candidates sought the endorsement of the tribal Big Men as this sometimes gave them an edge over their rivals.

Patronage politics had informalised the operations of Kenya's post-colonial governments. It rendered decision making a preserve of the President and few trusted allies. It was almost impossible for Kenyans to predict government policy.[7] In addition to the governance structures recognised by the Constitution, there was an informal clique surrounding the President. This group of individuals wielded immense power that they either arrogated to themselves or had free rein to exercise. They exclusively directed government programmes towards their political interests and to the benefit of their supporters alone, which had far-reaching consequences for citizens. The Kenyatta régime was dominated by the 'Kiambu Mafia', Moi's by what Ajulu called the 'Kabarnet Syndicate' (Ajulu 1995: 6) and Kibaki's and his successor, Uhuru Kenyatta's, by the 'Mount Kenya Mafia'.[8] These were groupings in charge of what Cooper referred to as the spigot economy in which 'whoever controls the tap collects the rent' (Cooper 2002: 172). Berman and other scholars have shown that endemic corruption thrived in such a political system because decision-making was predicated on the whims of the President and his close allies but not the rule of law (Berman et al. 2004: 2–3). One of the greatest forms of corruption under Jomo Kenyatta was the illegal acquisition of public land for Kenyatta's and his clients' benefit. Besides land, Moi exploited cabinet appointments, bank loans, luxury cars and cash to sustain patron-client politics (*Daily Nation* December 24, 2002). In 1971, the Kenyatta government officially sanctioned and embedded conflict of interest within Kenya's body politic, when it adopted a recommendation by the Ndegwa Commission that allowed civil servants to engage in business ventures to augment their income (Himbara 1993: 100). This decision, in effect, sanctioned corruption since politicians and bureaucrats extracted rents from the government and were at the same time ones to design and implement policies to regulate politics not to intrude into the economy. It was not coincidental that Kenya's successive Presidents were the country's wealthiest and leading 'businessmen' and owned large tracts of land (*The Standard* October 1, 2004).

The exploitation of patronage politics by the President did not work out successfully all of the time. There were elements of resistance and so there was need for a carrot and stick approach to ensure political loyalty by frustrating dissent and ensure that the opposition did not organise and mobilise (Gyimah-Boadi 2007: 29). In instances where the use of state largesse failed to lure dissenting voices, Moi resorted to state violence. On the threshold of multiparty politics in the early 1990s after Kenya legalised the formation of multiple political parties, some of the KANU defectors and those with wavering loyalty were intimidated back into the fold lest they suffer economic consequences and even face bankruptcy. Moi sacked defiant cabinet ministers to deny them opportunities for rents and forestall the formation of alternative centres of power. The centralised Constitution propped up personal rule, stymied policy-based politics, promoted authoritarianism and fundamentally frustrated reform. Personal rule and the interests of *ancien régime*[9] politicians were at odds with institutionalised politics.

CONCLUSION

This chapter proceeded from the premise that the 'ethnic group' is a fluid concept. The emergence of ethnic groups or tribes lay in the shift from the barter trade to the capitalist mode of production that brought about competition for resources between and among tribes. Kenya's politicians and the middle class defined the concept of citizenship in an insular, exclusionary and tribal manner ensuring that ethnicity was embedded in Kenya's body politic. These were mostly the beneficiaries of patronage, corruption and personal rule that made it impossible for Kenya's successive governments to deliver on public goods. This created a situation whereby the citizenry competed for scarce resources on the basis of tribal origin. Political competition during elections necessitated the use of state violence to suppress and even physically eliminate dissenting voices. Kenya could address these challenges through establishment of a rule-based system of government. The realisation of a Constitution in 2010 was a step towards this direction. If implemented, the Constitution would check the tendency among the politicians to mobilise for support on the basis of ethnicity. The single-party rule atrophied Kenya's institutions and impeded the democratisation process and holding of credible elections. These institutions were yet to unshackle from the legacy of personal rule. The irony is that politicians, civil society practitioners, the clergy, the media and academics were deemed to be the vanguard of devising alternative mechanisms for addressing ethnic politics yet these were the very people who benefitted from it. Kenya's politics remained beholden to the interests of the political class because this grouping had hindered Kenya's transformation and normative politics and ethically inspired oversight institutions. This had made it difficult for politics to transcend ethnic identity and be anchored in social, economic and political challenges that Kenyans encountered irrespective of creed, party or tribal affiliation.

NOTES

1. Atieno-Odhiambo stated that members of various tribes in Kenya at their work places in their offices, in public forums and in whispers along the streets and in the privacy of their homes did not speak of ethnicity. Instead they talked and thought about tribalism as they experienced it daily, 'in its many enabling capacities, incapacitating impact upon their hopes, and blocking of opportunities for whole communities. They use tribalism as a practical vocabulary of politics and social movements' (Atieno-Odhiambo 2002: 230).
2. Babafemi Adesina Badejo is a Nigerian scholar and as such the book benefitted from an outsider's view of Kenya's politics.
3. The rule of law refers to a situation whereby individuals and especially rulers in a self-binding way submit to 'the logic of abstract rules that regulate social interaction' (Hyden 2006: 11).
4. I use the word 'governance' to refer to 'responsible, accountable, transparent, legitimate, effective democratic government' (Cheru 2002: 35).
5. The Luhya, among few tribes, had not exhibited predilection to ethnic bloc voting since the advent of multiparty politics partly because of the absence of an ethnic chief to command the loyalty of the entire community. The Luhya was one of the tribes that had provided swing votes in presidential elections since 1992 except in 2002 when they, almost to a man, voted for Mwai Kibaki as the candidate of a broad tribal alliance, the NARC in which Kijana Wamalwa, a Luhya, was a luminary.
6. Kenya's Constitution promulgated in 2010 is a Presidential but with checks: it has horizontal checks in terms of Constitutional organs like the parliament, the Judiciary, and Constitutionally recognised oversight

commissions; vertically there are devolved systems of government and lastly there is the normative check, in the form of Constitutionalism principles and values. It was hoped that these reforms would reform the executive (*The Standard on Sunday* March 27, 2011: 29).

7. 'Policy' in this context refers to the ubiquitous usage of the word in any system of government but does not refer to a programme of action-oriented approach to governance.

8. The media coined the term to refer to Kibaki's and Uhuru Kenyatta's inner courts comprising Kikuyu and to some extent Meru politicians from ethnic communities inhabiting the region where the Mount Kenya is located.

9. The term *ancien régime* was 'coined by aspiring reformers in late eighteenth century France as a shorthand term for *those features* of the old social and political order which they hoped to be able to sweep away for their replacement by new more rational and enlightened arrangements' (Clark 1987: 197).

REFERENCES

Books & Book Chapters

Badejo, A. 2006. *Raila Odinga an Enigma in Kenyan Politics.* Nairobi: Yintab Books.

Bates, R. 1983. Modernization Ethnic Competition and the Rationality of Politics in Contemporary Africa. In *State Versus Ethnic Claims: African Policy Dilemmas,* ed. D. Rothchild, and V. Olorunsola. Boulder: Westview Press.

Berman, B., D. Eyoh, and W. Kymlicka (eds.). 2004. *Ethnicity and Democracy in Africa.* Athens: Ohio University Press.

Brown, D. 2000. *Contemporary Nationalism Civic, Ethnocultural & Multicultural Politics.* London and New York: Routledge.

Chabal, P., and J. Daloz. 1999. *Africa Works Disorder as Political Instrument.* Oxford: James Currey.

Chazan, Naomi, Peter Lewis, Robert Mortimer, Donald Rothchild, and Stephen John Stedman. 1999. *Politics and Society in Contemporary Africa.* England: Lynne Rienner.

Cheru, F. 2002. *African Renaissance Roadmaps to the Challenge of Globalization.* London: Zed Books.

Cheeseman, N. 2015. *Democracy in Africa: Successes, Failures, and the Struggle for Political Reform.* New York: Cambridge Univbersity Press.

Cooper, F. 2002. *Africa Since 1940.* Cambridge: University Press.

Cowen, M., and L. Laakso. 2002. Elections & Election Studies. In *Multiparty Elections in Africa,* ed. M. Cowen, and L. Laakso. Oxford: James Currey.

Geertz, C. 1996. Primordial Ties. In *Ethnicity*, ed. J. Hutchinson, and A.D. Smith. New York: Oxford University Press.

Gyimah-Boadi, E. 2007. Political Parties, Elections and Patronage: Random Thoughts on Neo-Patrimonialism and African Democratiztion. In *Votes, Money and Violence Political Parties and Elections in Sub-Saharan Africa*, ed. M. Basedau, G. Erdmann, and A. Mehler. Scottsville: University of Kwazulu-Natal Press.

Hay, M. 1976. Luo Women and Economic Change During the Colonial Period. In *Women in Africa: Studies in Social and Economic Change*, ed. J. Nancy, and G. Edna. Stanford: Stanford University Press.

Horowitz, D. 1985. *Ethnic Groups in Conflict*. Berkeley: University of California Press.

Hyden, G. 2006. *African Politics in Comparative Perspective*. New York: Cambridge University Press.

Kasfir, N. 1976. *The Shrinking Political Arena: Participation and Ethnicity in African Politics with a Case Study of Uganda*. Berkely: University California Press.

Leys, C. 1975. *Underdevelopment in Kenya: The Political Economy of Colonialism*. London: Heinemann.

Lonsdale, J. 2004. The Dynamics of Ethnic Development in Africa. In *Ethnicity and Democracy in Africa*, ed. B. Berman, D. Eyoh, and W. Kymlicka. Oxford: James Currey.

Mamdani, M. 1996. *Citizen and Subject*. New York: Princeton University.

Mamdani, M. 2004. Race and Ethnicity as Political Identities in the African Context. In *Keywords/Identity for a Different Kind of Globalization*, ed. N. Tazi. France: Alliance of Independent Publishers.

Meredith, M. 2006. *The State of Africa: A History of Fifty Years of Independence*. London: Free Press.

Morton, A. 1998. *Moi the Making of an African Statesman*. London: Michael O'Mara Books Ltd.

Posner, D. 2005. *Institutions and Ethnic Politics in Africa*. Cambridge: Cambridge University Press.

Wolff, S. 2006. *Ethnic Conflict: A Global Perspective*. Oxford: Oxford University Press.

Young, C. 1976. *The Politics of Cultural Pluralism*. London: The University of Wisconsin Press.

Young, C., and T. Turner. 1985. *The Rise and Decline of the Zairian State*. London: The University of Wisconsin Press.

Young, C. (ed.). 1993. *The Rising Tide of Cultural Pluralism the Nation State at Bay?* Madison: The University of Wisconsin Press.

Journals

Ajulu, R. 1995. The Transition to Multi-partyism in Kenya: the December 1992 Presidential, Parliamentary and Municipal Elections. Leeds: Centre for Democratisation Studies, Leeds University.

Ajulu, R. 2002. Politicised Ethnicity. *Competitive Politics and Conflict in African Studies* 61 (1): 251–268.

Atieno-Odhiambo, E. 2002. Hegemonic Enterprises and Instrumentalities of Survival: Ethnicity and Democracy in Kenya. *African Studies* 61 (2): 223–249.

Berman, B. 1998. Ethnicity Patronage and the African State: The Politics of Uncivil Nationalism. *African Affairs* 97 (388): 305–341.

Clark, J. 1987. Social History and England's "Ancien Régime". *Past & Present* 115: 165–200.

Daley, P. 2006. Ethnicity and Political Violence in Africa: The challenge to the Burundi State. *Political Geography* 25: 657–679.

Ekeh, P. 1975. Colonialism and the Two publics in Africa: A Theoretical Statement. *Comparative Studies in Society and History* 17 (1): 91–112.

Himbara, D. 1993. Myths and Realities of Kenyan Capitalism. *Journal of Modern African Studies* 31 (1): 93–107.

Jackson, R., and C. Rosberg. 1984. Personal Rule: Theory and Practice in Africa. *Comparative Politics* 4: 421–442.

Lentz, C. 1995. Tribalism' and Ethnicity in Africa. *Cahiers des Sciences Humaines* 31 (1), 303–328. Online: http://weblearn.ox.ac.uk/site/human/modhist/undergrad/final/modhist/further/further21/ht06w5w6/Lentz%20Tribalism%20and%20Ethnicity%20CSH.pdf. Accessed 10 Jan 2012.

Le Vine, T. 1997. Conceptualising 'Ethnicity' and 'Ethnic Conflict': A Controversy Revisited. *Studies in Comparative International Development* 32 (2): 45–75.

Lynch, G. 2006. The Fruits of Perception: Ethnic Politics and the Case of Kenya's Constitutional Referendum. *African Studies*. 65 (2): 233–270.

Mefeje, A. 1971. The Ideology of Tribalism. *The Journal of Modern African Studies* 9 (2): 253–261.

Ndegwa, S. N. 1998. The Incomplete Transition: The Constitutional and Electoral Context in Kenya. *Africa Today*. 45 (2): 193–212.

Oyugi, W. 1997. Ethnicity in the Electoral Process: The 1992 General Elections in Kenya. *African Journal of Political Science* 2 (1): 41–69.

Reports

ICC. 2012b. Situation in the Republic of Kenya in the case of the Prosecutor v. William Samoei Ruto, Henry Kiprono Kosgey and Joshua Arap Sang

(Decision on the Confirmation of Charges). http://www.icc-cpi.int/iccdocs/doc/doc1314535.pdf. Accessed 28 Jan 2015.

Newspapers

Daily Nation. 2002. The End of an Era-As the Curtain Falls on Daniel arap Moi's 24-year Rule, A Special Report on the Life and Politics of Kenya's Second President, December 24.

Daily Nation. 2010a. Churches are Missing the Big Picture, February 5. http://www.nation.co.ke/oped/Opinion/-/440808/856400/-/5qyk7p/-/index.html. Accessed 30 Oct 2015.

Daily Nation. 2010b. Ethnicity Rampant in Public Universities, May 17. Online: http://www.nation.co.ke/News/Ethnicity%20rampant%20in%20public%20varsities%20/-/1056/920402/-/i8emkqz/-/index.html. Accessed 21 Sept 2015.

Standard on Sunday. 2011. The Evolving Nature of the Presidency, March 27. Available online: http://www.standardmedia.co.ke/newdesign/news/article/2000032005/the-evolving-nature-of-presidency.smg. Accessed 5 May 2016.

The Standard. 2004. Who Own Kenya? October 1. Online: http://www.marsgroupkenya.org/pdfs/crisis/2008/02/large_landowners_in_Kenya.pdf. Accessed 7 Nov 2015.

Zeric Kay Smith, 2000. The impact of political liberalisation and democratisation on ethnic conflict in Africa: an empirical test of common assumptions. The Journal of Modern African Studies 38 (1): 21–39.

CHAPTER 3

Autocracy, Big Man Politics, and Institutional Atrophy

Abstract This chapter argues that although Jomo Kenyatta, Kenya's first president and his successor, Daniel arap Moi, publicly denounced tribalism, they presided over single-party authoritarianism and exploited ethnicity for political and economic advantage resulting in weak and even dysfunctional state institutions. The abuse of legitimate violence by the state under these two regimes normalised state sponsored violence directed against dissent. The interference with the judiciary and legislature by the executive removed trace of the doctrine of separation of powers, atrophied institutions and reinforced personal rule. Arbitrary constitutional amendments, impunity and flawed elections took hold under these two regimes. This legacy ensured that ethnicity, but not crosscutting interests, remained the major vector of political mobilisation and a fault-line for state violence.

Keywords Jomo Kenyatta · Daniel arap Moi · Authoritarianism
State violence · Separation of powers

INTRODUCTION

This chapter focuses on the personal rule of Daniel arap Moi, the second President of Kenya. Moi used personal patronage in a particular way to marshal support. It is a tactic that rendered almost everyone in his régime beholden to him because of being drawn into his networks

© The Author(s) 2018   51
W.K. Shilaho, *Political Power and Tribalism in Kenya*,
https://doi.org/10.1007/978-3-319-65295-5_3

of patronage and clientelism. I argue that the Moi régime, particularly within the monolithic single-party rule, typified personal rule. It was characterised by patron-client politics, corruption and authoritarianism. The contracted political space forced most politicians to pledge loyalty to Moi and the only political party in Kenya at the time, KANU. Moi exploited ethnicity and incumbency to prevent the emergence of alternative power bases. He used the notion of 'the tribe' as an element of governance and created tribal spokespersons in various parts of the country as well as distributing cabinet portfolios and posts within the KANU executive committee along ethno-regional lines (*The Weekly Review*, 2 December 1988: 4; *Weekly Review*, 22 July 1988: 20). The beneficiaries, in effect, became Moi's clients. This chapter analyses the *Nyayo* régime as an example of Big Man rule and its contribution to ethnicisation of politics under Moi. Jomo Kenyatta, Moi's predecessor had ruled in a similar fashion except that Kenyatta had more legitimacy and gravitas. He was seen as the face of the struggle for independence. *The Weekly Review* posited that Kenyatta used the might of the state to suppress resentment that other ethnic groups had against his Kikuyu-dominated government (*The Weekly Review*, 9 December 1988: 26).

Moi continued along the ethnic exclusion trajectory. The chapter uses the lens of personal rule to explore how Moi adroitly manipulated tribalism coupled with autocracy in order for him to remain in power for 24 years, ten of which under multiparty politics. This chapter forms the basis for understanding party politics in Kenya, first under one-party rule and then in the multiparty period. This encompasses the first fourteen years of Moi's dominance under one-party rule and the subsequent ten years. It explores Moi's involvement in the controversial land redistribution programme in the Rift Valley Province, the construction of the single-party state with its corollary, the weakening of the judiciary, parliament, and other institutions requisite for scaffolding democracy. In 1988, the Moi régime abolished the tenure of judges, and that of the members of the Public Service Commission (PSC) (Throup and Hornsby 1998: 40; *The Weekly Review*, 5 August 1988: 3). Although Moi restored judicial tenure in the early 1990s, Mutua suggested that this did not redeem the image of the judiciary. Judges remained subservient to the executive and invariably ruled against opponents of the régime in politically sensitive cases (Mutua 2009: 67). Moi also influenced the structure of the education system with mixed results. The admixture of ethnicity and education reinforced a process that created ethnically conscious Kenyans in the bureaucracy, academy, media, religious formations and other spheres of the society. He tried to afford education opportunities to previously marginalised parts of the country but at the same time exploited the education system to entrench ethnic politics.

SINGLE-PARTY TO MULTIPARTY POLITICS: THE CHANGING FACE OF ETHNICITY

Ethnicity was an integral part of Kenya's politics both during the single-party state and remained so after the country returned to multiparty democracy. Kenya's successive governments promoted tribalism and decried it at the same time—a factor that one might term the duplicitous nature of Kenyan political elites. What was the distinction between the manifestation of ethnicity during the single-party state and multiparty system? Posner suggested that the salience of a given dimension of ethnicity distinguished the single-party state from a multiparty state in some African countries. Posner argued that within a single-party state, people tended to identify themselves as 'members of small, localized groups based on tribe, sub-tribe or clan' (Posner 2007: 1303–1304). It was on the basis of these identities that Kenya's parliamentary elections were, in most cases, contested during the period of the single-party state. Posner observed that in a multiparty setting, political competition created incentives that forced people to identify themselves as large groups along religious, linguistic or regional bases (Posner 2007: 1304). The point Posner is making that the transition from a single-party state to multiparty politics shifted the locus of competition from the local constituency level to the national or Presidential one as voters identified themselves in terms of various dimensions of ethnicity as reflected by politicians (Posner 2007: 1307). In Kenya's multiparty political setting, ethnicity was a factor both in elections. Clan and ethnic differences featured during primaries in electing candidates for the county assembly, parliament, senate, women representative and governor. The sub-tribal differences were politicised among the Luhya and Kalenjin while clan differences influenced primaries and elections predominantly among the Luo, Maasai and Somali. In Presidential elections, these tribes tended to exhibit bloc voting.

Under the single party authoritarianism, ethnic delegations visited the President at the State House or rural home to pledge loyalty. The practice was witnessed under Uhuru Kenyatta, in office since 2013 until the time of writing, an indication of the endurance of the politics of autochthony that typified Jomo Kenyatta, Daniel arap Moi and Mwai Kibaki regimes. Multiparty politics saw a trend emerge in which ethnic Big Men organised public rallies within their ethnic homelands during which they were installed as tribal spokesmen. The ritual reinforced tribal politics by promoting bloc voting. It was also common for tribal barons to be installed as honorary elders in other communities across the country. In some cases, 'fake' elders performed the installation rituals. Later 'genuine' ones would then emerge and dismiss them and nullify the ceremony. Allegations of mercantilism in these rituals were rife. These rituals were meant to create the impression that the politician in question, although from a different tribe, had been co-opted as 'son of the soil' who the community had to accommodate and vote for as 'one of their own'. Politicians exploited it to overcome the othering autochthonous politics.

PERSONAL RULE

Although both the Kenyatta and Moi régimes were examples of personal rule, Moi's frenetic tours across the country and his penchant for giving 'instant' solutions to Kenyans' pressing challenges distinguished him not only as a neopatrimonial ruler but also as a demagogue. The distinction between the two régimes lay in the fact that Kenyatta was associated with the attainment of independence; thus, he did not have to contend with legitimacy issues, save in incidents of political assassinations. Besides Tom Mboya, other political murders in which the Kenyatta régime was implicated included Pio Gama Pinto 1965 and J.M. Kariuki who were assassinated in 1965 and 1975 respectively (Morton 1998: 22).[1] Pinto, a Kenyan of Goan ancestry, was a close ally of Oginga Odinga's and the theoretician behind Odinga's socialist leanings. Morton observed that his assassination was a precursor to Odinga's political woes (Morton 1998: 122–123). Moi had struggled against legitimacy issues not least because he was not widely regarded, particularly within Kenyatta's inner court, among the potential successors to Kenyatta (Ogot 1996: 187). The Kalenjin, his community, was lesser in number than the Kikuyu, but also less established in either the economy or the bureaucracy (Morton 1998). Upon ascendancy to power, Moi tried to make up for these setbacks through patronage that he disproportionately extended to fellow Kalenjin members and use of coercion to suppress dissent.

Moi began curving his presidency around 'a people's President' image. He preferred engaging people directly as opposed to going through his appointees. He had an interest in the details of government affairs not so much that he was efficient but that he was driven by paranoia and the need to facilitate the Kalenjin foothold in the economy. Bratton and van de Walle (1997: 61–62) suggested that in cases of personal rule, the ruler tries to ensure the stability of his system through distributing either material or financial favours to his followers who in effect are his clients (Bratton and van de Walle 1997: 61–62). They used the term 'neopatrimonialism' to refer to 'personal rule'. They described the neopatrimonial régime as one in which ruling is a right 'ascribed to a person rather than to an office, despite the official existence of a written Constitution. One individual (the strongman, "Big Man," or "supremo") often President for life, dominates the state apparatus and stands above its laws' (Bratton and van de Walle 1997: 62). The two scholars indicated that such a system is characterised by uncertainty for both the ruler and his followers thus the preoccupation with the efforts to gain financially and materially through 'access to various forms of illicit rents, prebends and petty corruption' (Bratton and van de Walle 1997: 61–62). Hyden used the term 'prebendalism' to refer to the relationship between the political decision-makers and their communities, where the benefits of office were shared. This is how he put it:

> Prebendalism refers to a practice, once prevalent in Europe, whereby public offices are competed for and then utilised for the personal benefit of office holders as well as their support group. This practice was pursued across Africa, but became particularly pronounced in countries such as Nigeria—the public revenue from oil provided an especially generous basis for dispensation of patronage (Hyden 2006: 64–65).

A régime in which personal rule prevails is not obliged to be responsive to the needs and wishes of the people as a whole, but rather to specific groups or constituencies. As shown before and will be demonstrated subsequently in the book, it was the political interests of the President and his close allies that mattered in Kenya rather than the welfare of the people. Despite the shift to multiparty politics, traces of personal rule persisted. Manifestations of personal rule under multiparty rule entailed appointments made on the basis of ethnic and personal loyalty to the President, failure to sanction those implicated in corruption and other egregious crimes because the President regarded them as dependable allies. Jackson and Rosberg pointed out that where personal rule prevailed, rulers had no regard for concepts such as 'the people', 'the public', 'the nation', 'the national interest' and 'public opinions' (Jackson and Rosberg 1984: 425).

Analysts hailed Kenya's competitive single-party elections that registered a high turnover of sitting MPs including members of the cabinet (Barkan 2009: 13; Jackson and Rosberg 1984: 440). However, this political competition ought to be read within the framework of personal rule. The President, in essence the patron, was beyond electoral challenge. The elections provided him with an opportunity to purge the system of disloyal clients and rehabilitate some of those he had previously jettisoned. The import of these elections had little to do with policy or programmes of action but the capacity to deploy patronage to buy loyalty through self help initiatives popularly referred to as *Harambee*-Kenyatta's clarion call. Jackson and Rosberg argued that there were no ideological differences among politicians within this system other than contestations for supremacy among the Big Men themselves (Jackson and Rosberg 1984: 436). In Kenya's single-party state, the President was not subjected to an electoral contest but elections were the occasion for him to ensure that he had leverage over the jockeying and jostling among his supporters and members of the inner court. Why would almost all politicians within a system of personal rule strive for the attention of the President? It is a matter of political and economic survival or damnation for a politician to either gain or lose the President's trust. The excerpt from Jackson and Rosberg below shows how critical it was in Africa to win the President's loyalty,

> In most African countries the political monopoly is a monopoly not only of power but also of wealth and status. Therefore to be deprived of membership in the ruling monopoly of African of an African country or to be restored to membership is to have one's life and fortune dramatically altered. For politicians everywhere the political wilderness is a lonely place; for African politicians it is also a misfortune. (Jackson and Rosberg 1984: 435)

Clientelism, then, was a significant aspect of personal rule. The political patron wielded authority through rewards he gave to his clients, this could be in terms of office or in prebends, or as van de Walle calls it, rent seeking (van de Walle, 1994, 133–134; Hyden 2006: 102). Odhiambo-Mbai pointed out that corruption thrived in a personal rule because through corruption, resources were illicitly mobilised to reward clients (Mbai-Odhiambo 2003: 65). van der Walle and other scholars understood rent seeking to be a system in which the ruler in concert with a group of allies run a political system from which they draw benefits referred to as prebends (van de Walle 1994: 133–134; Widner 1994: 53; Gyimah-Boadi 2007: 29). Under Kenya's single-party state, the country witnessed a quintessentially personal rule primarily because of lack of checks and balances on the executive. Moi appointed individuals to the cabinet and as heads of parastatals based on ethnicity and patronage just like Jomo Kenyatta although Kenyatta did not disregard competence entirely. Since these appointees were solely accountable to the President, Moi seldom sacked them despite cases of incompetence and corruption (Cohen 1995). Instead he shuffled them from one parastatal to another and the result was a string of non-performing and collapsed state corporations (Kanyinga 1998: 55).

Nyayo Era

Moi brought a lot of energy to the presidency and wasted no time in making himself popular as soon as he assumed power. His efforts to connect with people from all walks of life, especially the peasantry and lumpenproletariat, were reminiscent of a politician out to stamp his imprimatur on Kenya's politics. He had existed under Kenyatta's shadow since appointed Vice President in 1967. Moi's régime was popularly known as the *Nyayo*, Kiswahili for 'footsteps'.

> In his Presidential progress he would regularly swap his official Mercedes limousine for an old Volkswagen Kombi so that he could reach the more inhospitable regions of Kenya. He travelled from sunrise to sunset, spending nights under canvas, washing from a small basin and eating under the shade of a tree. In the first year of his presidency he visited more places and received more people than Kenyatta during his fifteen years as President. This peripatetic President sought to bring government back to the people, opening up administrative structures so that the public felt more comfortable in bringing their grievances to the state. On occasions when individuals spoke to him about their problems it was the President, rather than local

administrators, who relayed them back to Nairobi. Moi was proving himself to be a man of the people… (Morton 1998: 170)

Upon being sworn into office in 1978, Moi pledged continuity with the Kenyatta regime through *Nyayo nyayo* philosophy.[2] Katz stated that *Nyayoism*, the ideological variant of *Nyayo*, contained elements such as Christian morality, developmentalism, nationalism, anti-tribalism and African Socialism. However, he identified the oppressive side of *Nyayoism* that equated opposition to the régime as anti-*Nyayoism* (Katz 1985: 158). Throup and Hornsby pointed out that *Nyayoism* 'changed from Moi following Kenyatta to Kenyans following Moi' (Throup and Hornsby 1998: 38).

Throup and Hornsby observed that Moi ascended to power when economic times were difficult in Kenya. This context denied him the abundant state largesse that had been available to Kenyatta. They mentioned that at the time, international prices for coffee and tea, Kenya's main exports, had plummeted and the population had increased substantially (Throup and Hornsby 1998: 26). Ajulu averred that the régime resorted to plundering state coffers and dismantling the Kikuyu economic power base to be replaced by Moi's own (Ajulu 2002: 262–263). The *Nyayo* régime defied the rational-legal authority. Bratton and van de Walle defined the rational-legal authority as one in which 'the public sphere is carefully distinguished from the private sphere; written laws and bureaucratic institutions routinise the exercise of authority and protect individuals and their property from the whims of capricious leaders' (Bratton and van de Walle 1997: 62). In such a system, people's existence was precarious owing to lack of certainty vis-à-vis the decisions of the government. Personal rule was inherently an unequal system and some clients wielded disproportionate power compared to the positions they held within the patron-client network (Throup and Hornsby 1998: 45). These tended to be the most loyal clients of the patron. For instance, some cabinet ministers, KANU politicians from Moi's Baringo district, ethno-regional spokesmen and other party apparatchiks wielded more power disproportionately to the positions they occupied. Moi promoted *Nyayoism* as an embodiment of triple elements of 'peace, love and unity' through which he attempted to create a distinct régime.

Nyayoism succeeded *Harambee*. Kenyatta's rallying call was popularly known as the *Harambee* (pull together) régime. Nyong'o stated that the ideology of *Harambee* was a laissez-faire one that called on all the people, their social differences and positions in society notwithstanding to join forces and contribute to the country's development (Nyong'o 1989: 224). Kenyans had no connection with *Nyayoism* and as Throup and Hornsby observed, the citizenry identified with it because of the single-party authoritarianism and abandoned it once the country returned to multiparty politics (Throup and Hornsby 1998: 38). While power, Moi spoke about *Nyayo* in almost every speech, using it, as Khapoya and Morton suggest, to forge an image of the patriarch. He portrayed himself as a forgiving patriarch and statesman by pardoning and releasing political detainees whom Kenyatta had incarcerated (Khapoya 1988: 56; Morton 1998: 171).

THE POPULIST BIG MAN

In his early years in office, Moi portrayed himself as a benevolent leader. He introduced free milk for primary school children, abolished fees in primary schools, expressed his government's intention to fight against corruption and literally became the face of the government (Moi's speech on Jamhuri Day on 12 December 1978; *Daily Nation*, 24 December 2002). Morton, Moi's biographer, shows that there were distinct changes that came with the Moi régime like tackling inefficiency and corruption (Morton 1998: 168). However, these were nothing but statements of intent. Corruption and tardiness were some of the distinguishing features of the Moi régime because the régime hardly operated according to the rule of law and prized tribalism over meritocracy in bureaucratic appointments. As Morton observed, Moi may have given directives, but the government lacked the capacity to implement them (Morton 1998: 169).

Moi was given to making arbitrary roadside decisions since he was averse to record keeping. He communicated his directives orally either face to face or telephonically. This political behaviour showed how unaccountable the régime was. The logic was to deflect responsibility for excesses such as corruption to junior officers and make it difficult to be implicated in any malpractices under his régime once he left office. While in office, the President was immune from civil and criminal prosecution. Moi's long-serving former private secretary, Watson Murigo, recalled his days with him. 'When he was Vice president, I somehow managed to have him put in writing matters that I suspected might raise questions in future. I was not so lucky when he became President' (*Daily Nation*, 24

December 2002). Moi was known for making decisions on the spur of the moment during his numerous tours around the country. He would announce 'the building of a road here and a health centre there, all out of the blue' (*Daily Nation*, 24 December 2002: 10) and ordered the bureaucrats who accompanied him to implement the directives immediately. The financial and logistical implications of these directives did not matter.

Most of the roadside directives Moi made had economic implications. In 1979, without what a newspaper pullout called 'any research or professional advice', Moi ordered the introduction of primary school milk. However, while in primary school, this author invariably witnessed teachers hoarding the milk, indicative of the corroding effect of mendacity, impunity, and mistrust that hallmarked Moi's rule. In 1985, he phased out the 7-4-2-3 education system and replaced it with the 8-4-4 one (*Daily Nation*, 24 December 2002: 8; Moi's Speech on 15 Anniversary of the Kenya Independence Celebrations, on Tuesday 12 December 1978: 178). The 8-4-4 education system was bedevilled by numerous challenges such as inadequate facilities, a wide teacher–student ratio owing to insufficient teachers, workload for students and overemphasis on passing examinations hence rote learning at the expense of critical thinking. The opposition had cited the education system as part of reform required to jump-start the country's progressive transformation but had reneged on it after coming into power in 2002. However, in 2017, the government had started phasing out the 8-4-4 system to be replaced by the 2-6-3-3 one (Citizen Digital 30 January 2017). Moreover in 1986 Moi instructed government departments through the University of Nairobi to produce what he called a '*Nyayo* car' ostensibly to showcase Kenya's scientific and technological sophistication (Jamhuri Day Speech, 12 December 1988). Morton mentioned other ad hoc ventures that turned into white elephants all bearing the *Nyayo* imprint such as *Nyayo* buses, *Nyayo* tea zones and *Nyayo* hospital wards (Morton 1998: 206–209). All of them collapsed after costing enormous amounts of money that no one could account for. Morton cited the quixotic *Nyayo* car launched in 1990 that foundered after the production of only three cars depleting the public coffers of millions of Kenya shillings (Morton 1998: 207).

Moi involved himself in populist gestures described above because he lacked a transformational agenda hence the knack for wonder or grandiose projects. What often passed for government policy was not arrived at through a consultative and evidence-based process. Moi was driven by the urge to attract crowds, sustain patronage networks and maintain the patriarchal image of *Baba wa Taifa* (Father of the Nation) who traversed the country doling out goodies to impoverished communities. He directly engaged his followers by bypassing regional politicians. By doing so, he portrayed these politicians and bureaucrats as inefficient and prebendary misers whom his followers had to hold responsible for their plight. The propensity among pundits, and the media to blame the President's advisers and other minions for the President's flaws, state excesses, and an unresponsive government were pervasive in Kenya's political discourse. It highlighted self-censorship, and deference to the executive, specifically to the person of the president. Critically, it underscored the inability to appreciate leadership on the one hand and accountability and responsibility on the other. Disregard for consultation, the intrusion of the régime leader in all aspects of Kenyans' lives and the gifts he gave out to clients and followers were attributes reminiscent of a régime in which citizens were more like subjects at the beck and call of the patriarch. However, behind these avuncular gestures lay an iron-fisted régime that did not brook dissent and was distrustful of even supposedly close allies. Moi was a Janus-faced politician as attested to by Philip Mbithi, an academic turned bureaucrat who, as Head of Civil Service and Secretary to the Cabinet, was regarded as one of Moi's trusted lieutenants.

> I found President Moi to be the best case study in dual-personality. He could be so friendly yet so ruthless...On my last day in the Civil Service, President Moi called me very early in the morning to tell me that I should go to State House so that we could finalise on some changes he wanted to make in the Government. As we parted, the President gave no hint that he had any problem with my work. Then the shock. I heard of my sacking over the 1 pm news. After a moment of reflection, I decided not to take up the job in Arusha—Prof Philip Mbithi (*Daily Nation*, 24 December 2002).

THE CULTURE OF HANDOUTS

Moi liberally gave out wads of notes to indebted politicians and civil servants (*Daily Nation*, 24 December 2002). Almost the entire state apparatus owed him loyalty. He also extended this generosity to crowds that often awaited him and his entourage by the roadside and airstrips in far-flung parts of the country as he took 'the presidency to the people of the country' (*The Weekly Review*, 9 December 1988: 26–27). This used to trigger stampedes as people scrambled for the money flung at them. Moi gave out money to university students as well so much that by the time students completed their undergraduate studies, some of them had been inducted into the patronage networks. In 2000, this author witnessed Moi giving out wads of money to university students during the burial of a cabinet Minister, Francis Lotodo, in West Pokot, Rift Valley region. To the Pokot tribe, Lotodo was a hero who stridently stood by the marginalised tribe but to his detractors, he was a war monger and tribal warlord who encouraged cattle rustling and incitement to violence pitting the Pokot against the neighbouring tribes especially the Marakwet. Lotodo had been jailed twice and was at some point expelled from KANU (*Daily Nation* 1 December 2011). He personified impunity and virulent tribalism that characterised the Moi regime.[3] Moi was known to buy bananas, roast or boiled maize and vegetables from roadside traders and distribute these among the gathered crowd. It was one way of trying to show that the Presidency was 'accessible'. Moi's 'generosity' was legendary during *Harambee* (open-air fund raising gatherings for community projects) that became highly politicised. He gave money to clients to donate on his behalf during *Harambee* meetings that he could not attend. Some analysts argued that *Harambee*[4] was a conduit through which the Moi régime bribed voters with money illicitly obtained from the public coffers (Lynch 2006: 243; Mwangi 2008: 271–273). *Harambee* meetings were not meant to alleviate poverty and promote construction of projects such as schools and health centres, Moi's ostensible reasons for promoting them. They pandered to what Chabal and Daloz referred to as 'wonderment', in which, in a particular clientelistic network, it was politically logical '…to flaunt one's substance, to spend abundantly and instantly, without worrying about the future' (Chabal and Daloz 1999: 107). Moi's patronage networks gifted Kenya's political parlance with the word 'handouts' that referred to the act of a patron giving out money to allies and supporters to either buy or sustain their loyalty.

Moi's propensity to give out money either by the roadside or during *Harambee* meetings was in tandem with his notion that the public could only be guaranteed public goods if they supported KANU. This use of the state largesse to placate renegades and maintain loyal clients and punish dissent was not only indicative of the abuse of state resources for partisan politics but also exposed the personal character of the Presidential rule under Moi that survived his regime. Misuse of state resources for partisan politics was illegal as per the 2010 Constitution and even before but impunity ensured that it remained integral to Kenya's political culture. This behaviour was a legacy of Moi's politicisation and personalisation of the concept of 'development'. He read Kenya's politics through a Manichean lens that implied that support and loyalty for himself and KANU would translate into improved economic and political fortunes of politicians and ethnic groups deemed to be loyal while disloyalty and dissent elicited marginalisation and political ostracism that spelt economic and political woes to the victims. The régime's interpretation of 'development' meant loyal politicians being appointed to the cabinet and government bureaucracy to become part of 'the redistributive system' (Diang'a 2002: 74). Khapoya observed that Moi's visibility particularly in far-flung rural areas largely demystified the institution of the presidency since he presented himself as an accessible leader, unlike his predecessor who was almost a recluse. Khapoya attributed Kenyatta's aversion to travel not simply to old age but also to the anim0osity from certain communities, particularly the Luo (Khapoya 1980). Through his constant travels to rural areas, Moi intended to make the masses feel closer to the presidency.

THE DEFT MANIPULATION OF ETHNICITY

Moi railed against ethnicity and repeatedly preached coexistence among Kenya's ethnic groups under his slogan of 'peace, love and unity'. He went further and tried to 'abolish' tribalism through 'closing down institutions which in the past have had some tribal origin or flavour' (Moi's Speech on Kenyatta Day, 20 October 1980; Moi's Jamhuri Day Speech, 12 December 1980). The Attorney General, Charles Njonjo, forced clubs and organisations whose names were deemed to propagate divisive tribalism to change to ethnically neutral ones. Subsequently, Abaluhya Football Club and Luo Union Football Club (later Luo United Football Club) switched to All Footballers' Confederation Sports Club Leopards (simply AFC Leopards) and Reunion respectively. Ironically, Moi astutely exploited ethnicity to stay in power which exposed the outlawing of tribal entities as the beginning of the construction of a one party mono-lith under the ruse of building a sense of nationhood among Kenyans. Upon coming into power in 1978, Moi introduced into Kenya's politi-cal lexicon what the media referred to as the 'provincial strategy' or 'regional representation formula for the executive' (*The Weekly Review*, 2 December 1988: 4). The strategy entailed distributing KANU national positions on an ethno-regional basis. The approach defined his 24-year rule and even major political parties that emerged during the multiparty era were guided by this strategy in electing, or rather selecting, national office bearers. Moi would sack a cabinet minister and replace him with a fellow tribesman to retain the support of the community in question. Moi did not have a broad ethnic base like Kenyatta. He came from the Tugen community, one of the smallest sub-tribes within the wider Kalenjin ethnic group. The Kalenjin had internal divisions. Morton men-tioned that in the 1960s, there were fears among the Kalenjin sub-tribes, such as Moi's Tugen, that the bigger ones such as the Nandi and Kipsigis would dominate and subordinate them politically (Morton 1998: 120). These suspicions ceased when Moi became President because almost the entire Kalenjin community supported him and regarded his régime as a communal entity just as the Kikuyu had done under Kenyatta.

THE PERSONALITY CULT

The strongman, usually the President, occupies the centre of political life. Front and centre stage, he is the centrifugal force around which all else revolves. Not only the ceremonial head of state, the President is also the chief political, military and cultural figure: head of government, com-mander-in-chief of the armed forces, head of governing party (if there is one) and even chancellor of the local university. His aim is typical to iden-tify his person with the 'nation'. His physical self is omnipresent: ...picture plastered on public walls, billboards and even private homes. His portrait also adorns stamps, coins, paper money and even T-shirts and buttons often distributed to party 'faithful'. Schools, hospitals, streets, markets, air-ports and stadiums are named after him. The mass media herald his every word and action, no matter how insignificant (Sandbrook 1985: 90).

Kenyatta and Moi both tried to develop a strong cult of personality, linking their image to that of the nation's destiny. Their images and names loomed large in both public and private facets of the lives of Kenyans. Kenyans attended schools and universities named after them, got treated in hospitals named after them, used money bearing their images, walked and drove along roads named after them, took off and landed in airports bearing their names, had their portraits hung in public offices, schools and other institutions of learning, and even in homes. While they cultivated strong personality cults, where their lives were inextricably intertwined with the destiny of Kenya, there were, however, differences between their styles of rule. Initially, the Kenyatta régime relied on the alliance between the Luo and Kikuyu, but after the fall out between them, Kenyatta's support was restricted to the Kikuyu (*The Weekly Review*, 8 April 1988: 5). Moi, on the other hand, reached out to a broader based ethnic alliance for demographic reasons (*The Weekly Review*, 9 December 1988: 26–27). He began to solidify his rule by receiving ethnic delegations either at the State House or at his Kabarak home in Nakuru, Rift Valley region. Led by ethno-regional Big Men, these delegations deluged Moi with pledges of loyalty in much the same vein as occurred in Kenyatta's time (Mutua 2009: 23; Holmquist and Ford 1994: 11). These pledges took ritualistic form, in that they portrayed Moi as ordained to rule Kenya (Haugerud 1995).

It amounted to political heresy and a deficit of loyalty for politicians to appear unenthusiastic with regard to these exhibitions of showmanship and sycophancy. Indeed, it could easily imperil one's political career. Morton pointed out that Moi received delegations from different parts of the country during the interregnum following Kenyatta's death that affirmed their loyalty to him (Morton 1998: 167). He swiftly exploited the practice to stamp his authority on the presidency at a time when some Kikuyu politicians opposed his succeeding Kenyatta. Moses Mudavadi, a powerful Luhya Big Man, was the only other politician to receive delegations at his Mululu rural home in Western Province. Morton showed that as a schools inspector in the Rift Valley, Mudavadi had influenced Moi's promotion to headmaster. As a Luhya in a predominantly Kalenjin inhabited region, he declined nomination and urged Moi to enter the Legislative Council (Legco) in 1955 as the Rift Valley representative. Mudavadi assured Moi, who was reluctant to join politics, that he would not lose any benefits in case he did not like it in the Legco and decided to go back to teaching and so Moi seemed indebted to him (Morton 1998: 73–74). The cult of personality essentially remained the pillar of the Moi régime particularly in the 1980s and helped to entrench him in power. By the 1980s, so entrenched in power was Moi that KANU supporters would police one another which meant that Moi had little reason to worry about the possibility of disgruntled politicians plotting against him. In the event that a regional Big Man dissented, Moi would sponsor a rival from the same region and ethnic group. The aim was to check the emergence of alternative power bases. Despite Moi's strong control over KANU, however, there were voices of dissent that later snowballed into an indomitable agitation for multiparty politics.

Moi exploited song and dance to carve the omnipresent image. He set up the Presidential Music Commission whose brief was to coordinate the composition of praise songs. In later years, the media likened the role of music under Moi to a situation in communist régimes in which music was used to advance sycophancy (*Daily Nation*, 24 December 2002: 12). Until the early 1990s, the state-owned radio station, Voice of Kenya (VoK) later renamed Kenya Broadcasting Corporation (KBC) was the only one in the country, and it continuously played songs in praise of Moi, erroneously referred to as 'patriotic songs'. The intention was to indoctrinate the listenership to ensure that Moi was constantly in the imagination of Kenyans. In this case, the régime conflated patriotism with loyalty to Moi and sycophancy. Primary school pupils and high school students had to pledge loyalty to Moi by singing 'The Loyalty Pledge' during assembly, a form of indoctrination to encourage obeisance to Moi and lull critical minds among young Kenyans. Khapoya showed that the régime did not hesitate to punish anyone who did not respect these songs. He cited a case of a Kikuyu politician, Kimani wa Nyoike, who was suspended from KANU for a year for condoning the singing of a song '*Tawala*, Kenya, *Tawala*' (Swahili for 'rule') in his own name while it had been composed to exclusively praise the 'able leadership of the President' (Khapoya 1988: 61).

Moi exercised all power to the exclusion of everyone else in his government. Moi, as the President, had the prerogative to appoint the Vice President. Thus, the appointee served entirely at his pleasure and remained beholden to Moi. He could casually appoint and dismiss the holder as he wished (*Daily Nation*, 24 December 2002). The entire government revolved around him, and he did not delegate. The

2010 Constitution replaced the title 'Vice President' with the 'Deputy President'. This was significant because the Constitution spelled out the functions of the Deputy President reserved for a running mate of the candidate who emerged victorious during presidential elections. The Deputy President is the principal assistant of the President. He/she performs functions of the President in the absence of the latter. Significantly, he/she draws authority from the Constitution unlike previously. In the event the incumbent President either died in office or could not continue holding office for reasons stipulated in the Constitution, the Deputy President assumed office until the end of the term (Republic of Kenya 2010: 92). The 2010 Constitution did not envisage the Deputy President as a lackey of the President. In the multiparty period, Moi exploited the prerogative to appoint the Vice President to consolidate support along ethnic lines. He astutely dangled the post to multiple tribes during the 1997 election campaigns in exchange for political support. The elections marked his second and final term in office and so it was assumed that whoever Moi appointed his vice would be the heir apparent. The irony was that the Vice President occupied an office that, in principle, was the second most powerful in the land yet the occupant had no political clout or a power base and was dwarfed by Moi's larger than life political shadow.

The Weekly Review observed that the Vice President had some balancing act to perform in that Moi expected him not to betray any ambition by cultivating support countrywide neither did he expect him to act narrowly by confining himself to his region alone (The Weekly Review, 22 July 1988: 4–7). Morton showed that Kenyatta and his close allies, predominantly fellow Kikuyu tribesmen and others drawn from the cousinage tribes of Meru and Embu under the GEMA constellation, treated Moi with disdain (Morton 1998: 129). Arguably, Oginga Odinga remained the only influential Vice President in Kenya's political history who had a solid political constituency, conviction, and so challenged Jomo Kenyatta. The 2010 Constitution sought to dignify the office of the Deputy President in the sense that the occupier would no longer be a mere appendage of the President. The President could not sack the Deputy President as had been the case previously. In essence, the Deputy President was the quintessential second in command and heir apparent. William Ruto, the first Deputy President under the 2010 Constitution, was also influential by dint of the Constitution and also as a Kalenjin ethno-regional Big Man without whose support Uhuru Kenyatta could not have easily risen to power in 2013.

THE ETHNICISATION OF KENYA'S EDUCATION SYSTEM

In the 1980s, Moi expanded education opportunities by building schools by means of the *Harambee* system and granted charters to more universities. At the same time, the régime encouraged the formation of ethnic associations among students to fragment them. The intention was to prevent the emergence of a pan-Kenyan identity among university students. Klopp and Orina showed how these student associations were incorporated into the KANU patronage system on Moi's orders. They also showed that politicians, academics and civil servants served as patrons of these associations to underscore how politically significant these associations were (Klopp and Orina 2002: 53). They were springboards to student and national politics. Often riots broke out among university students over deadlocked student elections owing to tribalism. As such, the youth were as ethnically conscious as the elderly.

The flipside of expansion of education opportunities especially to areas and communities that had lagged behind in access to education was that it encouraged ethnic balkanisation because of a quota rule. In principle, the quota rule was meant to ensure that all communities accessed quality education. National schools, some of the best but just a handful and concentrated in Nairobi and Central Provinces, had to enrol students from all parts of the country, although still students from the most populous tribes dominated. This was a form of affirmative action or 'positive discrimination' according to Morton. It gave a chance to students from marginalised areas to gain admission in the best schools in the country. Thus it attempted 'to create a greater equality of opportunity so that every tribe, every community might have the chance to play a role in society by improving its position' (Morton 1998: 208).

There was a quota rule or '85% policy' that stipulated that this percentage of students attending the best schools in a province must come from the local community (Morton 1998: 209). The other downside of the quota rule was that most students grew up without having interacted with fellow youth from other tribes and by the time they met, either at the university or at the work place, certain perceptions and stereotypes would have already calcified (*Daily Nation*, 25 October 2010). However, interaction among youth per se could not enable national cohesion. Equity, justice, the rule of law and inclusive politics were among factors that promoted a sense of nationhood. Although Moi attempted to spread education to most parts of the country on the premise of reducing ethno-regional inequalities, critics faulted him for perpetrating inequalities, since most of the schools he helped build were concentrated in his native Rift Valley Province (*Daily Nation*, 24 December 2002: 8). Moi was also criticised for ignoring quality because he did not ensure that quality and standards were maintained. There was a shortage of qualified teachers, and educational facilities across the board at both high school and university levels, and the recruitment of head teachers and vice chancellors was compromised since it was based on political connections, tribalism and cronyism. There was also an element of personality cult, because most of the schools were named after him (*Daily Nation*, 24 December 2002: 8). Moi's successor, Mwai Kibaki, (2002–2013) arbitrarily issued charters to middle level colleges exponentially raising the total number of universities in the country to almost 40. The move was laudable in the sense that it potentially created more opportunities for access to higher education to Kenyans. However, these institutions suffered from similar challenges as those that afflicted universities that Moi set up the prominent being lack of infrastructure, personnel and the persistence of ethnicity given that most of these universities were created for political and ethnic considerations and did not develop organically and so the staff were almost exclusively hired from the local ethnic group in breach of the Constitution that stipulated ethnic diversity in recruitment to the state institutions to reflect 'the face of Kenya' (*Daily Nation*, 17 May 2010).

The effects of Moi's system of personal rule were likely to undermine the state for generations to come as they reproduced themselves through the education sector. It was one thing to interfere with political offices but an insidious one to politicise the education system. The tribal politics preponderant in Kenya's bureaucracy, politics and other sectors of the society deepened once Moi interfered with the educational affairs. Instead of Kenya's educational institutions aiding in the promotion of a sense of nationhood and the designing of a development vision, they were instrumental in the incubation and propagation of ethnic politics. How Kenyans were socialised both at home and in such institutions accounted for ethnic loyalty that had militated against social, economic and political transformation in the multiparty politics. Kenya's education sector stood in need of comprehensive reform to rectify the effects of the single-party legacy. This legacy had ensured that the education sector remained politicised. Kenyan politicians pursued self-serving ends masked under tribalism and had been lackadaisical in addressing educational issues directly related to the country's posterity and development agenda. The Kibaki régime had not accorded the education sector the attention it deserved. His régime responded to the problem of insufficient places in national schools for qualified students transitioning from primary schools by elevating more high schools to national school. Some of the 'upgraded' schools had been built through the efforts and resources of local communities while the missionaries established others. Consequently, most parents from the local communities could not afford the prohibitive fees that came with the national school status. The Kibaki government, in accordance with the NARC campaign pledge, implemented universal primary education in 2003 which meant that there would be an exponential increase in pupils graduating from primary school eight years later and beyond. This necessitated adequate preparations to ensure promotion rates into high school. The government failed to anticipate and address this challenge hence the crisis. Consistent with Moi's knack for whimsical decisions, Kibaki responded knee jerk style and proffered piecemeal and ephemeral solutions.

LAND AND VIOLENCE IN THE RIFT VALLEY REGION

Land became a cause of political instability in the multiparty Kenya because the Jomo Kenyatta, Daniel arap Moi, Mwai Kibaki and Uhuru Kenyatta régimes had exploited it for the benefit of these individuals and their supporters. As a result, there was no political will to address the land question yet land reform was a key to Kenya's political stability. Throughout Kenya's multiparty period, inter-ethnic violence was a constant in Kenya's Rift Valley region. It pitted 'aboriginal' tribes against 'interlopers'. Although these conflicts were rooted in the controversial land redistribution programme soon after independence, cynical politicians especially under the Moi rule, exploited genuine grievances for self-serving political and economic ends with catastrophic consequences. Invariably, the state instigated violence led to mass displacements, destruction of property and loss of lives in the lead up to, during and after elections. Kibaki set up the commission of inquiry into the illegal and irregular allocation of public land known as the Ndung'u commission whose report he received in 2004. The report implicated prominent individuals in the Kenyatta, Moi, Kibaki and Uhuru Kenyatta régimes in illicit acquisition of public land. The government did not act on its recommendations. This unprecedented report contained recommendations which, if implemented, would resolve the endemic land issue in Kenya's historiography (Republic of Kenya 2004).

In the 1970s, the Jomo Kenyatta régime resettled some members of the Kikuyu tribe in the Rift Valley region from Central region. Moi, who at the time was the Vice President, did not oppose this resettlement. Jean Marie Seroney was among Kalenjin politicians who interpreted Moi's elevation to the Vice Presidency in 1966 as a calculated move by Kenyatta to placate the Kalenjin community as the Kikuyu occupied the land previously occupied by British settlers (Morton 1998: 131 133). The Central region, home of the Kikuyu community, had faced the problem of land scarcity ever since the colonial period. The expropriation of land from the Kikuyu peasantry by Kenyatta and fellow Kikuyu elite exacerbated the challenge. Morton observed that owing to their economic, traditional, political and numerical advantage, the Kikuyu were able to access land from the departing British settlers in the Rift Valley. Morton suggested that unlike the Maasai and Kalenjin, traditionally the Kikuyu valued land but not animals and recognised individual land ownership (Morton 1998: 132). What Morton says here has to be nuanced. The Maasai and Kalenjin valued animals as well as land because without land for grazing, pastoralism as an economic activity is impossible to practise. The Maasai considered most of the land in the Rift Valley region as their heritage that the British settlers had dispossessed them through coercive treaties and were equally resentful of further dispossession by the post-colonial governments (Kantai 2007: 109; OMCT 2008: 15). Ethnic resentment elicited by the land issue in the Rift Valley region lingered more than 50 years after independence as attested to in the observation by one of my respondents:

> Kenyatta used Moi to acquire land for Kikuyu so that the Kenyatta family could acquire land in Kiambu. The Kalenjin were not consulted and so regard the Kikuyu as foreigners. The matter has not been addressed as it should be. Kalenjins should accept that they cannot live together with foreigners who should think about going back to their ancestral Province if there is space. There are large chunks of land in Central Province owned by Kenyatta. (Interview, Onyango, January 25, 2009)

The ethnic manner in which land transactions in the Rift Valley Province were conducted immediately after independence bolstered the grievances of the Kalenjin who were opposed to what Morton called the 'take over' of their land. Morton showed that the land transactions were conducted almost exclusively by the Kikuyu who specifically exploited the Kenyatta incumbency to transfer land from the British settlers into their companies. The people crucial to the conclusion of these transactions, which included bank managers who signed loans, lawyers who negotiated the deals and owners of the land-buying companies, were Kikuyu (Morton 1998: 132–133). These factors convinced the Kalenjin to view the whole process as ethnically skewed in favour of the Kikuyu.

Kagwanja, Southall and research by the Humanitarian Policy Group showed that the Kikuyu elite had grabbed land in Central region and decided to resettle the dispossessed peasant Kikuyu in other regions as a way of solving the landlessness problem in the community (Kagwanja 2009: 374; Kagwanja and Southall 2009: 269; Humanitarian Policy Group 2008: 3–4). The host communities such as the Kalenjin resented this action, and thus the seeds of cyclic ethnic strife that Kenya subsequently faced under multiparty politics were sown not long after independence. Oucho pointed out that Kenyatta allocated land to the Kikuyu in the Coast region as well (Oucho 2010: 511). An expose in *The Standard* newspaper suggested that Kenya's three successive Presidents had aggravated the land question across the country through greed, avarice and impunity. The exposé showed that the Kenyatta, Moi and Kibaki families in, that order, owned the largest chunks of land in Kenya, closely followed by multinational companies. According to the expose, the Kenyatta family owned 500,000 acres of land. This was equivalent to the size of formerly Nyanza Province (*The Standard*, 1 October 2004). This disproportionate concentration of land among these political families in effect denied many Kenyans access to land and condemned them to being squatters. *The Standard* newspaper article revealed that of Kenya's 17.3% arable land, 20% of Kenya's 40 million people owned more than half of it. The article further showed that 13% of the population were absolutely landless while 67% owned less than an acre per person (*The Standard* October 1, 2004). According to Oucho, Kenyatta's frequent 'working holidays' in Nakuru and Mombasa, major towns in the Rift Valley and Coast regions, respectively, were meant to ensure allocation of land 'to his kinsmen who were supposedly landless and had fought for Kenya's independence under the banner of Mau Mau and, therefore, deserved free land' (Oucho 2010: 511). As such, Kenya's successive governments had to contend with a conflict of interest regarding the emotive land issue.

The land question and the pervasive sense of rapacity under Jomo Kenyatta contributed to the fallout between Kenyatta and his supporters on the one hand and Oginga Odinga and his on the other. Odinga and his allies opposed this acquisitive behaviour that they opposed as being at variance with the spirit of the struggle for independence (Morton 1998: 121). While the land question split Kenya's politicians, Kenyatta publicly upbraided Bildad Kaggia, Odinga's close ally, through an infamous speech dubbed 'What Have You Done for Yourself Kaggia?' In this speech, Kenyatta openly supported the illicit accumulation of wealth by the political elite and wondered why Kaggia was concerned with inequitable redistribution of national resources while fellow politicians were amassing property such as land.

> We were together with Paul Ngei in jail. If you go to Ngei's home, he has planted a lot of coffee and other crops. What have you done for yourself? If you go to Kubai's home, he has a big house and has a nice shamba (*land*).[4] Kaggia, what have you done for yourself? We were together with Kungu Karumba in jail now he is running his own buses. What have you done for yourself? (Mazrui 1967: 234)

Ochieng' pointed out that Kaggia argued for a land policy that would be in the best interest of the economy, the landless and the poor but he faced opposition from Kenyatta and his allies. He also advocated a social welfare state in which there was provision of free medical care and free education (Ochieng' 1996: 94–95). Kaggia was among the few Kikuyu and Kenyan politicians whose political thinking and ethos went against the politics of accumulation and ethnicity. He was unpopular among his fellow Kikuyu politicians who taunted him not only because he refused to exploit his ethnicity to enrich himself but also for associating with Odinga whom the Kikuyu detractors disparaged for being uncircumcised. Kaggia was frustrated into resigning from the government in 1966 (Ochieng' 1996: 95). Unlike most of the first-generation Kikuyu politicians, he died a poor man. In comparison with most of Kenya's avaricious politicians, Kaggia's modest lifestyle was an aberration. The link between politics and wealth that Kaggia and his ilk decried had embedded itself in Kenya's body politic and condemned morality, principles, and ethical conduct to the margins. It had become difficult to address corruption in the country because of a perverted notion among Kenya's politicians and government bureaucrats that there was nothing improper in misappropriating *mali ya umma* (public property). It was for this reason that since independence in 1963 to date, no cabinet minister or any other senior government official had ever been convicted for corruption despite grand graft being the leitmotif of Kenya's successive governments. Low ranking officials had been arraigned in court as a way of calming the public ire and shielding their seniors from prosecution. These were the fall guys, as it were. Neither have proceeds of corruption and assets acquired corruptly been confiscated from the corrupt and forfeited to the state. Kenya's successive Presidents and senior government officials seemed to be more interested in the privileges and prestige attendant to power but eschewed taking responsibility for their decisions expected of those who held public office. They were detached from the plight of the populace. The maxim that the higher the office, the greater the responsibility and equally the higher the level of accountability, was nonexistent in this polity.

CONCLUSION

The *Nyayo* era was basically a system of personal rule that was a continuation from Kenyatta. Moi adroitly exploited tribalism to maintain power but schizophrenically denounced it publicly. Tribalism was the anchor of Moi's regime. The Moi régime was quintessentially a neopatrimonial Big Man one that had no regard for written laws. In this régime, loyalty counted more than meritocracy and professionalism. Moi's authoritarian style was both his strength and his weakness. It enabled him to suppress dissent but swelled the ranks of embittered opponents who in tandem with foreign actors pushed for multiparty politics. His deft manipulation of ethnic loyalties through regional Big Men accorded the régime some semblance of stability and a veneer of ethnic inclusivity but fomented tribal animosity that boiled over once the country returned to political pluralism. It was odd for Moi's clients to purport to 'eat'—benefit from state largesse—on behalf of their respective tribes. The violence that engulfed the country under multiparty democracy could be attributed to a sense of uncertainty that enveloped Moi and his cohorts used to operating in a political atmosphere with little or no challenge at all. Having been confined to the political wilderness for years through suppression, excluded tribes staked claim on the state but met violent resistance. Personal rule had deleterious effects on Kenya's social fabric and body politic. It entrenched tribalism, set forth the practice of pseudo competitive politics through the form that elections took, hobbled independent institutions crucial in a democracy, such as the judiciary and parliament, institutionalised corruption and violence and disregarded merit in employment and appointment of state officials. Insidiously, Moi corroded the education system by turning universities into incubators of ethnic bigotry which spectacularly defeated the role and relevance if these institutions in designing political ethos attuned to Kenya's diversity. Moi, like his predecessor and successors, was a political creature of land injustices and therefore lacked the political will to redress the pressing land challenge at the centre of Kenya's conflict prone multiparty politics. The inability to professionalise the bureaucracy under Jomo Kenyatta, Daniel arap Moi, Mwai Kibaki and Uhuru Kenyatta ensured that loyalty was accorded the person of the President but not the state. Tribalism became the bulwark for these errant state officials because it was the basis on which they were appointed and retained their positions. They invoked tribe to plead victimhood when asked to account and take responsibility. Although Moi left office in 2002, the characteristics of single-party rule such as corruption, tribal-based politics, impunity and arbitrary rule remained a powerful legacy in the years that followed. A shift to rational-legal approach to politics as opposed to spoils politics was the only one that guaranteed Kenya political stability.

NOTES

1. For an analysis of political assassinations in post-colonial Kenya, see Musila (2015: 33–48).
2. Moi's *nyayo* philosophy was based on 'peace, love and unity'. It was, however, dismissed by critics as a mere slogan used to propagate Moi's populism. Had Moi implemented his interpretation of *Nyayo* as captured in his speech to the nation in 1981, he would have guided Kenya to social economic and political progress. On paper, *Nyayo* was meant to guide the country in forging a sense of nationhood (President Moi Speech on Madaraka Day 1981: 83).
3. According to a survey, Kenyan youth fell short on integrity, "50% believe it doesn't matter how one makes money as long as one does not end up in jail; 47% admire those who make money through hook or crook, (including hustling); 30% believe corruption is profitable; 73% are afraid to stand

up for what is right for fear of retribution; only 40% strongly believe that it is important to pay taxes. 35% of the youth would readily take or give a bribe" (Awiti, A O and Scott, B. 2016).
4. Kenyatta downplayed the influence of tribalism in Kenya's body politic and cited *Harambee* as the antidote to tribalism. In his words: 'The people have destroyed tribalism through the unity and hard work which give living expression to the *Harambee* spirit of one united and progressive country' (President Kenyatta's speech on Jamhuri Day, 12 December 1969: 150). But there was a chasm between lofty rhetoric and the reality of a tribalised state and society.
5. My clarification.

REFERENCES

Books & Book Chapters

Barkan, J. 2009. African Legislature and the "Third Wave" of Democratisation. In *Legislative Power in Emerging African Democracies*, ed. J. Barkan. London: Lynne Rienner Publishers.

Bratton, M., and N. van de Walle. 1997. *Democratic Experiments in Africa. Régime Transitions in Comparative Perspective*. Cambridge: Cambridge University Press.

Chabal, P., and J. Daloz. 1999. *Africa Works Disorder as Political Instrument*. Oxford: James Currey.

Diang'a, J. 2002. *Kenya 1982 the Attempted Coup the Consequences of a Single-Party Dictatorship*. London: Pen Press Publishers.

Gyimah-Boadi, E. 2007. Political Parties, Elections and Patronage: Random Thoughts on Neo-Patrimonialism and African Democratiztion. In *Votes, Money and Violence Political Parties and Elections in Sub-Saharan Africa*, ed. M. Basedau, G. Erdmann, and A. Mehler. Scottsville, South Africa: University of Kwazulu-Natal Press.

Haugeraud, A. 1995. *The Culture of Politics in Modern Kenya*. Cambridge: Cambridge University Press.

Hyden, G. 2006. *African Politics in Comparative Perspective*. New York: Cambridge University Press.

Kanyinga, K. 1998. Contestation over Political Space: The State and Demobilisation of Opposition Politics in Kenya. In *The Politics of Opposition in Contemporary Africa*, ed. O.A. Olukoshi. Nordiska Afrikainstitutet: Uppsala.

Morton, A. 1998. *Moi the Making of an African Statesman*. London: Michael O'Mara Books.

Musila, G. 2015. *A Death Retold in Truth and Humour: Kenya Britain and the Julie Ward Murder*. New York: James Curry.

Mutua, M. 2009. *Kenya's Quest for Democracy: Taming the Leviathan*. London: Lynne Rienner Publishing.

Ogot, B.A. 1996. The Politics of Populism. In *Decolonisation and Independence in Kenya*, ed. B.A. Ogot and W.R. Ochieng. Nairobi: East African Educational Publishers.

Odhiambo-Mbai, C. 2003. The Rise and Fall of Autocratic State in Kenya. In *The Politics of Transition in Kenya from KANU to NARC*, ed. W. Oyugi, P. Wanyande, and C. Odhiambo-Mbai. Nairobi: Heinrich Boll Foundation.

Ochieng, W. 1996. Structural and Political Changes. In *Decolonization and Independence in Kenya*, ed. B.A. Ogot, and W.R. Ochieng. London: James Currey.

Oucho, J. 2010. Undercurrents of Post-Election Violence in Kenya: Issues in the Long-Term Agenda. In *Tensions and Reversals in Democratic Transitions*, ed. K. Kanyinga, and D. Okello. Nairobi: Society for International Development and Institute for Development Studies-University of Nairobi.

Sandbrook, R. 1985. *The Politics of Africa's Economic Stagnation*. Cambridge: University Press Cambridge.

Throup, D., and C. Hornsby. 1998. *Multiparty Politics in Kenya*. Oxford: James Currey.

Van de Walle, N. 1994. Neopatrimonialsim and Democracy in Africa with an Illustration from Cameroon. In *Economic Change and Political Liberalism in Sub-Saharan Africa*, ed. J. Widner. Baltimore: The John Hopkins University.

Widner, J. 1994. Political Reform in Anglophone and Francophone African Countries'. In *Economic Change and Political Liberalism in Sub-Saharan Africa*, ed. J. Widner. Baltimore: The John Hopkins University.

Journals

Ajulu, R. 2002. Politicised Ethnicity, Competitive Politics and Conflict. *African Studies* 61 (1): 251–268.

Cohen, J. 1995. Ethnicity, Foreign Aid and Economic Growth in Sub-Saharan: The Case of Kenya. HIID Development Discussion Paper No. 520. Online: http://www.cid.harvard.edu/hiid/520.pdf. Accessed 12 Jan 2017.

Holmquist, F., and M. Ford. 1994. Kenya: State and Civil Society and the First Year after the Election. *Africa Today*. 41 (4): 5–25.

Jackson, R., and C. Rosberg. 1984. Personal Rule: Theory and Practice in Africa. *Comparative Politics* 4: 421–442.

Kagwanja, P. 2009. Courting Genocide: Populism, Ethno-Nationalism and the Informalisation of Violence in Kenya's 2008 Post-Election Crisis. *Journal of Contemporary African Studies* 27 (3): 365–387.

Kagwanja, P., and R. Southall. 2009. Introduction: Kenya—A Democracy in Retreat? *Journal of Contemporary African Studies* 27 (3): 259–277.

Kantai, P. 2007. In the Grip of a Vampire State: Maasai Land Struggles in Kenyan Politics. *Journal of East African Studies* 1 (1): 107–122. Online: www.informaworld.com or www.scribd.com. Accessed 4 Oct 2016.

Katz, S. 1985. The Succession of Power and the Power of Succession: Nyayoism in Kenya. *Journal of African Studies.* 12 (3): 155–161.

Khapoya, V. 1980. Kenya Under Moi: Continuity or Change? *Africa Today* 27 (1): 17–32.

Khapoya, V. 1988. Moi and Beyond: Towards Peaceful Succession in Kenya? *Third World Quarterly* 10 (1): 54–66.

Klopp, J., and J. Orina. 2002. University Crisis, Student Activism, and the Contemporary Struggle for Democracy in Kenya. *African Studies Review* 45 (1): 43–76.

Lynch, G. 2006. The Fruits of Perception: Ethnic Politics and the Case of Kenya's Constitutional Referendum. *African Studies* 65 (2): 233–270.

Mazrui, A. 1967. The Monarchical Tendency in African Political Culture. *The British Journal of Sociology* 18: 231–250.

Mwangi, O. 2008. Political Corruption, Party Financing and Democracy in Kenya. *Journal of Modern African Studies* 46 (2): 267–285.

Nyong'o, P.A. 1989. State and Society in Kenya: The Disintegration of the Nationalist Coalitions and the Rise of Presidential Authoritarianism. *African Affairs* 88 (351): 229–251.

Posner, D. 2007. Régime Change and Ethnic Cleavages in Africa. *Comparative Political Studies* 40 (11): 1302–1327. Available online http://cps.sagepub.com/cgi/content/abstract/40/11/1302.

Reports

Awiti, A.O., and Scott, B. 2016. The Kenya Youth Survey Report. Nairobi. The Aga Khan University. January 18. Online: https://www.aku.edu/eai/Documents/kenya-youth-survey-report-executive-summary-2016.pdf or http://ecommons.aku.edu/eastafrica_eai/17/. Accessed 27 Aug 2017.

Humanitarian Policy Group (HPG). 2008. Crisis in Kenya 'land' Displacement and the Search for 'durable Solutions' In *HPG Policy Brief 31.* Online www.odi.org.uk/hpg. Accessed 5 Oct 2015.

OMCT (World Organisation Against Torture). 2008. The Lie of the Land Addressing the Economic Social and Cultural Root Causes of Torture and Other Forms of Violence in Kenya. Online: www.omct.org. Accessed 5 Oct 2016.

Republic of Kenya. 2004. *Report of the Commission of Inquiry into the Illegal/ Irregular Allocation of Land; Ndung'u Commission.* Nairobi: Government Printer.

Republic of Kenya. 2010. *The Proposed Constitution of Kenya.* Nairobi: Government Printer.

Newspapers

Citizen Digital. 2017. Matiang'i signals end of 8-4-4 system, announces roll out 2-6-3-3 structure. January 30. Online: Citizen Digital. 2017. Matiang'i signals end of 8-4-4 system, announces roll out 2-6-3-3 structure. January 30. Online: https://citizentv.co.ke/news/matiangi-signals-end-of-8-4-4-system-announces-roll-out-2-6-3-3-structure-156273/. Accessed 19 Aug 2017.

Daily Nation. 2002. The End of an Era-As the Curtain Falls on Daniel Arap Moi's 24-year Rule, A Special Report on the Life and Politics of Kenya's Second President, December 24.

Daily Nation. 2010. Ethnicity Rampant in Public Universities, May 17. Online: http://www.nation.co.ke/News/Ethnicity%20rampant%20in%20public%20varsities%20/-/1056/920402/-/i8emkqz/-/index.html. Accessed 21 Sep 2015.

Daily Nation. 2010. Yes, School Quotas Reduced Us All to Villagers, But Opened Doors for Many, October, 25. Online: http://www.nation.co.ke/blogs/Yes,%20school%20quotas%20reduced%20us%20all%20to%20villagers/-/446672/1040078/-/view/asBlogPost/-/xkxcjvz/-/index.html. Accessed 29 Nov 2015.

Daily Nation 2011. Feared in life, respected in death. December 1. Online: http://www.nation.co.ke/counties/west-pokot/Feared-in-life-respected-in-death/3444836-1281818-4e0g0a/index.html. Accessed 25 Aug 2017.

The Standard. 2004. Who Own Kenya? October 1. Online: http://www.marsgroupkenya.org/pdfs/crisis/2008/02/large_landowners_in_Kenya.pdf. Accessed 7 Nov 2015.

The Weekly Review. 1988: GG is Back, December 2.

———. 1988. Karanja's Options: A Very Narrow Tight Rope for the Vice President to Walk, July 22.

———. 1988. Man at the Helm, April 8.

———. 1988. Parliament Amends the Constitution with Surprising Alacrity, August 5.

———. 1988. The Evolution of the Presidency, December 9.

Presidential Speeches

Speech by H.E. the President, Hon, Daniel T. Arap Moi, CGH; MP; On the Occasion of the 15th Anniversary of the Kenya Independence Celebrations, on Tuesday 12th December, 1978. In Kenya Presidential Speeches 1963–1988 Jamhuri Day Speeches; Kenya National Archives Central Government Library: Nairobi.

Speech by H.E. the President, Hon, Daniel T. Arap Moi, CGH; MP; On the Occasion of the Jamhuri Day on 12th December 1980. In Kenya Presidential Speeches 1963–1988 Jamhuri Day Speeches; Kenya National Archives Central Government Library: Nairobi.

Speech by H.E. the President, Hon, Daniel T. Arap Moi, CGH; MP; On the Occasion of the 25th Anniversary of Independence (Jamhuri Day) Celebrations, on Monday 12th December 1988. In Kenya Presidential Speeches 1963–1991; Jamhuri Day Speeches at Kenya National Archives Central Government Library: Nairobi.

President Moi's Speech on Kenyatta Day on 20th October 1980. In Kenya Presidential Speeches 1963–1988: Kenyatta Day Speeches: Kenya National Archives Central Government Library: Nairobi.

Speech by H.E. Hon Daniel T. Arap Moi On the Occasion of Madaraka Day of 1st June 1981.

Interview

Onyango. 2009. Nairobi, January 25.

CHAPTER 4

Motion Without Movement: Kenya's Transition Without Transformation

Abstract The chapter argues that Kenya's founding multiparty elections in 1992 were not a harbinger of the envisaged state restructure. The Kenyan politics did not change substantively beyond the elections and so there was no transformation beyond formation of multiple political parties. Ethnicity, political opportunism, and abuse of the incumbency derailed the quest for transformative politics. In substance, the 1997 elections were similar to the founding ones five years earlier. The 1997 elections did not mark a qualitative leap in comparison to the 1992 ones. State violence, electoral irregularities, and tribal politics marred these elections. The challenge of holding multiparty elections in a political milieu defined by single party mentality, unreformed institutions as a result of a top heavy Constitution, tribal fragmentation, and impunity persisted. It rendered multiparty politics more about style than substance.

Keywords Incumbency · Mwai kibaki · Ethnic alliance
Multiparty elections · Reform agenda

INTRODUCTION

The chapter focuses on the period between 1992 and 1997, the first multiparty elections since Kenya's return to political pluralism to the second. The election in 1992 was a defining one in the sense that it was the

© The Author(s) 2018
W.K. Shilaho, *Political Power and Tribalism in Kenya*,
https://doi.org/10.1007/978-3-319-65295-5_4

first since the 'democratic turn' that led to multiparty elections. These elections saw new opposition parties line up to compete and possibly win power. The salient question here is: Did ethnicity and personality differences derail chances of the opposition leaders unseating Moi? This is the searching question in this chapter. The chapter argues that notwithstanding the change to multiparty politics within this period, Kenya's politics remained locked within the logic of ethnicity and thus did not change substantively which accounted for Kenya's inability to undergo transformation. Moi continued to have leverage upon Kenyan politics, although within a contestable political atmosphere. First, there was the persistence of the legal, Constitutional and institutional framework of the single-party state. KANU and Moi adroitly talked the opposition into acquiescing to multipartyism but retained a single-party structure. Wanjala contends that the single-party parliament was galvanised into making half-hearted and sometimes fallacious amendments to the Constitution ostensibly to prepare for a transition to multiparty democracy (Wanjala 1996: 92–93). Some of the amendments were deliberately crafted to suit KANU in the multiparty general elections that would follow. For instance, there was an amendment on Section 5(3) of the Constitution that required that a Presidential candidate garner majority votes besides twenty-five percent of the votes in at least five of Kenya's then eight Provinces. Other amendments were drafted in such a manner as to create the possibility of a constitutional crisis in the event that KANU lost. For example, the Constitution was silent on what would happen if there was no winner in the run-off elections (Wanjala 1996: 92–93).

Second, most of the leading politicians opposed to Moi were his former clients who had either defected or been purged from KANU (Ndegwa 1998). Save for Oginga Odinga, Martin Shikuku, Raila Odinga, James Orengo, Masinde Muliro, George Nthenge, Kijana Wamalwa, Ahmed Barmariz, Paul Muite, Wanyiri Kihoro, Gitobu Imanyara, Kiraitu Murungi to name but few, the rest of the other opposition politicians were similar to Moi in political socialisation hence their inability to devise an alternative political trajectory. One of the features of transitions of the late 1980s and early 1990s in Africa was the persistence of rulers drawn from the same social and political classes as their predecessors but which included an aging generation of old guard politicians who had served in previous régimes (Bratton and van de Walle 1997: 8). Third, structural challenges such as widespread poverty and economic difficulties made the realisation of reform difficult (Kibwana and Maina 1996: 463).

Fourth, and perhaps most significant, was the disunity among opposition parties. Owing to reasons related to but not confined to what Kenyans themselves term 'tribalism', Kenya's transition without transformation occurred (Nasong'o 2007: 101–102).

Conceptually, 'political transition refers to the passage from one type of political system to another. Often it refers to the passage from an essentially authoritarian régime to a basically democratic one, which ends with the introduction of the new democratic regime' (Ogot 1996b: 245). However, Ogot observes that transitions do not necessarily address the challenges that democratisation poses to the transformation of society. Indeed, Ogot suggests that the resolution of such societal problems such as ethnic fragmentation and the definition of the relationship between the state and civil society depend on consolidation of democracy (Ogot 1996b: 246). Ogot argues that for transition to be realised, democratic consolidation must meet four functions. First, democratic consolidation must entail redefining the development model because the neo-liberal one, that most champions of democracy advocate, easily promotes dependence and neo-colonialism. Second, democratic consolidation must redefine relations between the state and civil society and strengthen the latter. Third, it must entail establishment of strong political parties which are 'independent of the state and social movements and represent the real divisions of the society'. Fourth, Ogot argues for a new political culture to define the 'collective action' and ensure harmonious coexistence within a state (Ogot 1996b: 246). Murunga and Nasong'o averred that scholars, policy-makers and democracy advocates applied the concept of democratic transition to interpret the patterns of democratic change taking place in Africa, Asia, Eastern Europe and Latin America in the late 1980s and early 1990s, that was characterised by the shift from authoritarianism to more open systems of governance (Murunga and Nasong'o 2007: 6–7).

The opposition disunity prior to and after the 1992 elections made it possible for Moi to retain power first in 1992 and subsequently in 1997 against the expectations of reform-oriented Kenyans. Of critical significance is that tribalism interfaced with economic challenges, opportunism and the lack of a regulated political party system to make it difficult for multiparty politics to find traction in Kenya. To both Moi and the opposition politicians, tribalism carried political and economic value so much that even attempts at policy informed politics by a section of the opposition floundered. In spite of these setbacks, the 1992 elections were significant in Kenya's political history as they introduced a modicum of political competition, until then, unknown at the Presidential level. It brings out the logic of tribal politics and its destabilising effect through violence. Of importance is the role of the winner-takes-all electoral system on the survival of the KANU régime. KANU's political overtures to the opposition parties were couched in the language of development and cooperation. The influence of tribalism on political parties and the lack of commitment to reform made it difficult to distinguish between KANU and the opposition parties.

THE FORUM FOR THE RESTORATION OF DEMOCRACY (FORD)

Infighting and squabbles among opposition parties characterised the period before the 1992 elections, continued until 1997 and thereafter (*The Weekly Review* July 3 1992: 4–5). The FORD pressure group transformed into a political party in time for the 1992 elections, but degenerated into ethnic factions and splittered into a plethora of political parties based on ethnic identity, where politics was interpreted through what Bayart has termed 'the politics of the belly'. The new parties reflected the views of excluded groups that believed that it was 'our turn to eat', that is, the turn of 'our tribe' to have one of their tribesman in power in order to exclusively benefit from the state resources (Wrong 2009). The manifestos of these parties reflected the lack of substantive theoretical difference between them. There was no grand discussion of issues that were class based, although regional exclusion based on tribe was certainly an issue that raised its head. Manifestos of opposition parties were not different from KANU's (*The Weekly Review* July 3 1992: 21). Throup and Hornsby observed that FORD-Kenya, Democratic Party of Kenya (DP), Social Democratic Party (SDP) and Kenya National Democratic Alliance (KENDA) jointly released the most comprehensive manifesto called the *Post-Election Plan* sponsored by the Friedrich Neumann Foundation of Germany (Throup and Hornsby 1998: 343). Throup and Hornsby pointed out that although the document was 'too unfocused and not prioritised' it presented the most compelling economic statement among the opposition parties. FORD-K released its *Charter for the Second Liberation* which promised to restore Constitutionalism,[1] guarantee human rights and, more radically, abolish the Provincial administration, scale-down the civil service, end the 8-4-4 system of education, and privatise parastatals (Throup and Hornsby 1998: 343–344).

The FORD-Asili led by Ken Matiba, a former bureaucrat and cabinet minister, did not even prepare a manifesto and made no attempt to prepare a national programme of action. Neither did it have any printed copies of its Constitution. Unlike FORD-K, the party had few intellectuals in it. Throup and Hornsby pointed out that this accounted for its failure to spell out its programme of action. FORD-Asili's booklet, *Ken Matiba, Man of the People* comprised nothing but 'eulogies of Matiba as a natural leader' (Throup and Hornsby 1998: 344). The DP's manifesto was not any different from the others since it contained liberal economic policies too. It 'promised to end corruption and detention and reform the 8-4-4 education system' (Throup and Hornsby 1998: 344). Throup and Hornsby argued that all these manifestos were incoherent in offering an alternative programme of action because they were aimed at appeasing Western donors and the Kenyan elite (Throup and Hornsby 1998: 344).

These opposition politicians were more concerned about pleasing foreign actors and the local elite, an indication of the enduring challenge of forging a national identity in Kenya. They betrayed lack of sensibilities regarding sovereignty. Owing to ethnic balkanisation, it was almost impossible for Kenyan politicians to invoke patriotism and rally the citizenry around the imaginary of one Kenya in addressing the challenges besetting the country. Hence, regarding Kenya's socio-economic and political trajectory, successive governments often listened to and implemented recommendations by external actors specifically—the Bretton Woods institutions, Britain, the United States (US), and the European Union (EU) and lately China. Only when the incumbent was embattled, did he expediently invoke imperialism as Moi did to delegitimise the call for multiparty politics. Uhuru Kenyatta applied the same anti-imperialist rhetoric to discredit the International Criminal Court (ICC) during the 2013 elections as Chap. 6 demonstrates.

Divisions emerged within FORD before the 1992 elections pertaining to the fielding of a single Presidential candidate. Oginga Odinga, the Luo leader who at independence had split from KANU to form his own party, declared his interest in the FORD nomination, followed by Kenneth Matiba, a Kikuyu, then a veteran Luhya politician, Martin Shikuku. In December 1991, Mwai Kibaki, then the Health Minister in Moi's cabinet, resigned from the government and KANU and formed the Democratic Party of Kenya (DP) and declared his presidential candidature too. Moi and KANU looked at these declarations with some equanimity since they were signs that FORD was headed for a three way ethnic split (*The Weekly Review* July 3 1992: 5). These divisions not only rendered FORD rudderless but they also gave Moi a political lifeline. As a result, the threat that FORD initially posed to Moi's hold on power dissipated as the 1992 elections drew close. The disarray enabled Moi to outsmart a disjointed opposition and to reclaim the political initiative that he seemed to have lost as the groundswell in support of multiparty politics gained momentum. Following the splintering of FORD and for-mation of DP, the chances of the opposition dislodging Moi dimmed drastically (*The Weekly Review* July 3 1992: 5). It was curious that the Registrar of Societies acted in haste in registering the FORD parties lend-ing credence to the claim that the government had a hand in the squab-bles and eventual break-up of FORD (Kadima and Owuor 2006: 183).

The leading contenders for the FORD Presidential nomination, Matiba a Kikuyu and Odinga, a Luo, had personal handicaps that in effect fuelled tribalism within the party. The Kikuyu could not support a Luo while the Luo were convinced it was their turn to rule and expected the Kikuyu to reciprocate the support they had accorded them since before independence. A resurgence of the rivalry between politicians from the two communities ensued. Both politicians' supporters exploited the other's personal inadequacies to dismiss the Presidential ambition of the rival that exacerbated ethnic rivalry between the two factions. Matiba's critics, and supporters of Odinga, considered him unfit to lead the country due to a stroke that he had suffered while in detention while Odinga's critics, and supporters of Matiba, disqualified him for being too old and with failing eyesight not really capable of leading the country into democracy. Matiba's supporters observed that at 80,[2] Odinga was an octogenarian unfit to rule (*The Weekly Review* July 3 1992: 7). The Odinga faction pressed the point that the Kikuyu had their share of the presidency under Kenyatta. Odinga emphasised this issue: 'During inde-pendence I left the seat to Kenyatta; this time do you expect me to leave it to anybody?' (*The Weekly Review* May 8 1992: 4) Odinga's supporters dismissed Matiba as a Johnny-come-lately who joined opposition politics two years before the 1992 elections while Odinga had been a veteran of opposition politics for over 30 years. Matiba's supporters claimed that Matiba had better organisational and managerial capacity and the req-uisite personal financial resources and wealthy backers to withstand the rigours of a Presidential campaign (Throup and Hornsby 1998: 55). I argue that this was a handicap in itself. It disqualified him because he had been a long time beneficiary of the KANU patronage system that FORD claimed they would curb if they assumed power. Matiba joined the bureaucracy in his 30s after independence until 1989 when he resigned from the cabinet after being excluded through the controversial 1988 *mlolongo* or queue voting elections marred by widespread rigging. He was subsequently expelled from KANU (Throup and Hornsby 1998: 55). Although not poor, Odinga could not match Matiba's resource base (*The Weekly Review* May 8 1992: 5–6). Indeed the press opined that:

> According to some observers, the attitudes of both the Kikuyus and non Kikuyus on the matter is not a question of ignorance about the implications of their actions on the party's image. Rather it is a statement about the fact that when it comes to the crunch, tribalism becomes the single-most important factor in Kenyan politics. (*The Weekly Review* May 8 1992: 4)

The FORD internal differences proved irreconcilable in due course. The fragmentation of FORD into FORD-Kenya and FORD-Asili (original) led to the electoral competition between Odinga and Matiba, the respective leaders of the two factions. A section of media had predicted it: 'Both Odinga and Matiba want the country's presidency so badly, say sceptics that, whoever loses the bid for the FORD presidency will inevitably form a breakaway party as a means of realizing the Presidential dream' (*The Weekly Review* May 8 1992: 5).

These twin FORD parties bifurcated again into small entities of even less consequence. In the aftermath of the 1992 elections, a second split in the 'FORD family' gave rise to FORD-People and *Saba Saba Asili*. FORD-People was associated with the Kikuyu politician Kimani wa Nyoike, whom I referred to in Chap. 3. Matiba defected from FORD-Asili and formed Saba Saba Asili after losing control of FORD-Asili to Martin Shikuku. Kadima and Owuor opine that the Registrar of Societies exercised enormous discretion in registering more parties when it was advantageous to Moi and KANU (Kadima and Owuor 2006: 191). I analyse in detail FORD-Asili challenges below. These parties purported to be guided by national ideals while in essence they were ethnic enclaves for their 'ethnic barons' and their supporters (Mutunga 2002: 66).

The break-up of FORD and emergence of these parties had nothing to do with differences in ideology but a battle for political supremacy based on ethnicity. Matiba, Kibaki and Odinga the leading opposition candidates in the 1992 elections in that order, drew support largely from their ethnic groups (Ajulu 1993: 99). Owing to the lack of resources and clout, Shikuku and wa Wanyoike could not command the support of their tribes. Hence, FORD-Asili and FORD-People became fringe political parties in the period leading up to the 1997 elections. The FORD was a variegated entity comprising veterans of opposition politics, formerly KANU politicians inclined to reactionary politics who were elderly and younger politicians. Young political activists were referred to as Young Turks (Ogot 1996b: 248). A combination of these factors in addition to the ethnic rivalry pitting the Kikuyu against the Luo led to the disintegration of FORD (Mutua 2008: 90). According to Southall,

> It is axiomatic that, had the opposition been able to unite behind a single Presidential candidate or more realistically, if Kikuyu-Luo blocs had been able to forge a united front, Moi would have lost the recent election. The real conundrum of Kenyan politics, therefore, is quite why, having lost control of KANU under Moi and having been thumped in 1992, the politicians from these communities, who are scarcely divided by anything resembling a political principle, found it impossible to coalesce. The answer must clearly lie in the minutiae of ethnic politics: the lack of trust of politicians and voters of even (especially?) their near neighbours, the web of patronage-client relations, and the realization of individual politicians that membership of the political class brings access to the spoils system. (Southall 1998: 109–10)

Some *wananchi* (populace) attributed the loss of opposition parties to KANU in 1992 and 1997 to Moi's political adroitness, rigging and tribal divisions. I gathered this during a field research in Kenya. Ondari observed that Moi was too savvy for his competitors and so he disorganised them by encouraging formation of as many political parties as possible (Interview, Ondari, January 16 2009). The opposition leaders' inability to form an electoral alliance after they formed a myriad of parties meant in effect that they blew away the chances of régime change in Kenya. It was the fragmentation of the opposition that enabled Moi to rig the elections in his favour (Throup and Hornsby 1998: 454–455). In Nyanza region, some of Oginga Odinga's supporters such as Modi believed that Moi owed retention of power to astute divide-and-rule tactics. Modi, a 65-year-old asserted, 'Moi was not for multipartyism but Jaramogi (Odinga) succeeded in having Kenya return to multiparty politics. FORD was defeated because Moi divided the opposition, got votes from the Kalenjins and Luhyas and then isolated the Luo hence ruined Jaramogi's chances' (Interview, Modi, January 16 2009).

THE INCUMBENCY ADVANTAGE

Moi survived the 'wave of democratisation' (Huntington 1991) because of a Constitution that disproportionately vested too much power in the presidency. The 1963 Constitution was presidential and was arbitrarily amended many times to accent that fact. For instance, it stated in Section 23 (1) that 'The executive authority of the Government shall vest in the President and, subject to this Constitution, may be exercised by him either directly or through officers subordinate to him' (Republic of Kenya 1963). The judiciary and parliament were subservient to the executive. The judiciary could not impartially arbitrate accusations of electoral malpractices against Moi and KANU. The courts dismissed petitions against Moi's disputed victories in 1992 and 1997 on a technicality. Kenneth Matiba filed a petition against Moi's victory in 1992 but Justice Riaga Omollo dismissed it on grounds that he had not signed the petition form himself. Matiba had delegated the power of the attorney to his wife who signed it on his behalf given that he had stroke, he suffered while in detention, and so was paralysed in both hands (*The EastAfrican* 16 March 2013). Mwai Kibaki's petition against Moi in 1997 was dismissed too when a three judge bench ruled that he had not personally served Moi with the court documents (*Daily Nation* 23 July 1999; Brown 2001: 731, 734). It was bizarre that the judge expected Kibaki to go past a presidential security detail and hand over the court documents to Moi. The 2013 petition was also dismissed on a technicality, in a 'unanimous 5 minute' ruling after part of Raila Odinga's evidence was time barred and therefore rendered inadmissible. The verdict elicited criticism from the Law Society of Kenya (LSK). These rulings betrayed the judiciary beholden to the executive thus prone to making rulings informed by extraneous factors (Shilaho 2013: 99). Moi deployed patronage to placate some opposition members of parliament and he continued to dictate the pace and direction of the country's politics in much the same way as he did under single-party rule although he could be challenged openly by the media, civil society, sections of the clergy and some opposition politicians. After the legalisation of multiparty politics, the opposition leaders were in a hurry to defeat Moi and seemed to have overlooked the question of reform that would clip the heavily centralised executive powers that tilted the political playing field in favour of the incumbent (Kibwana and Maina 1996: 431; Wanjala 1996: 218). Most of the opposition leaders had been part of KANU for years and were aware of the benefits of such a constitutional structure and therefore what appeared like an oversight, was not.

In the run up to the 1992 elections, opposition parties divided along ethnic lines which meant that there was no strong campaign against the KANU monolith. In the aftermath of the elections, Moi exploited the patronage networks to entice some opposition MPs into defecting to KANU. Parliamentary losers in the 1992 elections were the most susceptible because 'they had no jobs, no prestige and no posts to compensate them for the risks they had carried out' (Throup and Hornsby 1998: 546). Consequently, some opposition MPs in Central, Nyanza and Western Provinces gave in to financial and material inducements and defected to KANU. DP's Protas Momanyi of Bonchari, in Kisii, opened the deluge of defections and crossed over to KANU even before he was sworn in. He retained the seat during the subsequent by-election. FORD-Asili MPs, Javan Omani of Lurambi, Benjamin Magwaga of Ikolomani, Japheth Shamalla of Shinyalu and Apili Wawire of Lugari, in Western Kenya, recaptured their seats. However, FORD-Kenya's Tom Obondo of Ndhiwa, Nyanza, FORD-Asili's Kiruhi Kimondo of Starehe, in Nairobi and Julius Njoroge of Makuyu, in central, defected to KANU but lost their seats to candidates of parties they had defected from. Kenya's winner-takes-all electoral system left the opposition leaders without any opportunities to extract prebends from the state. Demanding campaigns left most opposition leaders in a precarious financial situation. Therefore, they were faced with a stark choice: either cooperate with the government or budgetary allocations to their areas would be stopped (Throup and Hornsby 1998: 546: 464). But these politicians' behaviour should not be read purely through the rational choice lens. They also exhibited cynicism consistent with politics bereft of principle.

KANU thus retained its hold on power in 1992 mainly due to ethnic factionalism among the opposition parties (Southall 1998: 102). However, Kenneth Matiba, the runer up presidential candidate, disputed the credibility of the elections (Klopp 2001). Disunity among opposition politicians cost them but Moi exploited incumbency to aggravate the divisions by luring some of the opposition leaders with bribes and sine-cures (Khadiagala 2010: 70; Steeves 2006: 199). Had FORD fielded one Presidential candidate, KANU would not have won the elections given that FORD had massive support all over the country except the Rift Valley region, Moi's support base. The Kikuyu and Luo politicians could not agree to support a single Presidential candidate not because of ideo-logical but ethnic differences. However, ethnicity per se could not com-prehensively explain the inability of the opposition candidates to dislodge Moi from power in 1992. Electoral irregularities contributed to Moi's controversial victory as well. For instance, the voter registration process was riddled with irregularities in many parts of the country. Katumanga showed that the process of nominating candidates was flawed especially in the Rift Valley Province leading to KANU getting parliamentary seats without elections being held. In this Province, intimidation, violence and government-induced administrative bottlenecks made it difficult for the opposition to submit names of their candidates to returning officers. Consequently, KANU candidates were 'elected' without any electoral contest since many opposition candidates were disqualified at the nomi-nation stage (Katumanga 2002: 185–186). Consequently, forty one per-cent (18 out of 44) of the KANU candidates in the Rift Valley Province were returned to parliament unopposed (Nasong'o 2007: 96).

In spite of not having brought about the desired reform in Kenya's body politic, the 1992 elections were significant. It was the first time a political contest for the presidency since independence in 1963 had occurred, notwithstanding the allegations of irregularities by the oppo-sition. Previously it was considered almost treasonable for any politi-cian to contemplate challenging the President during elections. Before then, only parliamentary—within the parameters of openness defined by the regime—and civic elections for ward councillors, were open to elec-toral contest. Loyalty to Moi was a factor during parliamentary elections. Since the May 1963 General Elections that ushered in independence, in the sense that they were the last elections before Kenya's independence, Kenya held subsequent elections in 1969, 1974, 1979, 1983 and 1988 in which the incumbent was not challenged (KHRC 1998: 6).

The 1992 elections marked the beginning of the dismantling of insti-tutionalised authoritarianism. With the scrapping of Sect. 2A of the Constitution that had rendered Kenya *de jure* single-party state, there was euphoria reminiscent of independence (*The Weekly Review* July 3 1992: 4).

The elections signified the liberation of Kenyans from the shackles of 'political somnambulism into which they had been whipped by the many years of one party dictatorship' (Wanjala 2002: 107). However, the opening up of political space was accompanied by political practices that considerably stymied democratisation.

THE PERSISTENCE OF TRIBAL POLITICS

More than any other factor, the 1992 elections demonstrated what had long seemed to characterise Kenya's politics, the salience and influence of ethnicity. Cowen and Kanyinga put it differently when they argued that the elections brought to the surface 'the logic of communal politics' (Cowen and Kanyinga 2002: 130). The overarching influence of ethnicity in Kenya's politics cannot be minimised:

> The anti-Kikuyu sentiments subject was put across more forcefully by a Nairobi politician, Clement Gachanja. A Kikuyu himself, Gachanja said that "The Luhya, Luo and other Kenyans have regrouped themselves against the Kikuyu and it would be impossible for a Kikuyu to become the next President". Kibaki was quick to refute Gachanja's claims arguing that it was an individual's track record not his tribe that would influence the electorate. Kibaki's theory does not however explain why he has no following in Western and Nyanza Provinces or why Odinga has no support in Central Province. (*The Weekly Review* July 3 1992: 8)

Kenyans voted for Presidential candidates who originated from among their ethnic communities or those who formed pacts with politicians from their tribes. However, in 1992, a cross ethno-regional alliance produced results that attracted attention. Thus, in Kikuyu constituency in the predominantly Kikuyu inhabited Central Province, the FORD-K candidate and party's national Deputy Chairman, Paul Muite, received 38,416 votes which translated into 71.97% of the total votes cast but the voters cast their Presidential votes overwhelmingly in favour of Matiba, another Kikuyu. Matiba garnered 46, 277 of the total 53,137 votes while Oginga Odinga, a Luo and FORD-K's Presidential candidate, fared dismally emerging with a paltry 3, 246 (Badejo 2006: 169),[3] see Table 4.1 below. This result was significant. It underscored the persistent narrative in Kenya's politics that the Kikuyu bloc voting was

Table 4.1 Kikuyu constituency election results in 1992

Constituency	KANU		FORD-Asili		DP		FORD-Kenya		Others	
	Parl.	Pres.	Parl.	Pres.	Parl.	Pres.	Parl.	Pres.	Parl.	Pres.
Kikuyu	1%	2%	23%	87%	4%	5%	72%	6%	0%	0%

Source (Throup and Hornsby 1998: 494)

Table 4.2 Summary of the parliamentary and presidential voting in 1992

Candidate & party	Number of votes	Percentage
KANU	1,419,515	26.6
D.T. Arap Moi-KANU	1,964,867	36.8
FORD ASILI	1,170,874	22.0
K. Matiba-FORD-Asili	1,430,627	26.8
FORD KENYA	981,753	18.4
O. Odinga-FORD-Kenya	944,564	17.7
DP	1,064,700	20.0
M. Kibaki-DP	1,029,163	19.3
Other parliamentary	43,037	0.8
Other presidential	43,037	0.8
Registered voters	7,897,973	47.89 (of total voting pop'n)
Total votes	5,334,438	67.5 (of registered voters)
Total voting population	11,157,515	

Source (Ajulu 1995: 29)

the only one that had not shifted throughout the country's multiparty politics and before. Although tribe was pivotal in Kenyans' voting patterns, the Kikuyu tribe had never transferred their support to a presidential candidate from a different tribe in Kenya's post-colonial history. In 'the little general elections' held in 1966 and since the founding multiparty elections in 1992, the Kikuyu exhibited rigid ethnic bloc voting in favour of 'one of our own'. In 1966, Kikuyu voted for KANU led by Jomo Kenyatta against Oginga Odinga's KPU as highlighted in Chap. 1. In the 1992 presidential elections, Kikuyu voted for fellow tribesmen, Kenneth Matiba and Mwai Kibaki, who came second and third, respectively, after Daniel Arap Moi 'arap' with lowercase because it is not a name but means 'son of' (see Table 4.2). In 1997, Matiba was ineligible to run having refused to register as a voter leaving Kibaki to consolidate the Kikuyu vote that propelled him to the second position after

Moi (Southall 1998: 107). In 2002, Moi was ineligible to run having served two terms. Mwai Kibaki and Uhuru Kenyatta, both Kikuyu, were the two leading presidential candidates. Once again, the Kikuyu vote split between the two with Kibaki emerging victorious due to support by a broad ethnic alliance, NARC. In 2007, Kikuyu rallied behind Kibaki against Raila Odinga who this time round had a broad ethnic alliance, ODM. Having served the constitutionally mandated two terms, Kibaki did not run in 2013 upon which Kenyatta inherited the Kikuyu bloc vote and succeeded him as president. During the 2017 elections, the Kikuyu again overwhelmingly voted for Uhuru Kenyatta in his reelection bid. However, at the time of writing, the opposition coalition, the National Super Alliance (NASA) presidential candidate, Raila Odinga, had filed a petition before the Supreme Court disputing Uhuru Kenyatta's victory arguing that the elections were rigged in favour of Kenyatta. The case was ongoing.

THE ANALYSIS OF THE 1992 ELECTION RESULTS

Moi tended to exploit the tensions within the opposition parties by denouncing their differences as 'tribalism'. During his tenure in office, he had constantly argued against tribal difference. KANU secured votes from ethnic communities in the Rift Valley, his home Province, Coast and North Eastern Provinces (the other KANU bastions) plus swing votes from Kamba and sections of Luhya (*The Weekly Review* July 3 1992: 5). KANU had support from all over Kenya. The party had been in power uninterruptedly since independence and so it was entrenched through a combination of patronage politics and use of sheer violence. Kenyans did not sentimentally relate to KANU as a party that liberated them from colonialism as might have been the case elsewhere on the continent. At independence, KANU was rivalled by KADU which meant that some politicians and Kenyans did not agree with the KANU agenda for the country. KANU lost legitimacy immediately after independence, when it resorted to divisive and exclusionary politics. KANU was a metaphor for all that had gone wrong in post-colonial Kenya. More voters consistently voted against it since 1992 until they eventually voted it out of power in 2002. In 1992, Moi could then turn to that legacy of patronage and state-sponsored violence to retain KANU's hold on power. Moi had little difficulty in being able to meet the requirement that demanded that a Presidential winner should have majority votes in addition to securing

25% of votes in at least five out of Kenya's then eight Provinces (*The Weekly Review* July 3 1992: 9). There was also an amendment to the Constitution that prohibited the formation of a coalition government thus making it impossible for the sparsely supported opposition parties to consolidate their support and upstage KANU (Brown 2001: 727). The most plausible explanation is provided by Kadima and Owuor who argue that given that all Kenya's Provinces were ethnically heterogeneous, Moi was able to gain the mandatory 25% courtesy of small ethnic groups in opposition-dominated Provinces while maintaining his hold on KANU strongholds (Kadima and Owuor 2006: 192).

Moi abused state resources during campaigns which gave him an edge over the opposition. During the Cold War period, Moi repressed dissent using conventional instruments of violence, that is, the security forces. The global geopolitics of the time was more about ideological allies for the United States (US) and Union of Soviet Socialist Republics (USSR) than human rights and political and economic accountability. However, following the end of the bipolar world in 1989, the donor community invoked accountability and human rights rubric in aid disbursement (Berman et al. 2010: 479–480). Unable to fulfil these conditionalities, the Moi régime resorted to abuse of state resources such as money, relief food in famine-stricken areas, public land, cars and promises of cabinet and civil service appointments to win loyalty and curb defections from KANU (Mwangi 2008: 273–274). The media was yet to be as liberalised as it is currently and so Moi hoarded coverage by the national broadcaster, Kenya Broadcasting Corporation (KBC), which operated like the state media-the government mouthpiece. Owing to the fact that some prominent politicians and the power wielders, owned media companies in Kenya, the media perennially fell short of fulfilling its critical role in Kenya's democratisation. Bias against the opposition, deference to the government and the purvey of tribal bigotry were some of the accusations levelled against the Kenyan media. The British Broadcasting Corporation (BBC) observed that, 'As politics has become more factionalised along political and ethnic grounds, the media including much of the mainstream media, have been drawn into, and often aligned with different political interests' (BBC World Service Trust 2008: 9).

Patron-client networks developed and nurtured under KANU's domination of the politics, also advantaged Moi over the opposition parties. In 1992, the Moi régime shifted the electoral period as a boom-time for voters to a new height altogether whereby 'a substantial part of the Kenya's foreign exchange was converted into an election fund' (Cowen and Laakso 2002: 20–21). Throup and Hornsby provide evidence that the patronage of KANU went as far as to print fake money with which voters and politicians were bought through the infamous Youth for KANU '92 (YK '92). YK '92 was launched as a campaign organ for KANU (Throup and Hornsby 1998: 353–357) and responsible for distributing the fake money. Headed by Cyrus Jirongo, a presidential candidate in 2017, YK '92 was composed of upstart wheeler dealers, among whom was William Ruto, Kenya's Deputy President effective 2013. It lobbied and successfully campaigned for Moi's reelection against a formidable challenge posed by the opposition that would have dealt a blow to the ambitions of the then young politicians, had the opposition defeated Moi during the 1992 elections. KANU through YK '92 precipitated inflation and the economy took a nosedive after the elections. So awash with cash was the war chest of YK '92 that the 500 shilling note was christened 'Jirongo'. Despite this largesse, KANU was completely locked out of Luo and Kikuyu heartlands in 1992 and 1997 elections. These communities formed the bulk of the opposition against the Moi régime due to exclusion. Moi's fellow Presidential contenders performed abysmally outside of their 'ethnic homelands'[4] (Throup and Hornsby 1998: 463). The 1992 election results exposed how either policy or ideology seemed not to matter in the country's turn to multiparty politics. Kenneth Matiba, whose party did not even have a manifesto, emerged the second most popular Presidential candidate as shown in Table 4.2.

Although ethnicity influenced Kenyans' voting patterns in the 1992 elections, ethnicity alone could not account for the pattern of the 1992 election results. The First-Past-the-Post (FPTP) electoral system gave Moi an edge over a divided opposition because a presidential candidate only needed simple majority to be declared the winner. Following the legalisation of multiparty system, the opposition generated a lot of support and euphoria across the country to the extent that opposition victory appeared a real possibility. Indeed, the pressure against KANU was so great that the possibility of an early election was not farfetched either (*The Weekly Review* July 3 1992: 4). However, a combination of state resources owing to an unreformed political institution and ethnically and regionally fragmented opposition parties enabled Moi and KANU to prevail.

THE STATE VIOLENCE

Because of the manner in which the state had used its legitimate force to promote sectional interests, the ruling elites lost much of the legitimacy that governments hold in deploying force. Multiparty politics had ushered in a kind of 'organised disorder', where the idea of 'disorder as a political instrument' deployed by Chabal and Daloz has some salience (Chabal and Daloz 1999). Since the 1980s through the early 1990s following the advent of multiparty politics, the government lost monopoly over the legitimate use of force (Republic of Kenya 2008; Mueller 2008: 187–194). In the 1980s, KANU had used its youth wing to perpetrate violence against dissidents and ordinary citizens. In the early 1990s, the Moi régime gave free rein to the 'Kalenjin warriors' to attack tribes perceived to be supporting opposition politics in the Rift Valley and neighbouring provinces such as Western and Nyanza. In the mid-1990s, security forces allowed gangs such as *Jeshi la Mzee* (The old man's army) to break up protests by opposition activists agitating for reform along the streets of Nairobi (Kagwanja 2005: 56).

Official reports showed that at the height of the post-election violence in 2007–2008, the police acted unprofessionally as some of them stood by as atrocities were being committed, others exercised bias along ethnic lines while others engaged in rape (Republic of Kenya 2008: 56–57). Clearly, the police force no less than politicians was susceptible to partisan politics owing to the influence of ethnicity in recruitment. Consequently, the regular police, the administrative police and the paramilitary General Service Unit (GSU) tended to be biased in favour the government of the day. Despite the change of name of the regular police to the National Police Service (NPS), as opposed to the police force, there was no corresponding change in ethos. Probity, respect for human rights, and accountability had not set in. The police still acted with impunity, involved in partisan politics at the behest of the government, perpetrated extrajudicial executions and ranked among the most corrupt institutions in Kenya. In a nutshell, the police resisted civilian oversight as envisaged under the 2010 Constitution and remained an agent of state violence (Amnesty International 2013). Katumanga (2010) analysed the ethnicisation of the security sector in Kenya since the colonial period. He explored the process that led to the erosion of a sense of professionalism within the security sector under Kenyatta, Moi and Kibaki. Katumanga argued that these leaders made ethnically informed appointments to head the Defence and Internal Security dockets not in the interest of the state but that of these politicians and their political and economic allies. Competence was compromised giving rise to insecurity. This led to the emergence of militia groups to fill in the void (Katumanga 2010: 534–542).

Anderson also explored how Kenya's successive governments since Kenyatta's administration had exploited the illicit violence by gangs and militias to achieve political ends. He observed that some of these gangs sprung up to provide security in shanty and informal settlements (Anderson 2002). In the lead up to the 2002 elections, the *Mungiki* militia gang openly brandished machetes in the streets of Nairobi while demonstrating in support of KANU and its Presidential candidate, Uhuru Kenyatta (Kagwanja 2005: 63). Despite the Kenyan press and some politicians linking Kenyatta to Mungiki, Anderson observed that the politician did not respond to the allegations (Anderson 2002: 540–541). In January 2012, the ICC confirmed charges against Kenyatta whom it accused of mobilising *Mungiki* against ODM supporters in the Rift Valley towns of Nakuru and Naivasha during the 2007–2008 post-election violence. The Court ruled that there were 'substantial grounds to believe' that on 26 November 2007, Kenyatta, Kibaki and head of civil service Francis Muthaura held a meeting at State House in Nairobi with *Mungiki* leaders. During the meeting, *Mungiki* extracted concessions from the government such as, stoppage of extrajudicial killings against its members by the police, demanded recruitment in the security and armed forces and release from prison of its leader in support of Kibaki's re-election (ICC 2012). The case against Kenyatta collapsed for lack of evidence and interference by two successive governments as shown in Chap. 6.

The 1992 elections marked the beginning of a sombre chapter of tribal violence during elections. Subsequent government reports covering the period before and after the elections showed that there had been state sponsored violence in the Rift Valley and parts of Nyanza and Western Provinces (Republic of Kenya 1999, 1992). The government, however, blamed FORD of causing the tribal violence although one could not understand the reasons for why FORD would instigate it (*The Weekly Review* March 20, 1992: 8). There was no evidence to support this claim. Between 1990 and 1991, the state directed violence against the urban poor. KANU Youth vigilantes and City Commission *askaris* harassed the urban poor. The urban poor, including slum dwellers, *matatu* (taxi) owners, touts and hawkers engaged in demonstrations as political space seemed to open up with political pluralism (KHRC 1998: 8–10). It was the urban poor who bore the brunt of KANU's patronage driven politics that precipitated poverty.[5] The transition to multiparty politics triggered the cyclical electoral related violence that Kenya experienced since the reintroduction of multiparty politics the most intense one being the 2007–2008 post-election violence (HRW 2008; KNCHR 2008).

The electoral violence thus took on a tribal form and in effect, the elections became a tribal affair. This in turn made it difficult for the evolution of an effective pluralistic system in which tribal and other sectarian interests were subordinated to more ideologically based differences upon which national policy would be based (*The Weekly Review* March 13 1992: 18–19). The Kalenjin 'warriors' attacked members of the Kikuyu, Luo and Luhya tribes on accusation that they supported opposition parties. Kalenjin politicians identified these tribes as threatening to the 'Kalenjin' hold on power (Republic of Kenya 1992). They joined forces with other tribes in the Rift Valley under the aegis of Kalenjin, Maasai, Turkana and Samburu (KAMATUSA) and incited their tribal members to act against 'foreign' tribes whom they accused of trying to dispossess the Kalenjin, and by extension the KAMATUSA, of power. It became a dichotomous fight between pro-opposition tribes branded as 'alien' and 'foreign' oppressors of the pro-establishment 'natives' or 'indigenous' owners of the Rift Valley, the KAMATUSA (KHRC 1998: 12–13).

Majimboism and Incitement

The KAMATUSA politicians reignited *Majimboism* or regional federalism which the Kalenjin, Mijikenda and Maasai had embraced in the late 1950s and early 1960s as a way of defending their economic and political rights against encroachment by the larger tribes (KHRC 1998: 10–11). Then *Majimboism* was also meant to protect the economic and political interests of the white settlers against the KANU radicals. The KANU rival, KADU articulated the *Majimbo* policy (KHRC 1998: 10–11). However, in the 1990s under multi-partyism a renewed *Majimboism* ceased to be a policy of regionalism and became a virulent ideology of ethnic cleansing (KHRC 1998: 11). The government complicity in the atrocities was exposed,

If there is one thing that the select committee set up by parliament last May to probe ethnic clashes confirmed, it was the widely held public view that the clashes were politically motivated. It also legitimized charges that government administrators and law enforcement forces either abetted the clashes or were hesitant in dealing with perpetrators of the crime. (*The Weekly Review* September, 25 1992: 5)

In 1991, KAMATUSA politicians organised a series of meetings through which they condemned multiparty advocates and urged members of KAMATUSA tribes to arm themselves and fight against the opposition. The quote below encapsulates the culture of impunity among the political elite in Kenya. Despite evidence for incitement by politicians, inaction and complicity by government officials under the Moi régime, no one was held accountable for the heinous crimes that followed in which members of the Luo, Luhya and Kikuyu were killed, their homes set ablaze while others were displaced. The greatest blot to the 1992 elections was the massacre of 1500 people and the displacement of another 500 000 potential voters in the Rift Valley and Western Provinces due to KANU sanctioned ethnic clashes (Katumanga 2002: 186). Moi was adversely mentioned in connection with the 1992 ethnic violence but his name was expunged from the report by a judicial commission he appointed to inquire into tribal clashes (KHRC 2011). Nicholas Biwott, an influential Kalenjin politician under the Moi government, reportedly said,

FORD members would be "crushed" and added that KANU youth wingers and *wananchi* were ready to fight to the last person to protect the Government of President Moi. He said that Kalenjins were not cowards and that they were ready to counter attempts to relegate them from leadership. Hon. Mibei instructed *wananchi* in the Province to visit beer-halls and "crush" any government critic and later make reports to the police that they had finished them, while Hon. Kamuren said that the Kalenjin were ready to protect the government using any weapons at their disposal. Another Member said that FORD members would be "crushed" to serve as a lesson to other would-be dissenters. Hon Chepkok urged *wananchi* to arm themselves with pangas, rungus, bows and arrows to destroy any FORD member on sight. (Republic of Kenya 1992: 9–10)

The National Assembly set up a parliamentary select committee in 1992 to investigate ethnic clashes in Western and other parts of Kenya popularly known as the Kiliku Commission, named after Kennedy Kiliku, the then Changamwe MP. However, despite the commission naming individuals responsible for the clashes within the main text, it did not recommend that they are investigated further for possible prosecution. Moreover, some names appearing in the main text did not appear under 'perpetrators and abettors' of the clashes (KHRC 2011: 14, Republic of Kenya, 1992). The Kenya Human Rights Commission identified these two anomalies as the greatest failure of this commission. Moi appointed a judicial commission of inquiry on 1 July 1998 headed by the Court of Appeal Judge, Akilano Akiwumi, to inquire into what were referred to as 'tribal clashes' in Kenya. The commission submitted its report on 31 July 1999 but Moi shelved the report and released it three years later on 18 October 2002 following a court order. KHRC report pointed out that even then the executive exerted pressure on the Commission to have certain names deleted from the report before it was published. In addition, the Attorney General, Amos Wako, attempted to water down the report when he published it together with a parallel one in which he accused the commission of relying on 'extraneous evidence', failure to conduct evidence in open proceedings and being biased against the Maasai and Kalenjin communities (KHRC 2011: 26). Against a backdrop of impunity after the 1992 ethnic clashes, the ground had been set for a repeat of similar violence during the 1997 and 2007 elections.

VIOLENCE IN THE COAST REGION

In the run up to the 1997 elections violence erupted, this time, in the Coast region. Similar to the earlier violence in the Rift Valley, the targets were members of communities from elsewhere, termed *Wabara* (upcountry people) or *Wakirienge* (those who speak alien languages) (KHRC 1998: 56). In effect, the call was to attack fellow citizens from other tribes, legitimising this by appealing to a local belonging threatened by the invasion of 'others' from outside. These epithets referred mainly to the Luhya, Luo and Kikuyu whom the 'natives' within the Province suspected of being sympathetic to opposition parties. As in the Rift Valley violence, the intention was to change the political demography of the cosmopolitan Coast Province to ensure a KANU and Moi victory. The Coast region suffered from economic neglect in spite of being a tourist area. The region had been subject to extreme cases of 'land grabbing' that began during the Kenyatta régime and was perpetrated by both the political and the business elite under successive governments. Most of these land grabbers came from inland communities especially high-ranking officials from the Kikuyu and Kalenjin owing to their dominance of state organs during the Kenyatta and Moi régimes, respectively (Republic of Kenya 2004, KNCHR and Kenya National Land Alliance 2006, *Daily Nation* July 29 2009). Thus, the resentment by the local communities against their inland counterparts. KANU politicians ironically exploited genuine grievances to incite locals against the poor upcountry people whom the locals accused of taking their jobs (KHRC 1998: 64).

THE IDEOLOGICAL POLITICAL ORGANISATION?

In the run up to the 1997 elections, two parties tried to distinguish themselves on factors other than tribal interest. These were Safina and Social Democratic Party (SDP). Safina (Swahili for the biblical Noah's Ark) was formed in 1995. Among its founders was Paul Muite formerly of FORD-K and Richard Leakey, a Kenyan of British extraction from the world renowned Leakey family of palaeontologists. The inclusion of Leakey among its interim officials was meant to highlight the quest of Safina to transcend tribal and racial politics in Kenya. The government delayed the registration of Safina until close to the 1997 elections which contributed to a poor showing by the party since they had no time to set up party structures, recruit members and campaign. Moi, however, exploited what was supposed to be the party's strength and launched a scathing attack against it by playing the ethnic and racial cards. Moi publicly referred to Safina as an imperialist organisation led by 'unpatriotic Kenyans and former colonialists' (Cowen and Kanyinga 2002: 150). In 1995, Leakey visited Nakuru town, Rift Valley Province, to popularise Safina but goons affiliated to KANU set upon him by whips. The attack was consistent with the vilification campaign against him led by Moi owing to the perception that he represented Western interests in Safina. This was a somewhat ironic attack and perhaps pointed to Moi's rather schizophrenic approach not only to white Kenyans but also to politics generally.

Moi's actions spoke louder than words, and whilst condemning Richard Leakey in the opposition, until the 1992 elections, Leakey's brother, Philip, served as the MP for Lang'ata and was assistant minister for Environment and Natural Resources in Moi's government. Richard

Leakey entered parliament after the 1997 elections as a nominated MP representing the disabled being a double amputee having lost both feet following a near fatal air crash in 1993. Moi lured him out of opposition politics that occasioned his resignation from Parliament. Moi then appointed him as Head of Civil Service and Secretary to the Cabinet following the World Bank recommendation. Moi's political move perhaps above all shows how he co-opted political opponents and diluted any democratic transformation.

On paper, the SDP attempted to present itself as an ideologically anchored party. Since Oginga Odinga's KPU that Kenyatta banned in 1969, SDP was the only other party in Kenya's history to have attempted to pursue ideological as opposed to tribal politics. The SDP condemned free enterprise, argued for the provision of basic needs for all and called for a new land policy (Mutunga 2002: 82). The SDP's ideologues were Peter Anyang' Nyong'o and Apollo Njonjo both academics and seasoned critics of single-party rule. However, realising that the social democratic crusade on its own would not attract many votes, SDP recruited a woman, Charity Ngilu as its Presidential candidate during the 1997 elections. The party largely capitalised on the 'Ngilu wave', the euphoria that descended especially among the Kamba community since Charity Ngilu was the first woman to run for President in Kenya (Grignon 2001: 338). The SDP's campaign slogan was *Masaa ya Mama* (It is time for a Woman). Neither of the ideologues, had a solid ethnic base, however. They later fell out with Ngilu for coming up with stringent criteria for nomination of the party's Presidential candidate the foremost being that he or she must have a university degree that Ngilu did not have. Nyong'o was first elected to parliament in 1992 on a Ford-Kenya ticket, but he lost his parliamentary seat in 1997 when he changed parties thus defying the Raila Odinga influence among Luo, in his Nyanza backyard. Apollo Njonjo never held an elective post. Ultimately, even Safina and SDP could not cushion themselves against tribal politics.

In 1997 Moi was determined to retain power by means either fair or foul means (Brown 2001; Mitullah 2002: 133–134). Mitullah observed that the 1997 elections were characterised by some shortfalls such as some polling stations opening late, bribery and lack of transparency. In 48% of the polling stations voting materials such as ballot papers, ballot boxes and voters registers did not arrive at 6 am as required by the law (Mitullah 2002: 134). The Electoral Commission of Kenya (ECK) created confusion when it extended voting by a day but expediently

avoided stating unequivocally that it would apply only to those constituencies that were affected by late opening of polling stations (Mitullah
2002: 134; Brown 2001). Ajulu pointed out that in other areas voting
was extended by as many as two and even three days such that counting
was still in progress in some parts of the country long after Moi had been
declared the winner and inaugurated (Ajulu 1998: 275).

In multiparty Kenya, ethnicity thus became a shield from harm or a
marker for harm even for death. The definition of the 'enemy' was in a
constant state of flux in accordance with the fluid ethnic alliances. Since
1992, Kenya's politicians couched the competition for the presidency in
the idiom of the tribe as 'our power', the notion around which tribes
are mobilised either to defend the presidency or wrestle it from the
incumbent. Louis Moreno Ocampo, the former ICC Chief Prosecutor,
described the masterminds of the 2007 post-election in Kenya as individuals 'guided by political objectives either to retain or gain power' (*The
Standard* March 30 2010).

THE POLITICS OF DEVELOPMENT

Moi had deftly deployed a well-developed patron–client system which
took the form of 'development' during both periods of single-party
rule and that of the multiparty system. 'Development' was a by-word
for state largesse which the KANU régime distributed to clients and followers mostly through the *Harambee* system (Haugerud 1995: 45–50).
Once the political terrain was opened to multiparty competition, the
nature of previous regional exclusion saw the emergence of ethnic-
based opposition parties. This meant that in effect, the ethnic identity
of a Presidential candidate outweighed any other credentials that a candidate might have. Voters from a Presidential candidate's ethnic community would more likely vote for one of their own regardless of the
leadership qualities of those parliamentary candidates. Oloo suggests that
during the single-party state, the factors that were influential in the election of a candidate were individual leadership, skills, rhetoric, clan line-
age, development record, campaign funds and state patronisation. The
factors operated either singularly or in combination (Oloo 2005: 159).
Presidential candidates were overwhelmingly voted for by their ethnic
homelands.

In 1993, Moi reached out to opposition political parties. This was
politically prudent since it shored up the KANU tally in parliament

during crucial motions. Subsequently, Oginga Odinga, Kenya's doyen of opposition politics and Moi's erstwhile nemesis, surprised many when he led FORD-Kenya into what was referred to as 'a cooperation' with KANU. The ostensible reason for this volte-face was for the sake of development among the Luo community (Badejo 2006: 184). The Luo had felt politically and economically marginalised by both the Moi and Kenyatta régimes. This 'cooperation', however, was unpopular among fellow opposition leaders. The rapprochement showed how Odinga had mellowed, as he had previously had had a knack at confrontational politics. However, Odinga realised that Kikuyu politicians would not support him which convinced him to embrace Moi due to reasons highlighted earlier in Chap. 4 some of which were mere cultural stereotypes.

The cooperation between KANU and FORD-Kenya pointed to Moi's mastery of a politics of cooptation. Through the cooperation, Moi brought into the fold the Luo, arguably a community that personified opposition politics in Kenya. In as much as both Moi and Odinga portrayed the alliance as meant to bring development to the Luo community, they did not get into the details of what 'development' meant. It was not a structured political arrangement and did not enjoy the support of most FORD-Kenya membership. The Luo were taxpayers like other tribes and therefore were entitled to public goods regardless of their tribal and political affiliation. However, a centralised state, patronage politics and the selective allocation of national resources based on tribal considerations ensured that the state was used in promoting partisan politics.

Obligations and responsibilities governing the relationship between the governed and their leaders did not hold under Moi's rule and subsequently. 'Development' became a carrot and a stick that the government invariably dangled before and wielded against the opposition to extract acquiescence. At a rally on July 6, 1994, Moi reportedly derided parliamentary contributions by the FORD-Kenya MP from Kisii, Henry Obwocha. Moi warned him that there would be no 'development' in his constituency unless he defected to KANU (Badejo 2006: 183). The 2010 Constitution provided for county governments, an attempt to devolve power and resources to this second tier of government and mitigate zero-sum politics. But the rhetoric of linking 'development' to loyalty for the President and the government, in a quid pro quo manner, persisted under Uhuru Kenyatta, Moi's political protege, since the state retained 85% of the national revenue.

CONCLUSION

The period between 1992 and 1997 exposed the salience of ethnicity in Kenya's multiparty politics. Ethnicity thwarted any effort at devising an alternative form of politics as illustrated by Safina and SDP. Apart from the Big Man form of politics that Moi deployed, opportunism among the country's politics impeded establishment of competitive politics. The chapter shows that Kenya underwent transition but not transformation after both the 1992 and 1997 elections. Two reasons accounted for this. First, the KANU régime used tribal violence to displace opposition supporters in order to distort ethnic demographics especially in the Rift Valley Province and retained power in 1992. Five years later, the régime instigated violence again whose severest repercussions were felt at the coastal region. Second, the institutional framework of the single-party state and politicians, carryovers from the single-party era impeded Kenya's political, social, economic and constitutional reform. The chapter showed that ethnicity, opposition disunity and the winner-takes-all electoral system worked in Moi's favour. Significantly, the electoral body, ECK, lacked impartiality and deliberately disenfranchised voters in opposition bases. This highlighted the weakness of one of the institutions tasked with organising and conducting above-board elections. What I deduce from the politics of cooperation is that Kenya needed to rid itself of zero-sum politics that not only provided an incentive for the use of unorthodox means such as state violence to win elections, but also rendered losers in elections susceptible to financial and material inducements by the ruling party. Of concern was that in a zero sum political system, it progressively became extremely hard for the losers during presidential elections to upstage the winners subsequently. Power contests for the sake of it exposed KANU and opposition parties as entities devoid of principles. To both the opposition parties and KANU, manifestos were a mere formality. They sought to either attain power or retain it on the strength of ethnic demographics. Most politicians had been socialised within the single-party mould and were drawn to politics that safeguarded the interests of the *ancien régime*. The preponderance of opportunistic politicians and self-styled tribal spokespersons on the country's political landscape was the single most hindrance to reform in Kenya.

NOTES

1. Baregu defines Constitutionalism as 'a political culture that nurtures and sustains adherence to a Constitution as a social contract between the rulers and the ruled' (Baregu 2010: 28).
2. The gerontocracy politics surfaced again during the 2013 and 2017 presidential elections that pitted Uhuru Kenyatta against Oginga Odinga's son, Raila Odinga. Kenyatta's supporters dismissed Odinga's candidature on both occasions because of age. In 2017, Odinga was 72. But these critics had no issue voting for Mwai Kibaki who ascended to power at 71. Neither did they recall that Jomo Kenyatta became Kenya's Prime Minister at 72 and president at 73. Therefore, like Oginga Odinga's critics before, tribalism but not the age factor, was what inspired Raila Odinga's critics.
3. This voting pattern haunted Muite after the elections when some FORD-Kenya members questioned the wisdom of retaining him as First Vice Chairman in line to take over from Odinga in the event of the latter's departure in a party with "almost no Kikuyu support" (Throup and Hornsby 1998: 547).
4. In 1992 and 1997, the Kikuyu were divided along regional lines. In 1992, the Southern Kikuyu voted for Matiba while those from the northern part of Central Province voted for Kibaki. In 1997, with Matiba out of the Presidential race, the southern Kikuyu hesitantly supported Kibaki which accounted for Charity Ngilu's SDP winning some parliamentary seats in the region (Kariuki 2005: 104).
5. Kenya was one of the most unequal societies in the world. Its richest citizens earned 56 times more than its poorest citizens and 10% of its citizens controlled 42% of the country's wealth. The poorest 10% controlled 0.76% of the country's wealth making Kenya the tenth most unequal country in the world and the fifth in Africa (OMCT 2008: 7).

REFERENCES

Books & Book Chapters

Ajulu, R. 1995. *The Transition to Multi-partyism in Kenya: The December 1992 Presidential, Parliamentary and Municipal Elections.* Leeds Centre for Democratisation Studies. Leeds University.

Badejo, A. 2006. *Raila Odinga An Enigma in Kenyan Politics.* Nairobi: Yintab Books, Nairobi.

Baregu, M. 2010. The Legitimacy Crisis and the Resource of Military Coups in Africa the Limits of Democratisation In *When Elephants Fight: Preventing and*

Preventing and Resolving Electoral- Related Conflict in Africa, ed. K. Matlosa, G. Khadiagala, and V. Shale. Johannesburg: EISA.

Bratton, M., and N. van de Walle. 1997. *Democratic Experiments in Africa. Régime Transitions in Comparative Perspective.* Cambridge: Cambridge University Press.

Chabal, P., and Daloz, J. 1999. *Africa Works Disorder as Political Instrument.* Oxford: James Currey.

Cowen, M., and K. Kanyinga. 2002. The 1997 Elections in Kenya The Politics of Communality & Locality. In *Multiparty Elections in Africa*, ed. M. Cowen, and L. Laakso. Oxford: James Currey.

Cowen, M., and Laakso, L. 2002. Elections & Election Studies. In *Multiparty Elections in Africa*, ed. Cowen, M. and Laakso, L. Oxford: James Currey.

Grignon, F. 2001. Breaking the 'Ngilu Wave': The 1997 Elections in Ukambani. In *Out for the Count The 1997 General Elections and Prospects for Democracy in Kenya*, ed. Rutten, M. Mazrui A. & Grignon, F. Kampala: Fountain Publishers Ltd.

Haugerud, A. 1995. *The Culture of Politics in Modern Kenya.* Cambridge: Cambridge University Press.

Huntington, S. 1991. *The Third Wave: Democratisation in the Late Twentieth Century.* Norman: Oklahoma University Press.

Katumanga, M. 2002. Internationalisation of Democracy: External Actors in Kenya Elections. In *Electoral Politics in Kenya,* ed. Chweya, L. Nairobi: Claripress.

Kariuki, J. 2005. Choosing the President. In *The Moi Succession Elections 2002*, ed. H. Maupeu, M. Katumanga, and W. Mitullah. Nairobi: TransAfrica Press.

Kadima, D., and F. Owuor. 2006. The National Rainbow Coalition Achievements and Challenges of Building and Sustaining Broad-Based Political Coalition in Kenya. In *The Politics of Party Coalitions in Africa*, ed. D. Kadima. EISA: Auckland Park.

Katumanga, M. 2010. Militarised Spaces and the Post-2007 Electoral Violence. In *Tensions and Reversals in Democratic Transitions*, ed. K. Kanyinga, and D. Okello. Nairobi: Society for International Development and Institute for Development Studies-University of Nairobi.

Kibwana, K., and Maina, W. 1996. State and Citizen: Visions of Constitutional and Legal Reform in Kenya's Emergent Multiparty Democracy'. In *Law and The Struggle for Democracy in East Africa*, ed. Oloka-Onyango, J, Kibwana and Peter, C. Nairobi: Claripress.

Mitullah, W. 2002. Democratisation at Grassroots: Local Government Elections in Kisumu Municipality. In *Electoral Politics in Kenya*, ed. Chweya, L. Nairobi: Claripress.

Mutunga, W. 2002. The Unfolding Political Alliances and their Implications for Kenya's Transition. In *Building an Open Society The Politics of Transition in Kenya*, ed. L. Mute, W. Kioko, and K. Akivaga. Nairobi: Claripress.

Murunga, G., and Nasong'o S. (2007) (eds.). *Kenya The Struggle for Democracy*. Dakar: CODESRIA.

Ogot, B.A. 1996a. The Politics of Populism. In *Decolonisation and Independence in Kenya* ed. Ogot, B.A. and Ochieng', W.R. Nairobi: East African Educational publishers.

Ogot, B. A. 1996b. Transition from Single-Party to Multiparty System 1989–1993. In *Decolonisation and Independence in Kenya*, ed. Ogot, B.A. and Ochieng', W.R. Nairobi: East African Educational publishers.

Oloo, A. 2005. The Raila Factor in Luoland. In *The Moi Succession Elections 2002*, ed. H. Maupeu, M. Katumanga, and W. Mitullah. Nairobi: Transafrica Press.

Throup, D., and C. Hornsby. 1998. *Multiparty Politics in Kenya*. Oxford: James Currey.

Wanjala, S. 1996. Presidentialism, Ethnicity, Militarism and Democracy in Africa: The Kenyan Example. In *Law and The Struggle for Democracy in East Africa*, ed. Oloka-Onyango, J, Kibwana and Peter, C. Nairobi: Claripress.

Wanjala, S. 2002. Elections and the Political Transition in Kenya. In *Building an Open Society The Politics of Transition in Kenya*, ed. L. Mute, W. Kioko, and K. Akivaga. Nairobi: Claripress.

Wrong, M. 2009. *It's Our Turn to Eat The Story of a Kenya Whistle Blower*. London: Fourth Estate.

Journals

Ajulu, R. 1993. The Kenya General Elections: A Preliminary Assessment, In *Review of African Political Economy*, No. 56, 98–102.

Ajulu, R. 1998. Kenya's democracy experiment: The 1997 elections. *Review of African Political Economy* 25 (76): 275–285.

Anderson, D. 2002. Vigilantes, Violence and the Politics of Public Order in Kenya. *African Affairs* 101: 531–555.

Brown, S. 2001. Authoritarian Leaders and Multiparty Election in Africa: How Foreign Donors Help to Keep Kenya's Daniel Arap in Power. In *Third World Quarterly*, 22(5), PP. 725–739. Available Online: www.jstor.org Accessed Sep 13 2016.

Berman, J., J. Cottrell, and Y. Ghai. 2010. Patrons Clients, and Constitutions: Ethnic Politics and Political Reform in Kenya. *Canadian Journal of African Studies* 43 (3): 461–506.

Kagwanja, P. 2005. 'Power to Uhuru': Youth Identity and Generational Politics in Kenya's 2002 Elections. *African Affairs* 105 (418): 51–75.

Klopp, J. 2001. "Ethnic Clahes" and Winning Elections: The Case of Kenya's Electoral Despotism. In *Canadian Journal of African Studies*, 35(3). 473–517. Available Online www.jstor.org.innopac.wits.ac.za/stable/486297. Retrieved November 1, 2016.

Khadiagala, G. 2010. Political Movements and Coalition Politics in Kenya: Entrenching Ethnicity. *South African Journal of International Affairs* 17 (1): 65–84.

Mueller, S. 2008. The Political Economy of Kenya's Crisis. *Journal of Eastern African Studies* 2 (2): 185–210.

Mwangi, O. 2008. Political Corruption, Party Financing and Democracy in Kenya. *Journal of Modern African Studies* 46 (2): 267–285.

Nasong'o, S. 2007. Political Transition without Transformation: The Dialectic of Liberalisation without Democratisation in Kenya and Zambia. *African Studies Review* 50 (1): 83–107.

Ndegwa, S. 1998. The Incomplete Transition: The Constitutional and Electoral Context in Kenya. *Africa Today* 45 (2): 193–212.

Shilaho, W. 2013. Old Wine in New Skins: Kenya's 2013 Elections and the Triumph of the Ancien Régime. *Journal of African Elections special Issue The Evolving Role of Elections in Africa* 12 (3): 89–119.

Steeves, J. 2006. Beyond Democratic Consolidation in Kenya; Ethnicity, Leadership and 'Unbounded Politics'. *African Identities.* 4 (2): 195–211.

Stephen, Brown. 2010. Authoritarian leaders and multiparty elections in Africa: How foreign donors help to keep Kenya's Daniel arap Moi in power. *Third World Quarterly* 22 (5): 725–739.

Southall, R. 1998. Moi's Flawed Mandate: The Crisis Continues in Kenya. *Review of African Political Economy* 25 (75): 101–111.

Reports

Amnesty International. 2013. Police Reform in Kenya: 'A Drop in the Ocean'. London. Amnesty International Publications. Online: http://www.refworld.org/pdfid/510ba3de2.pdf. Accessed 23 Aug 2017.

BBC World Service Trust. 2008. 'The Kenya 2007 Elections and their aftermath: The role of the media and communication' in Policy briefing 1 Online: https://assets.publishing.service.gov.uk/media/57a08b8ee5274a31e0000c08/kenya_policy_briefing_08.pdf. Accessed 25 August 2017.

Daily Nation. 1999. Court dismisses Kibaki petition against Moi. July 23. Online: http://www.nation.co.ke/news/1056-389344-l787gez/index.html. Accessed 25 Aug.

The EastAfrican. 2013. Story of petitions has changed. March 16. Online: http://www.theeastafrican.co.ke/news/Story-of-petitions-has-changed/2558-1722140-xt6ad8/index.html. Accessed 25 Aug 2017.

Human Rights Watch (HRW). (2008). Ballots to Bullets Organised Political Violence and Kenya's Crisis of Governance, Vol 20 No 1 (A). Available online: http://www.hrw.org/sites/default/files/reports/kenya0308web.pdf. Accessed 10 Oct 2016.

ICC. 2012. Situation in the Republic of Kenya in the Case of the Prosecutor v. Francis Kirimi Muthaura, Uhuru Muigai Kenyatta and Mohammed Hessein Ali (Decision on the Confirmation of Charges). http://www.icc-cpi.int/icc-docs/doc/doc1314543.pdf. Accessed 28 Jan 2015.

Kenya Human Rights Commission (KHRC). 1998. Killing the Vote State Sponsored Violence and Flawed Elections in Kenya. Nairobi: KHRC.

Kenya National Commission on Human Rights. 2008. 'The Cry of Blood' Report of Extra-Judicial Killings and Disappearances. Online: http://www. marsgroupkenya.org/pdfs/2009/03/KNCHR_crimes-against-humanity-extra-judicial-killings-by-kenya-police-exposed.pdf. Accessed 9 Nov 2015.

KNCHR & Kenya National Land Alliance (KNLA). 2006. Unjust Enrichment The Making of Land Grabbing Millionaires in Living Large Series. Vol 2 No 1 The Plunder of Karura, Ngong and Kiptagich Forests. Online: www.knchr. org. Accessed 5 Oct 2016.

Kenya Human Rights Commission (KHRC). 2011. Lest We Forget: The Faces of Impunity in Kenya, Nairobi. Online: www.khrc.or.ke.

OMCT (World Organisation Against Torture). 2008. The Lie of the Land Addressing the Economic Social and Cultural Root Causes of Torture and Other Forms of Violence in Kenya. Online: www.omct.org. Accessed 5 Oct 2016.

Republic of Kenya. 1963. The Constitution of the Republic of Kenya (as amended to 2008). Online: http://www.unesco.org/new/fileadmin/ MULTIMEDIA/HQ/CI/WPFD2009/pdf/Kenyan_Constitution_ amended_2008.pdf. Accessed 11 March 2012.

Republic of Kenya. 1992. Report of Parliamentary Select Committee to Investigate Ethnic Clashes in Western and Other Parts of Kenya, 'Kiliku Commission.' Nairobi: Government Printer.

Republic of Kenya. 1999. Report of the Judicial Commission Appointed to Inquire into Tribal Clashes in Kenya, 'Akiwumi Commission'. Nairobi: Government printer.

Republic of Kenya. 2008. Commission of Inquiry into Post-Election Violence (CIPEV) or 'the Waki Commission'. Nairobi: Government Printer. Online: http://www.dialoguekenya.org/docs/PEV%20Report.pdf. Accessed 10 Nov 2011.

Republic of Kenya. 2004. *Report of the Commission of Inquiry into the Illegal/ Irregular Allocation of Land; Ndung'u Commission*. Nairobi: Government Printer.

Newspapers

The Weekly Review. 1992. A Constitution Much like the Rest July 3.
The Weekly Review. 1992. Now Comes the Hard Part May 8.
The Weekly Review. 1992. Ethnic Strife March, 20.
The Weekly Review. 1992. New Spate of Ethnic Clashes March, 13.
The Weekly Review. 1992. The Clashes Report September, 25.
Daily Nation. 2009. Mau list of shame, July 29. Online: http://www.nation.co.ke/News/-/1056/631968/-/uliiuc/-/index.html. Accessed 5 Oct 2015.
The Standard 2010. Ocampo tables 20 names for prosecution March 30. Online: http://www.standardmedia.co.ke/archives/InsidePage.php?id=20000047 82&cid=4&ttl=Ocampo%20tables%2020%20names%20for%20prosecution. Accessed 24 Sep 2016.

Interviews

Ondari. 2009. Sondu: January 16.
Modi. 2009. Nyakach: Janaury, 16.

CHAPTER 5

The State Ruptures

Abstract The chapter argues that the leadership transition from Daniel arap Moi to Mwai Kibaki in 2002, constituted a democratic reversal. The 2002 elections presented a watershed moment in Kenya's post-colonial history because it was the first time that an incumbent handed over power to a successor much as both Moi and Kibaki were establishment politicians. Thus Kibaki's ascendancy to power on a reform agenda and backed by a broad tribal alliance, did not lead to the anticipated reform but in fact blocked transformation. A resurgence of Kikuyu dominance of the political and economic spheres elicited resistance from marginalized ethnic groups that snowballed into the divisive 2005 referendum, then the equally divisive 2007 disputed presidential elections, and the subsequent post-election violence. The fear of losing control of the state by the plutocrats, entrenched impunity, ethnicity, historical injustices, especially land related, and weak institutions contributed to the violence. These issues were at the core of Kenya's fragility. The 2007–2008 post-election violence was not some atavistic "tribal" warfare. Although disputed Presidential elections were the proximate cause, a legacy of state-sanctioned injustices, impunity and institutionalized amnesia were some of the substantive causes.

Keywords Danial arap moi · Mwai kibaki · Kikuyu · Tribal warfare
Presidential elections

© The Author(s) 2018
W.K. Shilaho, *Political Power and Tribalism in Kenya*,
https://doi.org/10.1007/978-3-319-65295-5_5

INTRODUCTION

The power transfer from Moi to Kibaki following the 2002 elections was hailed in Kenya and internationally. This was largely because the rarity of peaceful transitions in Africa in which the incumbent lost to an opposition candidate and conceded defeat. Both KANU and NARC, an ethnic alliance that propelled Kibaki into power, were indistinguishable entities because of similarities in composition and political orientation and thus the 2002 elections marked the mere exchange of power between sets of political elite based on personal rather than competing visions for Kenya. The power shift was supposed to place Kenya along a sound path towards socio-economic and political renewal. However, the fallout within NARC accentuated ethnic consciousness in the country and set in motion a series of political events that resulted in the violently disputed 2007 presidential elections and the subsequent post-election violence (Branch and Cheeseman 2008).

The transition was an opportunity for the reform of Kenya's politics. Instead the baton of power merely passed over from Moi to Kibaki, without ridding the polity of tribalism, political intolerance, corruption and patronage perfected under the single-party state. Kibaki's political history cast doubts upon his ability to provide substantial leadership in the reorganisation of Kenya's politics. He had served in the governments of his predecessors in various prominent portfolios, including as Moi's deputy for 10 years from 1978. He was thus a creature of the system and would with difficulty bring a 'new' ethos into the management of politics in Kenya. The state remained a site for predatory[1] politics as it had been under both Kenyatta and Moi. In spite of the reformist agenda that contributed to NARC's victory, the Kenya's politicians especially close allies of Kibaki continued to exploit the state for personal benefit and that of their allies. The tribe remained the fulcrum of political mobilisation, the basis on which distribution of resources and government appointments was made and the avenue through which grievances were nursed and articulated. The continued exploitation of 'tribe' as the vector of political mobilisation served the interests of the politicians. NARC exploited it as a camouflage for opportunism, tardiness, corruption and inability to reform the state. Against this background, the chapter analyses the Janus effect of tribalism under NARC by which I mean tribalism was the glue that united NARC and the basis of its disintegration. The chapter further exposes the volatility latent in Kenya's status hitherto as the most stable country in a strife-torn region. NARC had its internal contradictions which, in large measure, explains why the NARC government constantly spoke at cross-purposes. NARC campaigned on an agenda of reform that went too far for most of its reactionary leaders. Its campaign message might thus be construed as a ruse to rally support from Kenyans desperate for change. However, most of the NARC members could not and had no intention of implementing it since they had opposed reform while under KANU and only opportunistically joined opposition politics. This was the case despite Kibaki's acknowledgement of the opposition unity and patriotism in his inauguration speech, 'Never in the history of this country have its leaders come together and worked so hard together as one indivisible entity with one vision. It is the love of Kenya that has brought us together. We chose to let go our individual differences and personal ambitions in order to save this nation' (Kibaki's Inauguration speech Daily Nation December 31, 2002). Incessant wrangles in NARC showed that prebendalism in the sense of the desire for the financial resources that office provided a fixation with ethnic arithmetic in political calculations and personality rather than policy-based politics characterised NARC, and would remain the bane of Kenya's multiparty politics unless a leader seized by the challenges besetting the citizenry but not diminished by insularity, got elected as President.

THE MOUNT KENYA MAFIA

Kibaki would not have been elected president in 2002 had it not been for the ethnically crosscutting NARC. However, Kibaki let his presidency be hijacked by Kikuyu and other politicians from GEMA community whom the media referred to as the Mount Kenya mafia. Mafia Kibaki had twice previously unsuccessfully run for President in 1992 and 1997 based on the GEMA support base. A respondent seemed to capture disgruntlement among communities that had voted for Kibaki but felt excluded,

> The 2002 dream was betrayed by Kibaki and the Kikuyu elite not the masses of the Kikuyu. 2002 was a turning point in Kenya's politics when Kikuyu history failed to turn. Kenyans voted against Moi and Uhuru but Kibaki reversed that history once he come into power. Anyway Michuki stated that they were interested in power not reforms 'since one of our own is in power' (Interview Muluka, January 23, 2009).

Despite its inherent weaknesses, its supporters essentially expected NARC to observe ethnic inclusivity in governance. The main NARC weaknesses were twofold: it was led by Kibaki, a non-reformer and was crafted on ethnicity. Paradoxically, given its multi-ethnic appeal, NARC fanned the embers of ethnic exclusion and exacerbated ethnic rifts that pre-existed Kenya's return to multiparty politics. NARC was a con-glomeration of ethnic Big Men despite some of the planks in its reform agenda that included economic improvement and constitutional review. Thus, as Barkan has shown, NARC's reform agenda partly accounted for the support it garnered across ethnic divides (Barkan 2004: 89–99). Unlike ethnically stand-alone opposition parties in 1992 and 1997, NARC represented Kenya's populous ethnic communities and had a semblance of national diversity. Yet reform pledges during the campaign masked the ethnic undertones within the coalition. After being sworn in, Kibaki reneged on all of NARC's campaign pledges apart from the intro-duction of the controversial plan for universal primary education.

Kibaki was involved in a road accident and severely injured weeks before the 2002 elections and was hospitalised abroad. Kijana Wamalwa, his running mate, was also taken ill and hospitalised abroad. Raila Odinga became the face of NARC and indefatigably campaigned for Kibaki and couched the NARC leadership in collegial terms. He urged Kenyans to vote three-piece suit style, that is, for a NARC councillor, MP and President. The landscape of political rivalry was turned upside down as Raila Odinga, a Luo, campaigned for Mwai Kibaki, not only a Kikuyu but also a politician who had seemed wedded to the *ancien régime*. In December 2002, Kibaki was sworn in while in a wheel chair and a neck brace. A period of convalescence followed during which there was a lag in establishing new government appointments which created the impression that Kibaki was not in charge. The GEMA politicians took advantage of the public sympathy for Kibaki to consolidate power by making cabinet appointments, appointments in the key sectors of the bureaucracy and ambassadorial postings in strategic capitals in the West skewed in favour of the Kikuyu and related GEMA tribes. This ethni-cisation of the state was reminiscent of the Kenyatta and Moi régimes. Oucho suggested that some of the appointees had long attained retire-ment age (Oucho 2010: 515).

Kibaki set up a committee, the *Integrity and Anti-Corruption Committee of the Judiciary in Kenya*, ostensibly to root out corruption within the judiciary in keeping with the NARC reform agenda. The then

Minister of Justice and Constitutional Affairs, Kiraitu Murungi, summed up its work as 'radical surgery'. The head of the committee, Justice Aaron Ringera, was Murungi's partner in a law firm and both were Meru by ethnicity. In addition, he had not himself been vetted having been part of the discredited judiciary under Moi. Justice Aaron Ringera was accused of hampering the fight against corruption as the head of the Kenya Anti-Corruption Commission (KACC) and therefore he lacked the requisite moral authority to head such a committee. He delivered death threats against John Githongo, while they both served under Mwai Kibaki. Githongo had been appointed by Kibaki as Permanent Secretary for Governance and Ethics, Kenya's anti-corruption czar, after the 2002 elections but was frustrated upon realising that the Kibaki regime, like the Moi one before, abetted the looting of public coffers through mega-corruption scandals. He resigned and went into exile in Britain (Wrong 2009: 218, 222, 245, 250, 327). In 2002, an Advisory Panel of Commonwealth Judges found Kenya's judiciary to be corruption riddled and recommended that it be reformed (The Advisory Panel 2002). However, Moi and Bernard Chunga, the Chief Justice, criticised the judges and ignored the report. Ringera did not therefore have the moral authority to assess the suitability of colleagues to serve on the bench. On the strength of the Ringera Judicial Report, Kibaki purged the judiciary of some judges under the guise of cleaning it up of corrupt and incompetent elements (Oucho 2010: 515). However, none of the sacked judges was ever prosecuted. This created the impression that Kibaki had wanted to replace the weeded out judges with those pliable and sympathetic to his régime and propagate the subservience of the judiciary to the executive. Justice Philip Waki[2] and other judges were reinstated after successfully challenging their sacking before a tribunal (Oucho 2010: 515).

Kibaki scuttled the reform process that had picked up pace during Moi's final years in office (Wanyande et al. 2007: 10). The quest to consolidate power became the single most important preoccupation of Kibaki and his allies. The NARC's ethnic Big Men had formed the coalition's top decision-making organ called The Summit before the 2002 elections. The Summit was instrumental in consolidating votes for Kibaki from diverse communities. However, once the Mount Kenya Mafia had appropriated the presidency they effectively blocked any new political luminaries within The Summit from reaching Kibaki. Consequently, The Summit collapsed. The Summit was NARC's idea of collegial leadership and an attempt to shift from the Kenyatta and Moi régimes whose hall-marks were arbitrary, whimsical, and unpredictable personal rule. Indeed, Kibaki stressed the idea of consultative governance in his inauguration speech:

> We want to bring back the culture of due process, accountability and transparency in public office. The era of "anything goes" is gone forever. Government will no longer be run on the whims of individuals. The era of roadside policy declarations is gone. My government's decisions will be guided by teamwork and consultations. (President Kibaki's Inauguration speech December 30, 2002)

THE NARC SPLITS OVER POWER SHARING

The NARC victory became yet another false start in Kenya's attempt at a break with the one-party legacy. The Kibaki-led National Alliance Party of Kenya (NAK) faction of NARC obstructed reform in the same way that KANU had done throughout its hold on power since independence. Raila Odinga's Liberal Democratic Party (LDP) faction was not entirely reform-oriented either. The veneer of ethnic diversity within NARC crumbled as it became mired in an ethnically based exclusionary politics. Kibaki lost legitimacy due to the erosion of the support across the country, except among Kikuyu coethnics. The LDP accused NAK of betrayal over the distribution of posts in the cabinet and government at large. Notably of NARC's 125 MPs, 69 MPs drawn from all the eight Provinces were affiliated to LDP which made LDP the senior partner in the coalition (Kadima and Owuor 2006: 212). Cabinet and parastatal appointments in 2003, however, were skewed in favour of Kibaki's DP. Of the 24 cabinet portfolios, the DP was allocated 12, the LDP 6, FORD-K 3 and NPK 1, a pattern that was reflected in other appointments in the bureaucracy (Kadima and Owuor 2006: 215). The acrimonious fallout regarding allocation of positions in the cabinet, the bureaucracy, and the stonewalling of reform by Kibaki, caused tension in the government, exacerbated tribal divided Kenyans and boiled over during the 2005 referendum on a draft Constitution.

Kibaki lost the 2005 Constitutional referendum—that I discuss later in the chapter—whereupon the government assumed a distinctly Mount Kenya hue. All the strategic appointments in the financial, security and defence sectors went exclusively to the Kikuyu and then other GEMA affiliates (Oucho 2010: 515). The fallout between Odinga and Kibaki spread to their supporters and polarised the country in ways similar to the previous era when KANU had been in power. At issue was the pre-election Memorandum of Understanding (MoU) that had spelled out power sharing on a 50–50 basis. NARC implosion was contrasted with Kibaki's exuberance during his inauguration,

> Some prophets of doom have predicted a vicious in-fighting in following this victory. I want to assure you that they will be disappointed. When a group of people come together over an idea or because of a shared vision, such a group can never fail or disintegrate. NARC will never die as long as the original vision endures. It will grow stronger and coalesce into a single party that will become a beacon of hope not only to Kenyans but to the rest of Africa. (President Kibaki's speech December 30, 2002)

A further and critical impediment to and consequence of the stalled transformation after NARC came into power was the continued conduct of multiparty politics under a one-party constitutional framework and mindset. In the absence of constitutional, institutional and legal reforms, the crux of governance upheavals stemming from systemic corruption, political assassinations, historical land inequities, interethnic clashes, exclusionary politics and impunity that threatened Kenya's social fabric remained intact. NARC lacked the will to change Kenya's political trajectory and follow the path of reform. Commenting on the revolution that never was in 2002, Ambunya, a youth in Nairobi, summed it thus, 'The electorate voted for change but to date no new Constitution since the politicians we have, have been there for many years. The forest may be different but the monkeys are the same' (Interview, Ambunya January 26, 2009). One of the distinguishing aspects of the Kibaki régime were the appointment and retention of civil servants aged at least 60 years to top-level positions effectively locking out 'younger, better qualified and energetic Kenyans' from power. Oucho suggested that the régime was unsure of what would become of the ill-gotten wealth of this group once they got out of power (Oucho 2010: 515).

The NARC had two political groupings that were intent on defending the status quo. The first group comprised elderly Kikuyu and Meru politicians whom Kibaki had recycled back into the government such as John Michuki, Matere Keriri, Francis Muthaura, George Muhoho and Njenga Karume. These politicians were nostalgic for the Kenyatta era, or as Badejo puts it, for 'the good old days of unbridled bleeding of the Kenyan State' (Badejo 2006: 197). This group blamed Moi for interfering with their predatory inclinations when he came into power (Barkan 2004: 92–93). The second group comprised 'Johnny-come-latelies' who fervently defended and benefitted from the one-party monolith, but who had opportunistically defected to the opposition after the legalisation of multiparty politics in 1991. Kibaki was the most prominent politician within this category much as he also fitted in the first category having resigned from KANU and the government as Minister of Health on December 26 1991 after Moi had acceded to multiparty politics on December 3 1991. These were essentially political opportunists and vacillators. These politicians ensured that Kenya remained hamstrung by the incongruence of 'effecting political liberalisation without democratising the political systems and the rules of the game' (Nasong'o 2007: 84). Nasong'o compellingly argued that Kenya's political liberalisation[3] merely brought forth the act of legalising opposition parties and accorded them freedom to contest political office (Nasong'o 2007: 84). However, democratisation and the restructuring of governance institutions that would entail redesigning the political architecture especially the electoral system to accommodate multiparty politics and to make it more responsive and accountable to the electorate did not take place (Nasong'o 2007: 84; Diamond 2008: 20).

The third NARC group comprised individuals who did not contribute at all to what was popularly referred to as the second liberation in reference to the struggle for multiparty democracy and respect for human rights since they were not only long serving KANU members but also high ranking. These politicians opportunistically defected from KANU over succession politics. They included Kalonzo Musyoka, Joseph Kamotho, George Saitoti, and Moody Awori to name but four. These politicians were affiliated to LDP. They were neither reformers nor had they been guided by the national interest in their opposition against Moi's preferred successor, Uhuru Kenyatta. I hasten, however, to add that in Kenya's politics characterised by vacillation, opportunism, tribalism and self-centredness, it was not possible to dichotomise politicians as either reformers or reactionaries. There were no ideological positions to necessitate such a separation and so I use the word 'reformer' guardedly. These formerly KANU politicians felt betrayed by Moi as most of them considered themselves politically senior to Uhuru Kenyatta who at the time was an unknown quantity and a political parvenue. Although

Raila Odinga was at some point the KANU Secretary General, and cabinet minister in Moi's administration, Raila Odinga was a seasoned opposition politician who had established an alternative centre of power in the party that rivalled Moi because he had joined KANU and the cabinet on his own terms backed up by a formidable ethnic constituency as leader of NDP in the lead up to the 2002 elections. Unlike Moi's clients who did not have the command of their respective tribes, Odinga was not vulnerable to Moi's 'use and dump' tactic (Badejo 2006: 211; Sunday Nation, February 17, 2002). Upon the collapse of the NDP-KANU entente over succession politics, Odinga corralled KANU renegades to defect to the opposition, a move that resulted in KANU implosion. Bar Raila Odinga, and previously National Development Party of Kenya (NDP) leaning politicians, and youthful politicians affiliated to FORD in the early 1990s, popularly known as Young Turks, NARC was composed of Moi clients who were sycophantic and timorous while in KANU.

The NARC was an unwieldy political organisation bereft of a coherent unifying philosophy. Significantly, most of its prominent politicians had a dubious political history. Some NARC politicians had been implicated in corruption and human rights violations including incitement to ethnic clashes in the early 1990s. Emmanuel Karisa Maitha, William ole Ntimama, George Saitoti and Joseph Kamotho were examples (KHRC 2011). Owing to their long-term affiliation with KANU, a disproportionate section of the NARC politicians identified with the single-party state and opposed reform. In the run-up to the 2002 elections, anyone who opposed Moi could style himself as a reformer. Ideology did not matter in the assembling partners within the NARC coalition. It would be misleading to state that the bar regarding principle was lowered. It simply did not exist. All NARC affiliate parties professed free market economy since as Kadima and Owuor observed most party representatives in Kenya conflated good governance principles such as transparency, accountability and national unity with ideology (Kadima and Owuor 2006: 205).

The NARC's opposition against Moi was as self-serving as Moi's rule that it pledged to reform. Rhetorical pronouncements about reform were consistent with an established duplicitous behaviour by Kenya's successive regimes.[4] It was therefore not possible for NARC, crowded by politicians devoid of ideological and moral conviction, to bring about reform in the post Moi political dispensation. The NARC projected a quest for power without the commitment to engineer the country socially, economically and politically. This had been an enduring inadequacy among the opposition parties in Kenya since the early 1990s (Nasong'o 2007: 95–96). The FORD pressure group turned political party had set this precedent in the early 1990s following the advent of multiparty politics (*The Weekly Review* July 3, 1992: 5). NARC was therefore virtually entirely composed of members of the *ancien régime* to whom reform was anathema. These politicians had been beneficiaries of the highly centralised political system which had allowed for attendant gatekeeping excesses. Thus early into Kibaki's tenure he emerged as quintessentially Moi-like and appeared to lack the will to take an audit of the country's post-independence politics. Even before getting elected, he had hinted at being unable to change the country's political trajectory. While accepting nomination as NARC Presidential candidate, he counselled against acting upon the report on state-instigated tribal clashes known as the Akiwumi report. He was reported to have cavalierly said, 'Do not waste time reading through every page of the report. Read it and leave the rest to historians because it is the nation's history and forgive. The truth is well known' (*Sunday Nation* November 24, 2002). Once in power he had resisted the formation of a Truth and Reconciliation Commission. It took the post-election violence in 2007 for the Truth Justice and Reconciliation Commission (TJRC) to be formed. Moreover, Kibaki commissioned an international firm, Kroll and Associates (UK), a private investigation and security firm, to track public money allegedly looted by Moi and his allies and possibly held in offshore accounts. However, he again shelved its report (*Daily Nation* December 11, 2010d). Besides the Ndung'u commission, the Kroll investigation was yet another initiative that Kibaki set up in 2003, early in his rule, ostensibly as proof that he was committed to addressing the corruption menace, endemic under Moi and Kenyatta. The failure to implement the recommendations contained in reports by these two bodies betrayed the lack of political will integral to the fight against corruption and other excesses that had undermined the Kenyan state since independence. Save for infrastructural development, this regime was an extension of the Moi and Kenyatta ones particularly its failure to appreciate ethnic inclusivity.

The Entrenched Plutocracy

Kenya's mostly election-linked quest for democratic transition has not produced a democratic public sphere, inclusive political systems, an accountable leadership and democratic institutions, and civilian controlled coercive arms of the state, but mostly an exclusionary and ethno conscious public sphere, predatory elite, militia rule and Praetorian coercive arms of the state. (Kanyinga et al. 2010: 15)

Although out of power, most leadership deficiencies associated with KANU such as patron-client politics survived it. Multiparty elections had not resulted in responsive and accountable leadership. The *ancien régime* was so entrenched that the legacy of Kenyatta and Moi single-party rule reproduced itself under Kibaki and then Uhuru Kenyatta. Elections *per se* could not neutralise vestiges of this legacy. The Kenyatta-Moi-Kibaki axis had vast economic interests and continued to frustrate efforts to reform Kenya's polity. For this reason, the Kenyan political elite, irrespective of party affiliation, regarded national politics as an opportunity to plunder the state. In this polity, the state was 'a site of eating' (Ogude 2009). This entailed looting of public coffers, land grabbing, nepotistic and tribally informed government appointments, questionable procurement and tendering processes and skewed national resource distribution in favour of the President's home region. There was a one-on-one relationship between inequalities and poverty in Kenya and exclusionary politics. A report by Society for International Development (SID) illuminated inequalities within the country. It significantly showed that Kenya's top 10% of the households controlled 42% of the total income while the bottom 10% controlled less than 1% (SID 2004: v). By 2002, children born in the then Nyanza Province, predominantly inhabited by Luo, were more likely to die within their first year of birth compared to those in resident in what was previously called Central Province dominated by Kikuyu (Cheeseman 2015: 165). As such, Ghai observed that, 'There was wide scale perception which statistics support, that the centralised state has, for the last 50 years, singularly failed to promote economic and political development and that only a few areas and a small elite had benefited from the policies of the government' (Ghai 2007). The bureaucracy was dominated by the Kikuyu followed by the Kalenjin whose percentages of the total civil service jobs were disproportionate to their population percentages. The Kikuyu constituted 17.7% of the population but occupied 22.3% of all jobs in the government. The Kalenjin occupied 16.7% of all civil services jobs disproportionate to their 13.3% of the population (*Daily Nation* April 6, 2011a). These inequalities stemmed from the fact that of Kenya's four presidents by 2017, three were kikuyu while the other Kalenjin.

The MPs perennially awarded themselves hefty salaries and perks yet Kenya's parliament was inefficient, tribally divided and corrupt making Kenyan MPs among the highest paid in Africa and even in the world (*Daily Nation* April 25, 2011b). This remuneration was in stark contrast to the pay that politicians in Europe and America received yet these economies were far bigger than Kenya's. This prebendalism picked up in pace soon after NARC came into power. 'Joe Khamis', a former NARC MP, detailed acts of corruption in the administration of parliament. Excerpts from his memoirs serialised by one of Kenya's dailies showed the extent to which MPs turned parliament into a cash cow through dubious tendering processes, receipt of perks, overseas junkets among other untoward acts aimed at self-aggrandisement (*Daily Nation* 25, 2011b).

The composition of NARC leadership appeared to be a reincarnation of KANU, although not as institutionally entrenched. Ajulu described NARC as a new clan of 'kleptocrats' similar to the old KANU predators (Ajulu 2003: 8). It was, however, difficult to distinguish KANU from NARC under the 'old' and 'new' binaries of predatory politics. A high school teacher I interviewed was of the view that almost the entire NARC political clan had been so '*Kanunised* that they could not shed the KANU slough and therefore could not bring change' (Interview, Machanja, January 15, 2009). The neologism in this context refers to corruption, malfeasance, impunity, ethnicised politics and anti-reform tendencies that were the hallmarks of KANU rule. Ultimately, the political histories of most of the NARC politicians belied the optimism of supporters in the party's capacity to transform the country.

It was credulous that its supporters could expect NARC to devise a better political path primarily because NARC was composed entirely of political turncoats formerly associated with KANU. Compounding matters was the fact that most of those who participated in the struggle for multiparty politics lacked economic resources and hence vulnerable to the privileges associated with power because they had been excluded from opportunities to extract rents from the state. GEMA politicians such as Kiraitu Murungi, Martha Karua, and Paul Muite who agitated for reform previously while Moi was at the helm, abandoned the reform rhetoric after they were either appointed as ministerial positions or simply supported the Mwai Kibaki and then Uhuru Kenyatta regimes on the basis of tribalism. John Michuki, a Kikuyu politician and cabinet minister under Kibaki, publicly confessed to the press that the Kikuyu were only interested in a share of the executive powers while Moi was in power. However, with the ascendance of Kibaki to power, they were no longer interested in constitutional reforms (*Saturday Nation* January 30, 2010). These politicians realised that a reformed state would be at odds with politics of wealth accumulation. In Mutua's words, they were lured by the politics of 'power, ethnicity and self-interest' and the language of reform was a subterfuge (Mutua 2009: 184).

Moreover civil society was depleted when some of its members were appointed to the judiciary and other government bodies (Mutua 2009. 208–209). This, however, did not affect its 'high institutional capacity' since it continued being critical and exposed the excesses of the Kibaki government (EU EOM 2008: 29–30). However, the act of joining the government by some members of civil society pointed at pervasive opportunism and unprincipled politics. Murunga and Nasong'o argued that the notion that civil society is the antithesis of the authoritarian state and an agent for change and transformation was flawed because there were elements of corruption and authoritarianism within civil society too (Murunga and Nasong'o 2006: 15). The religious fraternity appeared no better. During the Kibaki régime, religious groups had become embroiled in partisan politics (Ghai 2008: 213; Lynch 2006: 250; Cheeseman 2015: 84; *Daily Nation* February 5, 2010a). Some of them a declared preference for various presidential candidates during the 2007, 2013 and 2017 elections on the basis of self-interest couched under tribalism and sectarianism while still some accepted presidential appointments to statutory bodies.[5] Rev Mutava Musyimi changed from a critic of the Moi regime excesses to a reactionary; an apologist for the government of the day upon Kibaki's election in 2002. He was elected to parliament in 2007. It robbed them of the requisite moral gravitas and impartiality to mediate during disputes as happened in 2007. It was imperative that attitudinal shifts should take place at the leadership level in order for the country to transform. However, Kenya's leadership proved unable to attain attitudinal renaissance because of the insularity of individual interest nestled in ethnicity.

Completion of the constitutional review process was supposed to be the point of departure for the NARC administration in its attempt to transform the country. Moi had pledged a review of the Constitution during his New Year speech in 1995 but repeatedly reneged on this pledge (Ndegwa 1997: 612). Once the constitutional review process started, Moi scuttled and scuppered it. During the 2010 referendum campaigns on a draft Constitution, Kenya's second in as many years, in an ironic twist, Kibaki lambasted Moi who campaigned against it, for trying to mislead Kenyans on the contents of the draft, while he blocked reform throughout his tenure of office. Moi in turn lambasted Kibaki asking whence he got the moral authority to falter his legacy while he, Kibaki had failed to deliver on NARC's pledge of a new Constitution within 100 days of assuming power (*Daily Nation* July 29, 2010c). The spat served to expose the depth of leadership crisis in the country since each exposed the mendacity of the other.

Both the opposition politicians and KANU expediently exploited the Constitution issue to their advantage. Neither side was committed to ensuring that there was a new set of laws in Kenya. In the 1990s both Moi and the opposition had accorded the reform debate rhetorical support and had prioritised individual interests above national well-being (Lynch 2006: 239). Moi in collaboration with sections of the opposition had scuppered efforts at constitutional review in the run-up to the 1997 elections. Despite the expectant atmosphere that greeted Kibaki's election, he in turn 'stonewalled and torpedoed' the review process altogether (Mutua 2009: 14). It would take the 2007 post-election violence for Kibaki to face up to his own complicity in and the gravity of the divisive politics under the kind of weak institutions that he had elected to pursue.

KENYA: THE BASTION OF STABILITY?

The 2002 transfer of power pointed to an attempt to consolidate democracy in Kenya. Kenya passed muster in terms of the 'power transfer test' (Beetham 1994: 160) in which the opposition peacefully replaced an independence political party. This kind of power transfer is one of the tests of a consolidated democracy because in a representative democracy 'political authority must be based on a limited mandate, with citizens reserving the right to renew it periodically in free and fair elections' (Nasong'o 2007: 85). Since the advent of multiparty politics in the wake of the end of the bipolar world in 1989, Africa had witnessed elections marred by violence of which Kenya's and Zimbabwe's in 2007 and 2008, respectively, were among the most emblematic. The disputed Ivory Coast Côte d'Ivoire Presidential elections in 2010 followed by post-election violence were yet another illustration of democratic reversals in Africa. Yahya Jammeh, Gambia's autocrat in power for 22 years, was defeated in Presidential elections on December 2016 but refused to concede. Eventually, he was forced out of power by the threat of military intervention by the regional body, the Economic Community of West African States (ECOWAS). Africa's democratisation has to contend with the challenge posed by incumbents determined to win elections by hook or crook, and some who extend their tenures of office beyond the two term limit by tinkering with Constitutions. Yet some rulers stay in power in defiance of the law such as Joseph Kabila of Democratic Republic of the Congo (DRC) whose mandate ended in December 2016 but continued exercising authority under the pretext that the country was not ready for elections.

As the cases of Kenya, Zimbabwe Ivory Coast Côte d'Ivoire and Gambia showed, some incumbents in Africa were unwilling to concede defeat after losing elections because they had vested economic and political interests in the existing power arrangement structures. Some feared being held accountable for inequities gross human rights violations associated with their regimes. The Kibaki régime did not bring any lawsuit against Moi despite the litany of inequities that characterised the latter's régime ranging from corruption egregious human rights violations to political assassinations. The murder of Dr Robert Ouko in 1990, who was at the time the Minister of Foreign Affairs and International Cooperation, was one of the high profile political assassinations witnessed under the Moi regime. The Truth, Justice and Reconciliation Commission Report, recommended that Daniel arap Moi and his powerful irony, Nicholas Biwott—mentioned in Chap. 4 in connection with state violence—be investigated for the death of Ouko (The Final Report of the TJRC of Kenya 2013). Moi did not address inequities by Kenyatta either which institutionalised impunity and amnesia. The deduction was that Kibaki expected his successor to gloss over inequities under his watch. The Kibaki régime abetted corruption and perpetrated extrajudicial executions too (KNCHR 2008). Philip Alston, the UN Rapporteur on extrajudicial, summary and arbitrary killings (Alston Report 2009) and the Kenya National Commission on Human Rights report entitled '*The Cry of Blood' Report on Extra-Judicial Killings and Disappearances* documented summary executions by security agencies under Kibaki. The Kenyatta, Moi and Kibaki families illegally and irregularly acquired land as shown in Chap. 3. In a word, the transfer of power from Moi to Kibaki was a democratic reversal.

The successful 2002 elections in Kenya reinforced its image as an island of stability in a sea of turmoil within the East African, the Horn of Africa and Great Lakes regions (Human Rights Watch 2002: 3). The incident-free elections were conspicuous in the East African subregion known for its damaging internecine wars. In 2002, the then larger Sudan was making efforts towards a peace agreement following years of civil strife that had pitted the Khartoum government against rebels based in the southern part of the country. Sudan officially split into two countries on July 9, 2011 which saw the coming into being of South Sudan. Ethiopia had a history of civil strife and authoritarian regimes. In 2000, the semi-autonomous island of Zanzibar degenerated into violence following disputed elections. The eastern region of Democratic Republic of the Congo had become a theatre of war since the overthrow of Mobutu Sese Seko, one of Africa's prototype plunderers, in 1997. Both Uganda and Burundi straddled socio-economic and political reconstruction following years of intermittent civil wars and political uncertainty. Rwanda was still reeling from the horrifying events of the 1994 genocide. Somalia was closer to what a failed state looked like and had never experienced peace since the overthrow of the clan based régime of Siad Barre in 1991. NARC's victory was therefore a great boost to Kenya's standing internationally and a beacon of hope in the conflict-ridden subregion. Accordingly, George W. Bush invited Kibaki for a state visit ten months into office. Barkan pointed out that Kibaki was the first African head of state he had honoured as such (Barkan 2004: 87). The alien legitimacy upon which post-colonial African rulers relied on, as argued by Peter Ekeh (1975), was evident here.

The 2002 elections were iconic and a watershed in Kenya's post-colonial political history in the sense that they ended KANU's entrenched hold on power since independence. Both international and local observers hailed the elections as untypically free and fair compared to the previous ones of 1992 and 1997 (Ajulu 2003: 5; Barkan 2004: 90). Uhuru Kenyatta, the KANU Presidential candidate conceded defeat and Moi subsequently handed over power to Kibaki during a public ceremony before a mammoth crowd at Uhuru Park, a recreational park next to the Nairobi's central business district. Kenya had not held controversy-free Presidential elections before. As demonstrated in Chap. 4 Kenneth Matiba and Mwai Kibaki had filed petitions against the credibility of the election results in 1992 and 1997 respectively but the petitions were dismissed on a technicality (Brown 2001: 731, 734). The culture of disputed elections persisted in 2013 when Raila Odinga filed a petition against Uhuru Kenyatta's win but the Supreme Court, a jurisprudential innovation under the 2010 Constitution, dismissed it on a technicality. At the time of writing, a case was ongoing at the Supreme Court in which Odinga had yet again filed a presidential petition challenging the declaration of Kenyatta as the presidential winner during the 2017 elections arguing that the elections were fraudulent (Republic of Kenya 2017).

THE 2005 CONSTITUTIONAL REFERENDUM

Throup suggests that the 2005 referendum symbolised, by a banana for approval and an orange for rejection, did not pose any direct threat to Kibaki's hold on power (Throup 2008: 292). Both the existing and proposed constitutions retained a powerful presidency.[6] Yet Kibaki vigorously campaigned for the draft Constitution. His government arbitrarily created ethnically 'homogenous' administrative units called districts to woo communities to vote for the draft Constitution. While in the opposition, he had opposed the idea on the grounds that the units were economically unviable and a tax burden onto the people (Ogude 2009: 13). Moi devised this approach on Kenya's return to multiparty politics. Moi arbitrarily created districts, now defunct upon the promulgation of the 2010 Constitution, such as Suba, Teso, Mount Elgon, Kuria, and Mbeere to pander to tribal anxieties. Except for Mount Elgon, these districts were named after ethnic groups that previously belonged to districts in which they were minorities. Mount Elgon was hived off formerly Bungoma district to separate Sabaots from the dominant Luhya. John Michuki, (earlier mentioned) as an opposition politician had petitioned the courts to outlaw the districts that Moi had created but did not raise such concerns under Kibaki. Like the KANU régime, Kibaki deployed state resources such as vehicles and helicopters in the campaigns eliciting criticism from opponents. Despite this abuse of state resources, the government lost the referendum with 43% of the vote against 57% (EU EOM 2008: 7; Republic of Kenya 2008a: 93). Upon losing the referendum, Kibaki dissolved the cabinet and prorogued parliament. He reconstituted the cabinet after sacking disloyal cabinet ministers allied to the Orange camp including Raila Odinga, the lodestar of the 'No' campaign.

But the aftershocks of the referendum almost brought Kibaki's government down as more than 20 ministers and assistant ministers declined to take up their appointments. Superficially, this appeared to be innovative political behaviour in Kenya as most politicians considered appointment to the executive as the apogee of their political careers. Yet, as Whitaker and Giersch have shown, Ngilu and Musikari Kombo only momentarily declined appointments to the cabinet in order to twist the arm of a politically weakened Kibaki to appoint more of their allies to ministerial posts (Whitaker and Giersch 2009: 13). To plug the void created by the sacked ODM rebels, Kibaki replaced them with MPs from KANU and FORD-People to form the Government of National Unity (GNU) despite NARC having competed against the two in 2002. The GNU, however, was a convergence of reactionary politicians. Simeon Nyachae, the FORD-People leader, one of those included in the cabinet, was a wealthy politician and the personification of the discredited provincial administration. He had risen through the ranks beginning as a clerk in 1954 in the colonial service, and retired in 1986, at the apex, as Chief Secretary, Head of Civil Service and Secretary to the Cabinet. In between he had risen from district officer to provincial commissioner (*Daily Nation* November 19, 2002: 3). Nyachae was elected to parliament in 1992 and served until 2007 when he lost his seat during that year's elections. He was the quintessential system's man; a plutocrat. The co-optation of KANU and FORD-People in the government was testament to the fact that principle and ideology were absent in Kenya's highly fickle, insular, and idiosyncratic politics. Kibaki had uncharacteristically hit out hard at KANU during his inauguration in 2002: 'Fellow Kenyans, I am inheriting a country which has been badly ravaged by years of misrule and ineptitude. There has been a wide disconnect between the people and the Government, between people's aspirants (sic) and the government's attitude toward them' (Kibaki's Inaugural Speech December 30, 2002).

The 2005 referendum was a dress rehearsal for the 2007 Presidential election.[7] The referendum outcome shaped the incendiary path towards the 2007 elections. Buoyed up by the plebiscite victory, the Orange camp transformed into a political party, the Orange Democratic Movement (ODM) and began preparations for the 2007 elections. Raila Odinga, its de facto leader and the face of the opposition against the draft Constitution, formed an ethnic alliance modelled on the NARC Summit. Initially, the Orange camp comprised the big ethnic groups, Luhya, Kamba, Luo, Kikuyu, Kalenjin and less populous ones from the Rift Valley, North Eastern and Coast Provinces. Uhuru Kenyatta, though, pulled out of the Orange camp after the referendum ostensibly to maintain the KANU identity, since he was the KANU national Chairman at the time. Kenyatta's disassociation from ODM removed any trace of Kikuyu support that the Orange Camp might have had.

When Raila Odinga and his supporters tried to register a party called the Orange Democratic Movement (ODM), they discovered that a party by a similar name had already been registered allegedly by people acting at the behest of the Kibaki government. The intention was to frustrate attempts by the victorious Orange camp in morphing into a political party. At issue was the word 'orange', a brand then associated with the referendum victory. To side-step this hurdle, the Odinga group registered a party with a similar name but with the addendum 'Kenya' (ODM-K) whose registered office bearers were individuals loyal to Kalonzo Musyoka. At different times Musyoka served as the KANU Organising Secretary and Vice Chairman and had been a long time cabinet minister under Moi. He was one of the 'Johnny-come-latelies' into opposition politics in 2002. ODM-K officials led by Kalonzo's tribesman, Daniel Maanzo, refused to step down in favour of those perceived to be allied to Raila Odinga when a power struggle between Musyoka and Odinga ensued over the mode of nominating the party's Presidential candidate. The two parted ways. Odinga and his allies decamped ODM-K and took control of the 'original' ODM after individuals who had secretly registered it surrendered the party to him. Wanyama suggested that the Odinga group bought ODM from one Mugambi Imanyara in whose name ODM had been registered (Wanyama 2010: 71). Raila Odinga then transformed ODM from a briefcase political entity into a formidable mass movement.

The 2005 referendum outcome exemplified another step towards the consolidation of democracy in Kenya. It appeared to build on the 2002 elections in which the electorate voted against choices favoured by incumbents and prevailed. However, for Kibaki and his coterie, the 2005 referendum did not raise the stakes. They could afford to lose. The flipside was that the referendum exposed campaigns saturated by ethnic stereotyping and innuendoes (KNCHR 2006). Kadima and Owuor observed that although the contents of the draft Constitution were discussed and debated, the referendum campaigns showed that politicians canvassed for support along ethnic lines with the major tribes being galvanised against the Kikuyu and related ethnic groups in Mount Kenya region (Kadima and Owuor 2006: 220). Hate speech[8] became rife and resurfaced in the 2007 election campaigns both among politicians and in the media. The substance of the draft Constitution was lost as politicians sensationalised and personalised the debate on the content of the document (*Daily Nation* October 15, 2010b). According to the Kenya National Commission on Human Rights (KNCHR),

> ...the referendum was about a new Constitution only in name. Rather, it was a moment to settle various political scores, up-end different political layers, and assert political superiority. And in this zero-sum game between politicians, ethnicity, patronage, and incitement became the preferred tools of the trade, with the people of the country bearing the brunt of their antics. (KNCHR 2006: 5)

Politicians implicated in making inflammatory speeches got away with obnoxious behaviour despite the KNCHR furnishing the Attorney General with detailed evidence of law breaching by the offending politicians. Amos Wako, the Attorney General, frustrated efforts by those who sought to bring the offending individuals to justice (KNCHR 2006: 6). By the time elections were held in 2007, Kenya's political landscape was a powder keg. The controversial re-election of Kibaki was the spark required to ignite the polarised country into violence.

THE NARC FALLOUT AND THE DISPUTED 2007 ELECTIONS

Kibaki's decision to renege on the implementation of the MoU aggravated mistrust among Kenya's political elite and within the society. It defeated the sense of unity among opposition parties captured in his inauguration speech. It led to the disintegration of NARC and an unstable polity prior to the 2007 elections. The MoU was meant to act as a guide in the formation of an inclusive government based on the political strengths of LDP and NAK. The trashing of the MoU took the country back to the 1960s polarisation between the Kikuyu and Luo, a precursor to elite fragmentation that had characterised Kenya's post-independence period (Cheeseman 2009: 3). The siege mentality among the Kikuyu was so intense that Uhuru Kenyatta, who doubled as the KANU Chairman and Official Leader of the Opposition at the time, did the unthinkable by not running for President but instead chose to campaign for Kibaki, a fellow Kikuyu. Kenyatta's strategy was to tie up his position in order to inherit the mantle of leadership and support of the Kikuyu ethnic bloc after Kibaki. So unsettled was Kenya's oligarchy in 2007 that Moi had no time for KANU, the party he invariably spoke in support of, and endorsed Kibaki, the Party of National Unity (PNU) candidate for re-election. Moi, Kibaki and Kenyatta were *ancien régime* members wary of the possibility of Raila Odinga defeating Kibaki. Besides Odinga had threatened to punish previous corruption and recover money stolen from the Exchequer (Mueller 2008: 201).

However, unlike previous splits, the NARC fallout snowballed into a series of political duels about such issues as the 2005 referendum and culminated in the unprecedented inter ethnic violence of 2007–2008 following disputed presidential results in which Raila Odinga and his supporters accused Mwai Kibaki and the electoral body of robbing him of victory. The 2007–2008 post-election was not some primordial tribal warfare, a vestige of a bygone era. It was in tandem with cyclical state violence euphemised as tribal clashes that had characterised Kenya since 1991, when Kenya returned to multiparty politics due to blocked reform and exclusive politics. For the analyses of Kenya's 2007 elections (see Throup 2008; Mueller 2008, Branch and Cheeseman 2008, Khadiagala 2008). The opportunity to lance Kenya's festering post-colonial abscess, comprising perfidy, mendacity, impunity, native-foreigner politics related to land ownership, opportunism and corruption, was squandered with the tossing out of the MoU. Consequently, cynical practices among Kenya's politicians manifested through setting one ethnic group against another for political capital prevailed and set the country lemming-like towards collective disaster. The Independent Review Commission (IREC) painted a combustible atmosphere preceding and during the 2007 general elections:

Civil society was accused of partiality; the faiths abandoned the true message, instead of leading their flocks to their respective nests. Observers to some extent assumed the role of participants, with regrettable consequences. The electoral environment was expectant and fully charged. (Republic of Kenya 2008a: 53)

The next chapter analyses the politics of the Kenyan cases at the International Criminal Court (ICC) following the indictment of six prominent Kenyans suspected to be the masterminds of the atrocities committed in the wake of the violently disputed elections in 2007. The lack of transformative politics not only threatened Kenya's stability but also entrenched political dynasties (Shilaho 2015a). Uhuru Kenyatta, Jomo Kenyatta's son, controversially ascended to power in 2013 following yet again disputed elections and despite crimes against humanity charges against him and his running mate, William Ruto. Uhuru Kenyatta's presidency was illustrative of dynastic power transfers in Kenya and in other countries in Africa, that inhibited the nurturing of visionary leadership by ensuring that power was restricted within a tiny plutocracy related by blood ties and whose view of the state was infracted by self-interest and tribalism. Beneficiaries of this politics defined the state narrowly along familial ties, ethnicity and spoils politics. Political dynasties were entrenched in Kenya's politics and enduring because they reified, and exploited ethnicity to retain power and with power they dominated the economy and amassed more capital. Straddling both politics and the economy, they compromised the democratisation process by stone walling reform. Inspired by a sense of self-preservation, they ensured that no political level playing field existed that could lead to their possible loss of power and the attendant economic benefits. Dynastic power inheritance at the presidential, parliamentary and other tiers of representation underscored the relationship between patronage, familial ties and political office (Dal Bo et al. 2009: 16).

Moi entrenched a 'feudal practice' in which relatives inherited membership to his inner court. It became normative when a member of parliament died in office, his son, brother, cousin or even a wife was declared the sole candidate for the seat. Sometimes there were protests but Moi never listened to them (The Weekly Review, November 10 in Himbara 1994: 142–143). For instance, Vincent M'Maitsi inherited a parliamentary seat from his fallen father in 1988 as MP for Hamisi constituency in Western Kenya, at 23 while still an undergraduate student. Thereafter Moi appointed him Assistant Minister of Planning and National Development (Himbara 1994: 120). Politicians such Uhuru Kenyatta, Noah Katana Ngala, Musalia Mudavadi, and Vincent M'maitsi, were thrust into politics entirely on the basis of what the press referred to as 'officially sanctioned political inheritance' (Sunday Nation March 3, 2002). The trend persisted under multiparty politics across the political spectrum.

CONCLUSION

The 2002 elections constituted one of the most significant phases of Kenya's political history. KANU was defeated after being in power since 1963. Although the 2002 elections appeared out of sync with the two previous ones, the ethnicity factor still played a role. The Luo, Kikuyu and Luhya and other small communities overwhelmingly voted for Kibaki under the NARC ethnic alliance making it impossible for KANU to win. The Kalenjin and a section of Kikuyu voted for KANU. The NARC turned out to be KANU in almost every aspect but in name. The NARC was bedevilled by tribal polarisation, arbitrary rule, ethnicisation of the government bureaucracy, corruption and anti-reform tendencies. Moi attempted to outwit the opposition by appealing to ethnicity. He manoeuvred the succession politics on the basis of tribalism in the sense that he tried to build a broad tribal alliance for Uhuru Kenyatta but it collapsed once he tried to impose him on the KANU and Kenya. The opposition responded in a similar fashion and prevailed. The KANU renegades defected and backed Kibaki together with their respective tribes. The Big Man politics had ensured that Kenya's politicians related to power exclusively for selfish ends. There was no place for accountability, transparency, justice and vision for a progressive state and society. Ethnic Big Men ran for president repeatedly since they owned their parties and counted on ethnic support. As long as they hailed from the most populous tribes, they believed they were guaranteed support. It was almost impossible to replace them as heads of these parties. Having been socialised under single-party rule, to which most of them owed their political and economic fortunes, a disproportionate fraction of NARC politicians were not only incapable but actively resisted state reform. Until Kenya's politicians outgrew provincialism and internalised the notion that power was entrusted to these politicians and was exercised in their interest, it would be difficult to reform the state for inclusivity.

In 2002, Kenyan and foreign observers witnessed Kenya's 'free and fair' elections. However, it was one thing to replace Moi the embodiment of neopatrimonial politics but a totally different one altogether to rid the system of attributes associated with this system of rule. Ironically, the 2002 elections were a benchmark for a series of events stemming from the disintegration of NARC that culminated in the post-election violence in 2007. The acclaimed 2002 elections and the 2005 Constitutional referendum were to be flashes in the pan rather than solid markers of a consolidated democracy. They were indications not of ideological definitiveness and directed policy, but rather illustrated the fickleness of Kenya's politics. Kenya was unable during this period to overcome the stranglehold of Big Men and patrimonial politics that perpetuated the ethnicisation of politics. The opportunity that reform of the one-party state presented towards the institutionalisation of the rule of law to strengthen multiparty democracy, regulating political parties, opening Constitutional reform and creating independent oversight bodies was hoist on the petard of tribal politics. One lesson that Kenyans ought to have learnt from this period is that intitutionalisation of politics would be in the best interest of all as opposed to emotionalism associated with the tribal identity of the President.

NOTES

1. Gatekeepers under Kibaki popularly referred to as 'Mount Kenya mafia' Mafia attempted to monopolise power and resisted setting up strong independent institutions. Diamond argued that this cabal sought to restrict access to political power and exploited their consolidated power to stifle economic competition so as to appropriate profits thus maintaining a predatory state (Diamond 2008: 24).

2. Justice Philip Waki chaired the Commission of Inquiry into the Post-Election Violence (CIPEV) following the disputed 2007 Presidential elections. The Waki commission was revolutionary in the sense that it set in motion the process of curbing impunity in Kenya's body politic. It recommended that the masterminds of the 2007–2008 post-election violence be held accountable which resulted in six Kenyans, including Uhuru Kenyatta, and William Ruto being indicted by the International Criminal Court in December 2010 for crimes against humanity.

3. Political liberalisation in this context means the 'opening up of the public political space for a multiplicity of social actors to participate freely' (Nzomo 2003: 189).

4. Jomo Kenyatta himself denounced tribalism and urged Kenyans to embrace nationalism (Mzee Jomo Kenyatta; Kenyatta Day Speech 20 October 1965: 361). But under Kenyatta, there was a gap between speech and practice a pattern that Moi exhibited as well. Early into his rule, Moi not only railed against ethnicity but also 'banned' tribal institutions in 1980 (President Moi's Speech on Kenyatta Day 20 October 1980: 424–425). Moi cautioned that ethnicity posed a serious threat to Kenya's political stability. Yet Moi exploited tribalism for his political advantage throughout his 24 years in power (Moi's Jamhuri Day Speech 12

December 1980: 184–185). This duplicitous and schizophrenic approach to Kenya's challenges survived Kenytta and Moi as evidenced through NARC's climb down on the reformt agenda.

5 Eliud Wabukala, the former head of the Anglican Church of Kenya (ACK), took up the position as head of the Ethics and Anti-Corruption Commission (EACC) in January 2017. The EACC was previously known as the Kenya Anti-Corruption Commission (KACC). Ironically the EACC was widely seen as a hindrance in the fight against corruption owing to perceived government interference, and in some instances, was headed by individuals who had been implicated in corruption.

6. The Independent Review Commission (IREC) was formed to, 'inquire into all aspects of the general elections held on 27 December 2007, with emphasis on the Presidential election', observed that 'State power in Kenya, harking back to the country's colonial past and decades of single-party rule, remained vested in a centralised executive exercising control through a network of provincial administrators/district commissioners, a vocal but relatively powerless legislature and a compliant judiciary exercising few checks and balances. Therefore the presidency was rightly seen as the ultimate political prize' (Republic of Kenya 2008a: 1).

7. The CIPEV report noted that although the 2005 referendum was peaceful and that the results were accepted without being contested, the battle lines were drawn as the ethnic fault lines widened thereafter. The significance of the Presidential victory in 2007 could not be overemphasised hence tensions began to rise (Republic of Kenya 2008b: 30).

8 Hate speech is defined as "a form of speech that degrades others and promotes hatred and encourages violence against a group on the basis of religion, race, colour, or ethnicity. It includes speech, publication or broadcast that degrades, as inherently inferior or degrades, dehumanizes and demeans a group" (KNCHR 2006: 37).

REFERENCES

Books & Books Chapters

Badejo, A. 2006. *Raila Odinga An Enigma in Kenyan Politics.* Nairobi: Yintab Books.

Cheeseman, N. 2015. *Democracy in Africa: Successes, Failures, and the Struggle for Political Reform.* New York: Cambridge University Press.

Kadima, D., and F. Owuor. 2006. The National Rainbow Coalition Achievements and Challenges of Building and Sustaining Broad-Based Political Coalition in Kenya. In *The Politics of Party Coalitions in Africa*, ed. D. Kadima. EISA: Auckland Park.

Kanyinga, K., D. Okello, and A. Akech. 2010. Contradictions of Transition to Democracy in Fragmented Societies: The Kenya 2007 General Elections in Perspective'. In *Tensions and Reversals in Democratic Transitions*, ed. K. Kanyinga and D. Okello. Nairobi: Society for International Development and Institute for Development Studies-University of Nairobi.

Mutua, M. 2009. *Kenya's Quest for Democracy: Taming the Leviathan*. London: Lynne Rienner.

Nzomo, M. 2003. Civil Society in the Kenyan Political Transition: 1992–2002. In *The Politics of Transition in Kenya from KANU to NARC*, ed. W. Oyugi, P. Wanyande, and C. Odhiambo-Mbai. Nairobi: Heinrich Boll Foundation.

Oucho, J. 2010. Undercurrents of Post-Election Violence in Kenya: Issues in the Long-Term Agenda. In *Tensions and Reversals in Democratic Transitions*, ed. K. Kanyinga, and D. Okello. Nairobi: Society for International Development and Institute for Development Studies-University of Nairobi.

Shilaho, W. 2015a. Political Dynasties and Political Opportunism: Impediments to Kenya's State Restructure. Presented during University of Johannesburg/South African Association of Political Studies (UJ/SAAPS) Colloquium, 31 August-1 September 2015, University of Johannesburg.

Wanyande, P., M. Omosa, and C. Ludeki. 2007. Governance Issues in Kenya: An Overview. In *Governance and Transition Politics in Kenya*, ed. P. Wanyande, M. Omosa, and C. Ludeki. Nairobi: University of Nairobi.

Wanyama, F. 2010. Voting Without Institutionalised Political Parties: Primaries, Manifestos, and the 2007 General Elections in Kenya. In *Tensions and Reversals in Democratic Transitions*, ed. K. Kanyinga, and D. Okello. Nairobi: Society for International Development and Institute for Development Studies-University of Nairobi.

Journals

Ajulu, R. 2003. Kenya: A Reflection on the 2002 elections: Third Time Lucky or More of the Same? IGD Occasional Paper No. 39. Braamfontein: Institute for Global Dialogue.

Barkan, J. 2004. Kenya After Moi. *Foreign Affairs* 83 (1): 87–100.

Beetham, D. 1994. Conditions for Democratic Consolidation. *Review of African Political Economy* 21 (60): 157–172.

Branch, D., and N. Cheeseman. 2008. Democratisation, Sequencing and State Failure in Africa: Lessons from Kenya. *African Affairs* 108 (430): 1–26.

Brown, S. 2001. Authoritarian Leaders and Multiparty Election in Africa: How Foreign Donors Help to Keep Kenya's Daniel Arap in Power'. In *Third World Quarterly* 22 (5): 725–739. Available online: www.jstor.org. Accessed 13 Sep 2016.

Dal, BO, E. Dal Bo, P., and Snyder, J. 2009. Political Dynasties. *The Review of Economic Studies* 76 (1): 115–142.

Diamond, L. 2008. The Democratic Rollback: The Resurgence of the Predatory State. In *Foreign Affairs* March/April 87 (2): 36–48.

Ghai, Y. 2007. Devolution: Restructuring the Kenyan State. Lecture for the African Research and Resource Forum, Nairobi. Online: http://www.arrforum.org/publications/occasional-papers/40/94-devolution-restructuring-the-kenyan-state.html. Accessed 7 Mar 2017.

Ghai, Y. 2008. Devolution: Restructuring the Kenyan State. *Journal of East African Studies* 2 (2): 211–226.

Khadiagala, G. 2008. Forty Days and Nights of Peacemaking in Kenya. *Journal of African Elections Special Issue: Kenya* 7 (2): 4–32.

Lynch, G. 2006. The Fruits of Perception: Ethnic Politics and the Case of Kenya's Constitutional Referendum. *African Studies* 65 (2): 233–270.

Mueller, S. 2008. The Political Economy of Kenya's Crisis. *Journal of Eastern African Studies* 2 (2): 185–210.

Murunga, G., and S. Nasong'o. 2006. Bent on Self-Destruction: The Kibaki Régime in Kenya. *Journal of Contemporary African Studies* 24 (1): 1–28.

Nasong'o, S. 2007. Political Transition without Transformation: The Dialectic of Liberalisation Without Democratisation in Kenya and Zambia. *African Studies Review* 50 (1): 83–107.

Ogude, J. 2009. The State as a Site of Eating Literary Representation and the Dialectics of Ethnicity, Class and the Nation State in Kenya. *Africa Insight* 39 (1): 5–21.

Throup, D. 2008. The Count. *Journal of Eastern African Studies* 2 (2): 290–304.

Whitaker, B., and J. Giersch. 2009. Voting on a Constitution: Implications for Democracy in Kenya. *Journal of Contemporary African Studies* 27 (1): 1–20.

Reports

Alston, P. 2009. Press Statement by Prof Philip Alston UN Special Rapporteur on Extrajudicial Arbitrary or Summary Executions Mission to Kenya 16–25 February 2009. Available online: http://www.eastandard.net and http://www.unhchr.ch/huricane/huricane.nsf/view01/52DF4BE7194A7598C125756800539D79?opendocument. Retrieved 29 Oct 2015.

European Union Election Observation Mission (EU EOM). 2008. Kenya Final Report General Elections 27 December 2007. Available online: http://www.scribd.com/doc/3869389/EU-observer-mission-Final-Report-on-the-Kenyan-General-Election-2007. Accessed 3 Aug 2016.

Human Rights Watch. 2002. Kenya's Unfinished Democracy: A Human Rights Agenda for the New Government *14* (10)(A). Online: https://www.hrw.

org/report/2002/12/12/kenyas-unfinished-democracy/human-rights-agenda-new-government. Accessed August 26 2017.

Kenya Human Rights Commission (KHRC). 2011. Lest We Forget: The Faces of Impunity in Kenya, Nairobi. Online: www.khrc.or.ke.

KNCHR & Kenya National Land Alliance (KNLA). 2006. Unjust Enrichment The Making of Land Grabbing Millionaires in Living Large Series 2 (1). The Plunder of Karura, Ngong and Kiptagich Forests. Online: www.knchr.org. Accessed 5 Oct 2016.

Report of the Advisory Panel of Eminent Commonwealth Judicial Experts. (2002). Online: http://www.commonlii.org/ke/other/KECKRC/2002/8. html. Accessed 10 Aug 2015.

Republic of Kenya. 2008a. Report of the Independent Review Commission on the General Elections held on 27th December or 'the Kriegler Commission'. Nairobi: Government Printer.

Republic of Kenya. 2008b. Commission of Inquiry into Post-Election Violence (CIPEV) or 'the Waki Commission'. Nairobi: Government Printer. Online: http://www.dialoguekenya.org/docs/PEV%20Report.pdf. Accessed 10 Nov 2011.

Society for International Development. 2004. Pulling Apart: Facts and Figures in Kenya: Nairobi: Society for International Development. Online: http://www.sidint.net/docs/pullingapart-mini.pdf. Accessed 15 Nov 2016.

Newspapers

Daily Nation. 2002. 'Nyachae Long March in Race for State House to Test His Organisational Ability' November 19. Kenya National Archives and Documentation Centre: Nation Newspapers 8.11.2002, 14/15, Continuation, Years included 2003.

Daily Nation. 2010a. 'Churches are Missing the Big Picture' February 5. http://www.nation.co.ke/oped/Opinion/-/440808/856400/-/5qyk7p/-/index.html. Accessed 30 Oct 2015.

Daily Nation. 2010b. 'Machage Still in Court Over Suspension Over Ethnic Slur' October 15. Available online: http://www.nation.co.ke/News/politics/Machage%20still%20in%20the%20cold%20after%20suspension%20over%20ethnic%20slur%20/-/1064/1033828/-/vgi6h1/-/index.html. Retrieved 29 Oct 2016.

Daily Nation. 2010c. 'Moi Fires Back in Row with Kibaki' July 29. Online: http://www.nation.co.ke/-/1148/1148/-/xvvu7uz/-/index.html. Accessed 1 Aug 2016.

Daily Nation. 2010d. 'Wikileaks First Rattled Kenya with Report on Moi' December 11. Online: http://www.nation.co.ke/News/

politics/-/1064/1070892/-/item/1/-/xj6i7rz/-/index.html. Accessed 23 Dec 2015.

Daily Nation. 2011a. 'Shock of Kenya Rufled by Ethnicity' April 6. Available Online: http://www.nation.co.ke/News/politics/-/1064/1139782/-/7qbrhk/-/index.html. Accessed 24 Apr 2016.

Daily Nation. 2011b. 'When Parliament Turned into Sodom' April 25. Available online: http://www.nation.co.ke/News/politics/When+Parliament+turned+into+Sodom±/1064/1150796/-/item/2/-/x5ih8hz/-/index.html. Accessed 25 Apr 2016.

Saturday Nation. 2010. 'The Road We've Travelled in Search of Reform' January 30. Available Online: http://www.nation.co.ke/oped/Opinion/-/440808/852626/-/5qvtjv/-/index.html. Accessed 26 Oct 2016.

Sunday Nation. 2002. 'Confidence in Moi Camp Source of Worry for Rivals' November 24. Kenya National Archives & Documentation Section: *Daily Nation* Newspapers-8.11.2002, 14/15, Continuation Years Included 2003: Microfilm No. 282.

The Weekly Review. 1992. A Review of the Last Six months', July 3.

Presidential Speeches

President Kibaki's Speech to the Nation on His Inauguration as Kenya's 3rd President 30-12-2002. Online: http://www.statehousekenya.go.ke/speeches/kibaki/2002301201.htm. Accessed 29 July 2010.

President Moi's Speech on Kenyatta Day on 20th October 1980. In Kenya Presidential Speeches 1963–1988: Kenyatta Day Speeches: Kenya National Archives. Nairobi: Central Government Library.

Speech by H.E. The President, Hon, Daniel T. Arap Moi, CGH; MP; On the Occasion of the Jamhuri Day on 12th December 1980. In 'Kenya Presidential Speeches 1963–1988 Jamhuri Day Speeches'. Nairobi: Kenya National Archives Central Government Library.

Speech by H.E. Mzee Jomo Kenyatta during Kenyatta Day Celebrations in 1965. In Kenya Presidential Speeches 1963–1988. Kenyatta Day Speeches: Kenya National Library Archives Central Government Library.

Interviews

Ambunya. 2009. Nairobi, January, 26.

Himbara, D. 1994. Kenya Capitalists, the State and Development. Nairobi. East African Educational Publishers.

Machanja. 2009. Nyanndo, January, 15.

Muluka. 2009. Nairobi, January 23.

Ogude, J. 2009. The State as a site of eating Literary representation and the dialectics of ethnicity, class and the nation state in Kenya. *Africa Insight*. 39 (1), 5–21.

Peter P. Ekeh. 1975. Colonialism and the Two Publics in Africa: A Theoretical Statement. *Comparative Studies in Society and History* 17 (01): 91.

Republic of Kenya 2017. In the Supreme Court of Kenya at Nairobi. Election Petition No. (blank) of 2017. Online: https://drive.google.com/file/d/0B2rMMQJiqMB8VVBOb1NEcjBlUEE/view. Accessed August 23 2017.

Stephen N. Ndegwa, 1997. Citizenship and Ethnicity: An Examination of Two Transition Moments in Kenyan Politics. *American Political Science Review* 91 (03): 599–616.

Sunday Nation. 2002. 'Dynastic angle in Succession' March 3. (Kenya National Archives and Documentation Services Daily Newspapers 13.3.2002-7.3.2002: Microfilm No. 370).

Sunday Nation. 2002. 'How Kanu and Odinga's party will share the cake' February 17. (Kenya National Archives & Documentation section: Daily Nation Newspapers-13.2.2002-7.3.2002: microfilm No. 370).

The Final Report of the TJRC of Kenya 2013. Online: http://digitalcommons.law.seattleu.edu/tjrc/. Accessed 11 December 2016.

The Weekly Review 1989. November 10.

CHAPTER 6

The International Criminal Court (ICC), Impunity, and the Elusive Justice in Kenya

Abstract The chapter argues that ICC's indictment of six prominent Kenyans in 2010 for crimes against humanity committed during the 2007–2008 post-election violence was the first frontal attack against impunity deeply entrenched in the country's body politic. The controversial victory by Uhuru Kenyatta, the most prominent member of the 'Ocampo six', during the 2013 elections was also a democratic reversal just like Kibaki win in 2002. It ensured continued dominance of Kenya's political and economic spheres by an enduring plutocracy. A combination of mobilisation for support ethnically, regionally, and internationally, non-cooperation by the Kenyan government with the ICC, state interference in the cases, and shoddy investigations by the ICC led to the collapse of the cases. The chapter analyses Kenya's indigenous capital, in effect surrogates of foreign capital, violence and elusive justice. It underscores a treacherous terrain in which realpolitik, geopolitics and international criminal justice coalesce.

Keywords International criminal court · Crimes against humanity Uhuru Kenyatta · Post-election violence

INTRODUCTION

How had the ICC influenced Kenya's politics following the naming of six prominent Kenyans in 2010 that the local media referred to as the 'Ocampo Six', suspected masterminds of the 2007–2008 post-election

© The Author(s) 2018   143
W.K. Shilaho, *Political Power and Tribalism in Kenya*,
https://doi.org/10.1007/978-3-319-65295-5_6

violence? The chapter argues that the entry by the ICC into Kenya's violently disputed elections in 2007 unsettled Kenya's political elite attuned to impunity so much that Uhuru Kenyatta and William Ruto presented a joint presidential candidacy during the 2013 elections under Jubilee coalition, cynically referred to as the 'alliance of the accused', so as to have leverage over the ICC. The attempt by the ICC to accord justice to victims of atrocities committed during the disputed elections in 2007 was unprecedented. It was the first frontal confrontation against impunity deeply entrenched in Kenya's body politic owing to ethnicised politics, a compromised judiciary and weak and even dysfunctional institutions. Kenya's judiciary is yet to evolve into an independent institution following years of interference by the executive dating back to the single-party autocracy. However, despite expectations among a section of Kenyan populace that the ICC would deliver justice for the sake of the victims of egregious human rights violations, this was not to be. The hope that the ICC would dent impunity normative in the body politic remains a mirage. Kenyatta and Ruto politically exploited their charges at the ICC and by so doing exacerbated ethnic polarisation. Confronted by an unprecedented legal hurdle, Kenyatta and Ruto formed an ethnic alliance, ascended to power on a joint presidential ticket and reinforced ethnicity, a vector for political mobilisation and consequent violence since Kenya's return to multiparty politics in 1991. Since December 2010, when the six Kenyan suspects were named as masterminds of the 2007–2008 post-election violence, the ICC remained an overarching variable in Kenya's politics owing to elusive accountability for atrocities committed in the wake of the disputed presidential results in 2007.

The disputed 2013 presidential victory by Kenyatta and Ruto, at the time indicted by the ICC, raised questions pertaining to the rule of law, normative and inclusive politics based on accountability and probity that the 2010 Constitution was expected to make part of Kenya's political culture. Implementation of the Constitution had faced impediments since promulgation because Kenyatta, an offshoot of Kenya's plutocracy, stood to lose in the event a reformed state came into being. Ruto had mobilised the Kalenjin, his tribe, to vote against the proposed Constitution during the 2010 referendum. Kenya's stability depended on the establishment of the rule of law and justice. The collapse of two cases before the ICC, the first against Uhuru Kenyatta and the second against William Ruto and Joshua Sang, preceded by dropping of charges against three other suspects, two indicted as Kenyatta's co-perpetrators while the other as a co-perpetrator of Ruto and Sang, was two pronged. It exposed the deficiencies of the ICC, a legal as well as political institution. It also illustrated the vulnerability of the

ICC before suspects that were at the same time powerful state actors. Such suspects easily maximised control of state apparatus to derail the course of justice for victims of mass atrocities. Kenyans who initially had confidence in the ICC regarding justice had to wait further.

The inability by the ICC to afford justice to the victims of the 2007–2008 post-election atrocities exacerbated the threat that impunity posed to Kenya's stability and democratisation process. As the Court of last resort, the ICC intervened following the failure by Kenya to hold to account those liable for funding, organising and perpetrating the atrocities. Lack of political will to try the masterminds within Kenya's judiciary stemmed from Kenya's unresolved historical injustices such as political assassinations, state sponsored violence, land dispossession and related ethnic violence, economic crimes and endemic corruption. The realisation of the Constitution of Kenya 2010 was a culmination of efforts for state restructure spanning the entire post-colonial period. But resistance against its implementation, and reform imperilled Kenya's cohesion and progress. Uhuru Kenyatta's reluctance to facilitate implementation of the Constitution and the Truth Justice and Reconciliation Commission (TJRC) report were illustrations of hostility against both retributive and restorative justice. The TJRC was formed in 2008 and its broad mandate included: 'To look into gross violations of human rights and historical injustices that occurred in Kenya from 12 December 1963 when Kenya became independent to 20 February 2008 when the National Accord was signed' (The Final Report of the TJRC of Kenya 2013). The signing of the National Accord brought to an end the post-election violence triggered by fraudulent elections and anchored the grand coalition government-with Mwai Kibaki as President and Raila Odinga as the Prime Minister respectively. The TJRC had to probe 'Looters of public funds, land grabbers, political assassinations, and gross violators of human rights' (*The Standard* July 23, 2009). It was hoped that implementation of the recommendations contained in the TJRC report would promote national unity, healing and reconciliation. The TJRC submitted its report to Kenyatta in 2013 amid allegations of doctoring. The office of the president was accused of exerting pressure on local commissioners to expunge sections of the report that adversely implicated Kenyatta's father, Jomo Kenyatta, in historical land injustices across the country (*The Star* June 4, 2013, *The Star* June 3, 2013). By the time the 2017 elections were held, the report lay in abeyance yet the TJRC was part of agenda four item of the National Accord that spelled out long-term issues such as redress of land injustices to ensure lasting peace. Neither has the report been widely circulated to the public as stipulated by the law. Therefore, the report presents a case of conflict of interest to Uhuru Kenyatta. The report adversely mentions Uhuru Kenyatta and William Ruto in relation to the 2007–2008 post-election violence although no recommendations were made against them (The Final Report of the TJRC of Kenya 2013; *The Star* June 3, 2013).

The notion that resolution of Kenya's post-colonial upheavals might lie with the international community through institutions such as the ICC or even the local judiciary, was misplaced. In fact a legalistic approach resolving Kenya's disputes caused by enduring injustices could prove inimical to Kenya's stability, a country historically sharply divided along ethnic lines. At the same time, institutionalised impunity owing to disregard for the rule of law, a judiciary that could not hold the political elite and their cronies to account and exploitation of violence for political and economic advantage was detrimental to Kenya's peace and stability. Impunity manifested itself through state violence. Of concern was that Kenya's judiciary had proven ineffective throughout the country's independence to the extent that it was complicit in entrenchment of impunity by focusing on crimes by the poor and other less influential people while ignoring crimes by powerful politicians, government bureaucrats and other influence peddlers. In extreme cases, the judiciary tended to shield such people from accountability despite evidence of errant behaviour. In what seemed to be an inversion of its role, the judiciary seemed to protect the powerful against the powerless. Kenya's democratisation was precarious because of a legacy of bias in the application of the rule of law. Despite some judicial reform following the post-election violence, the judiciary had not yet won wider appeal among Kenyans as a disinterested arbiter of political and other disputes because of corruption, tribalism and partisanship (IWPR April 17, 2014).

The chapter analyses the nexus of Kenya's indigenous capital, spoils politics, violence and elusive justice. It shows how this linkage played itself out in the ICC cases and Kenya's international relations following the naming of Uhuru Kenyatta, William Ruto, Henry Kosgey, Francis Muthaura, Mohammed Hussein Ali and Joshua arap Sang as masterminds of crimes against humanity during the 2007–2008 post-election violence. Kenya's engagement with the ICC prominently thrust Kenya's domestic politics into African and international politics owing to the indictment of these high profile politicians except Sang, a former radio presenter with a Kalenjin FM radio, hardly known beyond his Kalenjin listership prior to being indicted. Within the group, Sang was not only small in stature but also in social standing. Mwai Kibaki, as the incumbent, backed Kenyatta and Ruto for the presidency in 2013 and simultaneously canvassed for support abroad to have them freed of the charges, an expression of a siege mentality among Kenya's plutocracy. The Kenyatta-Moi-Kibaki axis Jomo Kenyatta-Daniel arap Moi-Mwai Kibaki dominated Kenya's politics and economy and therefore was the nucleus of the local capital owing to its vast economic interests traversing the entire economic gamut. Kenya's political and economic control was in the grip of a tiny coterie of individuals related by blood ties, economic interests and more insidiously by their ability to mobilise ethnically for further economic and political gain. This plutocracy was resistant to accountability and so wary of the ICC. In Kenya's political system, the personal, here used to mean selfish economic interests, the communal or tribal, and the political intertwined and reinforced neopatrimonialism and blocked justice. Kenya's political elite exploited local and communal anxieties, cultural, and even primordial differences, and genuine concerns for personal gain. It was against this background that Kenyatta and Ruto easily mobilised their respective tribes against the ICC and their nemesis, Raila Odinga, turning individual legal responsibility into communal and then national threats and burdens. The indictees interpreted the charges as an affront to Kenya's sovereignty. Kenyatta and Ruto easily entered into an entente ahead of the 2013 elections because other than being united by adversity, both were of the *ancien régime* extraction and Moi's protégé (Shilaho 2013).

The chapter highlights a treacherous terrain in which politics and international criminal justice coalesce. A legal analysis of the Kenyan cases before the ICC is not what this chapter is about. It is confined to the politics of the cases specifically the cynical manipulation of the charges by self-styled tribal barons at the expense of justice. The legal threat presented by the ICC thrust Kenya's politicians into a siege mentality. It compelled Kenyatta and Ruto, who were on opposing sides during the disputed 2007 elections, to form an ethnic alliance between Kikuyu and Kalenjin, their respective tribes. It did not matter that these politicians were indicted for allegedly mobilising militias from their respective ethnic groups to commit atrocities against 'enemy tribes', in effect each other's supporters, during the ensuing ethnic violence. Ruto was indicted for mobilising 'Kalenjin warriors' to drive Kikuyu out of the Rift Valley region while Kenyatta was indicted for mobilising and sponsoring a Kikuyu militia, *mungiki*, to retaliate against opposition supporters, who included members of Luhya, Luo Kisii, and Kalenjin ethnic groups in Naivasha and other Kikuyu dominated parts of the Rift Valley. Consequently, the two were separately charged as co-perpetrators in crimes that included organising and financing murder, displacement, persecution, rape and other inhuman acts committed during the post-election violence (ICC 2013b, 2015a).

Kenyatta and Ruto could not afford to lose the 2013 elections. Victory was indispensable to their efforts to salvage their political careers, evade possible incarceration and defend the economic and political interests of Kenya's plutocracy. A combination of these three factors trumped the Constitution, and specifically Chapter 6 on leadership and integrity that demanded high moral and ethical standards for aspirants for and occupiers of public office. Once the High Court and the electoral body, the Independent Electoral and Boundaries Commission (IEBC) cleared Kenyatta and Ruto to vie for the presidency despite facing egregious criminal charges at the ICC, the moral bar that the Constitution spelled out fell off. The ICC intervened in Kenya under the principle of complementarity, because Kenya was 'unable and unwilling' to prosecute high ranking state officials implicated in atrocities committed during the 2007–2008 post-election violence in which an estimated 1333 people were killed and over 600,000 displaced (Republic of Kenya 2008a). Even among the low- and middle-level perpetrators none had been prosecuted (Brown and Sriram 2012; Human Rights Watch 2011).

In the subsequent sections, I focus on the nexus between politics and international criminal justice, the Kenyan situation at the ICC and highlight duplicity among Kenya's politicians. Opponents of a local mechanism for resolution of the conflict expediently changed tune and identified scapegoats once the ICC swung into action. They accused the Court of imperial tendencies and meddling in Kenya's internal affairs, thus its sovereignty. In Kenya's deeply ethnically divided society, 'truth' concerning the narrative of the post-election violence was lost during the 2013 elections campaigns that, like previous ones, dangerously split the country into ethnic enclaves. Kenyatta and Ruto took the ICC cases to the court of public opinion through highly charged political rallies to the extent that the question of justice for victims became disputable, if not, non-existent in the whole controversy.

THE ICC AND TRIBAL MOBILISATION

Owing to the influence of neopatrimonialism, and the salience of tribalism in Kenya's politics, it was not possible for Kenyan politicians to regard the ICC cases as strictly legal issues. This does not imply that the ICC is a purely legal institution. Being a multilateral institution and given that the Rome Statute allows the United Nations Security Council (UNSC) to refer cases to the ICC and defer those before it, it is untenable to describe the ICC as a purely legal institution. In Kenya, owing to weak institutions, politicians cynically invoked identity and, specifically, ethnicity, to plead victimhood and evade accountability. The practice had precipitated institutional atrophy and impunity as shown in Chap. 3. Kenyatta, Ruto and supporters accused the ICC of targeting Kikuyu and Kalenjin ethnic groups hence they reduced the 2013 elections to a referendum on the ICC. They interpreted their victory as repudiation of the ICC and an affirmation of Kenya's sovereignty. Kenyatta and Ruto easily mobilised ethnically because the society spilled over into the state in Kenya (Shilaho 2016: 109–122). Tribalism coupled with patronage-clientelism, a variant of neopatrimonialism, defined Kenya's political system.

THE ICC AND ITS DISPUTED LEGITIMACY

The Nuremberg and Tokyo trials, ad hoc international criminal tribunals, such as the International Criminal Tribunal for Rwanda (ICTR), the International Criminal Tribunal for Yugoslavia (ICTY), among other judicial processes preceded the ICC, a permanent Court to address war crimes, crimes against humanity and genocide. The Nuremberg and Tokyo trials showed that international criminal justice helps in securing peace by delegitimising and incapacitating spoilers. This very aspect of international criminal justice, however, makes the ICC a portent instrument of warfare that escalates rather than mitigates conflict (Nouwen 2013: 177). Kastner shares the same position and observes that the ICC '... has the potential to contribute to ending grave crimes but also bears the danger of prolonging a conflict by adding to the insecurity of the warring parties' (Kastner 2010: 134). Nouwen argues that the ICC judicial system is inherently flawed in the sense that unlike the Nuremberg and Tokyo Tribunals, the ICC does not deal with those who have been vanquished thus providing a battlefield over which protagonists seek to defeat one another (Nouwen 2013: 177). It was ironic that the ICC expected successive Kenyan governments, Kibaki's and then Kenyatta's, to cooperate and avail incriminating evidence against the suspects while Kenyatta was a suspect and Kibaki headed a government some of whose high ranking members had been indicted for crimes against humanity.

Kenyatta and Ruto were free to pursue their political ends as long as they met their obligations as the ICC suspects. It reduced the ICC cases against them to a political duel between ethnically fragmented political camps. The Court did not remove suspects and later the accused from Kenya's political matrix. The argument was that as long as the suspects obeyed summonses and did not abscond, there was no reason to detain them. The 2013 elections therefore provided yet another stage for ethno-regional political elite to contest for power against a background of the unresolved historical injustices and specifically the accusations of electoral theft in 2007. Kenyatta and Ruto delegitimised the ICC and cast it as the enemy of Kenya's sovereignty. They accused their main presidential challenger, Raila Odinga, of working in concert with a section of civil society and 'imperialists'—the ICC and the Western powers—to fabricate charges against them. These politicians exploited the ICC charges and accelerated tensions in Kenya during the electioneering period. However, had the ICC removed the two from the local political scene, it would have inflamed anti-ICC passions among their supporters still. The Rome Treaty provided for suspects and accused persons to be free as long as they honoured summonses and had no arrest warrants against them. However, never before had the Court allowed indicted persons to attend court proceedings via video link on account of their status. This vindicated the ICC critics that accused it of geopolitical considerations.

The Rome Statute that provides a legal framework for the ICC came into effect on 1 July 2002, and like most laws, does not apply retroactively. Significantly, the AU's 2004–2005 Strategic Plan underscores commitment to ensure ratification of the Rome Treaty by all AU member states (Coalition for the International Criminal Court-CICC, n.d.). The AU Constitutive Act Chapter 4(h) recognises intervention amidst grave human rights violations in a member state. It reads thus, 'the right of the Union to intervene in a Member State pursuant to a decision of the Assembly in respect grave circumstances, namely: war crimes, genocide and crimes against humanity' (Constitutive Act of the African Union 2000). The AU Constitutive Act is consistent with the Rome Statute that Kenya voluntarily signed on 11 August 1999 and ratified on 15 March 2005 thus becoming the 98 State Party. Moreover, Kenya domesticated the Rome Statute through the International Crimes Act 2008, effectively becoming part of Kenya's laws (Republic of Kenya 2008b, 2010). The ICC targets the masterminds of egregious crimes including war crimes, crimes against humanity and genocide while middle- and low-level perpetrators must be tried in local courts. These masterminds are too powerful to be tried by judicial systems in their respective countries (Human Rights Watch 2014a).

The ICC addresses mass atrocities committed by individuals. To avoid prosecution ruthless national leaders too often threaten, corrupt or compromise judges and prosecutors at home, but those in The Hague should be beyond the reach of such obstructionism. The ICC is meant as a Court of last resort for victims and survivors who cannot find justice in their own country and as a deterrent to leaders who have little to fear from domestic prosecution (Human Rights Watch 2014a).

The ICC and Africa

The ICC is perennially on a collision course with most African rulers primarily because it targets prominent state actors and non-state actors and most of the atrocities under its jurisdiction disproportionately occur in Africa principally owing to weak states characterised by institutional atrophy, tribal politics and local judiciaries too compromised to impartially dispense justice thus pervasive impunity. Although there are no legal mechanisms to bring high profile criminal suspects to justice, the legacy of slavery, colonialism and apartheid makes some African rulers suspicious of the intentions of the Western-dominated multilateral bodies such as the ICC. Africa forms the largest bloc among countries that have ratified the Rome Statute but is does not minimise the perception that the West has a greater say in the politics that affect the ICC especially within the UN Security Council and the Assembly of States Parties (ASP). The move by the AU to expand the mandate of the yet to be established African Court of Justice and Human Rights (ACJHR) to have jurisdiction over the Rome Statute crimes as well as transnational crimes, is laudable. However, it is not clear, where the AU will source funding to operationalise the court given that the AU itself relies on donors. Moreover during the AU summit in Equatorial Guinea in 2014, the AU member states voted and adopted the Malabo Protocol that grants immunity to sitting heads of state and government and senior government officials before the envisaged court, an aberration in international criminal justice that historically had no immunity for suspects regardless of their social status (Amnesty International 2016).

However, Africa needs to strengthen its judicial systems to obviate the need for the ICC to intervene in its conflicts. Some African rulers accuse the ICC of unfairly targeting them while ignoring atrocities elsewhere in the world such as Palestine, Iraq, Afghanistan and Sri Lanka. The accusation evokes the spectre of imperialism and encroachment on the sovereignty of African countries by the ICC, an institution that these politicians regard as an adjunct of the West to keep them in check. Sovereignty, however, is not an absolute because by acceding to regional and international norms, a state cedes part of its sovereignty. The concept of sovereignty has evolved and the notion that a state has exclusive mandate over its domestic affairs, including in cases of human rights violations, no longer holds. The concept of 'Sovereignty as responsibility' (Deng 2010, 354) is the norm in international relations. 'This means that where large numbers of populations suffer extreme deprivation and are threatened with death, the international community obligated by normative standards of humanitarian and human rights-cannot be expected to watch passively and do not respond. Humanitarian intervention then becomes imperative' (Deng 2010, 354). Therefore, in a case in which a state cannot protect its citizens from harm and gross violation of their human rights, due to lack of capacity or is itself the perpetrator of ethnic cleansing, war crimes, crimes against humanity or genocide, the international community is obliged to intervene, through a multilateral sanction, to protect life and restore sanity. But in situations in which it is impossible to obtain a multilateral sanction through the UNSC because of competing interests as the case in Syria showed, a humanitarian crisis could easily spiral out of control.

The accusation that the ICC is biased against African rulers is a self-serving criticism and therefore its nuance is lost. Of the 124 that have ratified the Rome Statute, 34 are African states, forming the largest bloc. African judges serve within the Court. Africa is also represented by officials in the Office of the Chief Prosecutor headed by a Gambian, Fatou Bensouda. Therefore, the ICC could not dismissed as an anti-African institution based on the composition of its personnel (Human Rights Watch 2014a). Moreover, more than 800 civil society groups from Africa are members of the Coalition for the International Criminal Court

(CICC) that translates into one third of its global membership (CICC n.d). Importantly, victims of atrocities and human rights groups in Africa support the intervention by the ICC in Africa since it creates hope for justice that is elusive in local judiciaries (Human Rights Watch 2014b). Put it differently, these victims are as African as those who perpetrate the crimes against humanity. But the ICC is more than the demographics of its personnel.

Proponents of the ICC intervention in African conflicts dispute the notion that the Court was formed with rogue African states in mind. Out of the nine African situations under investigation, that is, African countries whose citizens currently have cases before the ICC, or have had before or on whose soil the crimes within the ICC jurisdiction were committed, five are self-referral in the sense that the state in question asked the Court to intervene. The wholesale dismissal of the Court as an imperial institution is political and the only way the Court can address it is by being even handed to maintain universal legitimacy. The ICC has not been enthusiastic in dealing with mass atrocities in other parts of the world such as Palestine/Israel, Sri Lanka, Myanmar and Iraq thus lending credibility to its critics. Self-referral situations are Uganda, Mali, Central African Republic (CAR) I and II and the Democratic Republic of the Congo (DRC). But self-referral cases do not necessarily mean the states concerned are supportive of international criminal justice. These self-referral cases involve rebels fighting against governments and so do not necessarily indicate confidence in the Court by the governments in question. The duplicity with which some Africa rulers relate to the Court is indicative of self-preservation rather than confidence in the ICC. In referring cases involving rebels to the Court, the government runs the risk of having its officials investigated and prosecuted as well; thus the word 'Situation' refers to the whole gamut of the conflict as opposed to individual cases of wrong doing (Simmons and Danner 2010, 230–231).

Yoweri Museveni, the Ugandan leader, referred ringleaders of the Lord's Resistance Army (LRA), a terror ragtag army that for years committed atrocities in northern Uganda, to the ICC and had LRA's commander Dominic Ongwen handed over to the ICC in 2015 upon surrendering. However, Museveni was not keen on the Court investigating atrocities by Uganda People's Defence Force (UPDF). He was Uhuru Kenyatta's most vociferous backer in the latter's tirades against the Court and is one of the most acerbic critics of the institution. He is on record having described the ICC as 'a bunch of useless people' (BBC News May 12, 2016).

The Darfur, Sudan and Libya situations are exceptions because the United Nations Security Council (UNSC) referred them to the Court as permitted by the Rome Statute (Hoile 2014, 66–67). In principle, the ICC has jurisdiction over a crime committed by a citizen of a member state or on the territory of a member state or if the situation is referred to the Court by the UNSC (Human Rights Watch: 2014a). This, in effect, means the ICC 'may potentially assume jurisdiction over war crimes, crimes against humanity and genocide committed anywhere in the world' (Kastner 2010, 131). Kenya was the first country in which the ICC Chief Prosecutor initiated investigations on his own volition under the *proprio motu* powers granted by Chapter 15(3) of the Rome Statute that allows the Prosecutor to initiate an investigation without a referral to the State Party or the UNSC (Rome Statute of International Criminal Court 2002, Hoile 2014, 312). Ivory Coast was the second such situation. However, the ICC critics observe that European countries are the greatest funders of the ICC that gives them leverage over the Court and this calls into question its impartiality (Hoile 2014, 15–18, 37). Critics take issue with the three veto-wielding members of the UNSC, that is the US, Russia and China for having the power to refer cases to the ICC, as part of the Permanent 5 (P5), yet do not recognise the ICC since they have not ratified the Rome Statute. Furthermore, although most European countries are signatories to the Rome Treaty, the fact that major nations, such as Russia, Israel, China and India are not, denies the Court international legitimacy and emboldens critics' accusation of selective justice. As such, the critics of the ICC are not merely apologists of impunity or génocidaires.

THE KENYAN CASES AT THE ICC

Kenya and most other African countries ratified the Rome Statute apparently as an expression of aversion against impunity and affirmation of the rule of law.

In 2005, the African Commission on Human and People's Rights issued a resolution on ending impunity in Africa and on the domestication and implementation of the Rome Statute of the ICC. It called on civil society organisations in Africa to work together and develop partnerships that further respect the rule of law internationally and strengthen the Statute (CICC, n.d.).

Kenya's successive governments beginning with that of Mwai Kibaki and then Uhuru Kenyatta tried to have cases facing Kenyan suspects either deferred or terminated. The African Union (AU) launched a strident attack against the Court that threw the credibility and legitimacy of the court into doubt. Kenya ratified the Rome Statute against a background of its post-colonial history characterised by a culture of impunity. Political assassinations, state violence, politically instigated ethnic violence, extra-judicial executions, land grabbing and official grand larceny blot Kenya's post-colonial period but the masterminds and perpetrators had not faced justice (Kenya Human Rights Commission (KHRC) 1998, 2011; Republic of Kenya 1992, 1999, 2008a, b). Significantly, Kenya's laws do not accord immunity to the country's president accused of crimes covered by the Rome Treaty under Chapter 143(4) of the Constitution of Kenya (Republic of Kenya 2010, 88–89). In spite of this fact, the local judiciary had no capacity or political will to try Kenyatta and his deputy.

The charges against Kenyans at the ICC highlighted the fact that the institution had a delicate balancing act to do in navigating a dicey terrain of politics, the law, and geostrategic interests in an attempt to ensure justice for victims of mass atrocities in Africa. It is instructive that since inception in 2002 to date, the ICC had convicted only nine suspects, warlords one of whom, Jean Pierre Bemba, served as the Vice President of DRC an indication that international criminal justice is skewed, intractable and protracted. This abysmal conviction rate could dent the confidence victims had in the Court. However, the reputation of a judicial process lies in its capacity to convict suspects as much as in its impartiality and ability to adjudicate cases based on evidence.

Although Kenyatta had the dubious distinction as the first sitting president to appear before the Court when he was summoned for a 'status conference' in October 2014, the withdrawal of charges against him in December 2014 and subsequently against Ruto in April 2016 for lack of sufficient evidence to ensure successful prosecutions is two pronged. It dampens hopes of the victims of ever finding justice. It also implies that state power indeed provides ammunition with which to fight against the Court since most of the witnesses inexplicably recanted their testimonies while potential ones, ringleaders of the *mungiki* militia died through extrajudicial executions or were disappeared. These people attended a State House meeting and other meetings in which retaliatory attacks against opposition supporters were planned (ICC 2012a, 2015b). The ICC judges and Chief Prosecutor decried witness tampering in the Ruto case as well (KHRC April 7, 2017). A climate of witness interference in which the government was implicated contributed to the collapse of the two cases besides loopholes in investigations carried out by the prosecutor's office under Luis Moreno Ocampo coupled with a porous witness protection unit. Human Rights Watch observed that, 'with the Kenyatta case closed, the scope of justice the ICC can deliver to Kenya's victims is greatly reduced' (HRW 2014). Witness interference in the William Ruto case was so sustained that it compelled the Court to issue arrest warrants against three Kenyans-Paul Gicheru, Philip Kipkoech Bett, and Walter Osipiri Barasa (ICC 2013a, 2015c). Worth noting is that the ICC vacated charges against Kenyatta, Ruto and Ruto's co-accused, Sang, but did not acquit them. It means that in the event new evidence is found in both cases the charges could be reinstated. The inconclusiveness of the cases and nonresolution of the 2007–2008 post-election violence cements the ICC in Kenya's politics.

The Local Tribunal Versus the ICC

Kenyatta and Ruto voted for a Constitutional amendment bill meant to facilitate the formation of a special tribunal in February 2009. However, they were not committed to a local resolution to the 2007–2008 post-election atrocities. Before he was indicted, Ruto publicly expressed preference for The Hague judicial process as opposed to a special tribunal (*The Standard* April 5, 2011). Led by Chepalungu MP, Isaac Ruto (not a relative of William Ruto), the MPs allied to William Ruto and predominantly Kalenjin in ethnic affiliation and drawn from the Rift Valley region, voted against and defeated the motion while singing in rhyme, 'Don't be Vague, let's go to The Hague' (*Standard Digital* February 16, 2012). Kenyatta's allies, almost exclusively from the Kikuyu tribe, also voted against the bill (*The Star* March 12, 2011). These politicians and a section of civil society preferred the ICC option but for different reasons. This section of civil society argued that the government had neither the capacity nor political will to set up a credible special tribunal while William Ruto and his supporters feared that such a tribunal would be biased against them. At the time, Ruto had not closed ranks with Kenyatta and Kibaki having been on the opposing sides of the 2007 electoral contest, and thus the post-election violence. He feared that Kibaki and allies would turn the special tribunal into a witch-hunt having been unofficially widely adversely mentioned as the mastermind of atrocities against Kikuyu resident in the Rift Valley region. So strong were the allegations against Ruto that he voluntarily travelled to The Hague to 'clear his name' and possibly pre-empt being named among the suspected masterminds of the violence but was unsuccessful in meeting the Chief Prosecutor (*CapitalNews* November 4, 2010).

Mutual suspicion among Kenya's political elite and a legacy of impunity paved the way for the ICC intervention in Kenya's conflict. Ruto and allies preferred the ICC not so much because they believed in the rule of law and justice for victims of the 2007–2008 post election violence as because they thought that it would take as long as '90 years' before the cases were concluded. Ruto was on record as saying that by that time 'we shall all be dead' (*Daily Nation* October 16, 2013). Kenyatta, Kibaki and supporters imagined that the ICC would implicate Raila Odinga and other prominent ODM party politicians for having called for mass action in protest against what Odinga and his supporters were convinced was a stolen presidential victory in 2007. This politics of recrimination, suspicion, blame casting and expediency saw mass action, a constitutionally guaranteed form of protest, criminalised. Blame shifting played itself out during Ruto's trial. Through his defence, Ruto tried to shift blame and responsibility to Kibaki with regard to the 2007–2008 post-election violence. He accused Kibaki of polarising the country through tribalism after he ascended to power in 2002 that snowballed into violence in 2007–2008 (*Daily Nation* October 31, 2013). Furthermore, through his defence and then close ally Charles Keter, Ruto accused some officials in the government in which he served as the Deputy President, carryovers of the Kibaki administration, of scouting for witnesses, bribing and coaching them so as to testify against Ruto before the Waki commission and then at the ICC (*CapitalNews* October 16, 2013). The Waki Commission defied the culture of setting up commissions of inquiry as formalities perfected by successsive regimes and recommended that masterminds of the post-election violence be tried either before a special tribunal or at the ICC. Arguably the commission had the greatest impact in Kenya's quest for justice.

An ally of Kenyatta, a loquacious and divisive fellow Kikuyu politician, Moses Kuria, sensationally publicly confessed in 2015 that he and Martha Karua procured and coached ICC witnesses against Ruto

(*CapitalNews* September 24, 2015). Karua, a presidential candidate in 2013, was as hawkish as Kuria. She was Kibaki's hatchet woman at the height of the 2007–2008 post-election violence and a hardliner during the mediation talks led by Kofi Annan, the former United Nations Secretary-General. Hence politicians' support for The Hague was neither about justice for the victims of the atrocities nor aversion against impunity. Ruto and supporters feared being implicated in the post-election crimes and so hoped to buy time through the ICC judicial process while Kibaki, Kenyatta and their supporters hoped that the ICC would implicate their opponents in the ODM. The ICC seemed to have been aware of these undercurrents. It was even handed in its indictment in the sense that of the 'Ocampo six' three were from each side of the political divide during the 2007 electoral contest. Uhuru Kenyatta, Francis Muthaura, and Mohammed Hussein Ali belonged to the Kibaki side and were indicted as part of case one, while William Ruto, Henry Kosgey and Joshua arap Sang, were Odinga's allies in 2007 and were indicted as part of case two. This decision also seemed more political than purely legal and its zero conviction rate in Kenya underscored the view. After the confirmation of charges hearings in September 2011, Uhuru Kenyatta, Francis Muthaura, William Ruto, and Joshua Sang were committed to trial. Charges against Mohammed Hussein Ali and Henry Kosgey were not confirmed for lack of evidence then charges against Muthaura collapsed too. The indictment of these individuals aroused panic and catalysed the closing of ranks by erstwhile protagonists during Kenya's cyclic tribal clashes, the Kalenjin and Kikuyu.

Conclusion

The ICC was initially hailed across Kenya's ethnic groups as a welcome intervention in the country's violently disputed presidential elections in 2007. However, Kenyatta and Ruto as ethno-regional Big Men, exploited their influence in their respective ethnic groups, Kikuyu and Kalenjin, to whip up ethnic sentiment and mobilise against the ICC and their local political rivals. Once in power, they took advantage of control of state apparatus as leverage over the ICC. The result was derailment of justice for the victims of the 2007–2008 post-election violence. The cases demonstrated how difficult it was for the ICC to operate in a polity in which impunity and tribalism held sway. For the first time, Kenya's plutocracy appeared vulnerable before a judicial system they could not directly influence and interfere with. However, the collapse of the cases affirmed the capacity of Kenya's plutocracy to derail efforts towards attainment of sustainable peace, justice, healing and reconciliation. Although the Rome Statute established the ICC as a legal institution to address the egregious crimes: war crimes, crimes against humanity, and genocide, the Court had to grapple with realpolitik. The controversial election of Kenyatta and Ruto into the presidency in 2013, while indicted, the first the world over, exposed the limitations of the ICC until then viewed not only in Kenya but also elsewhere as the bulwark against impunity. The challenge that Kenya faced was the inability to institutionalise compromise and remove zero sum politics from elections. The rule of law must inform Kenya's public life to ensure resolution of long-standing disputes. Once more, the 2013 elections illustrated the fact that Kenya was so tribally balkanised that it lacked collective norms, and a sense of national identity to guide citizens in electing leaders.

For practical and logistical reasons, the ICC could only do so much in Kenyans' quest for justice and nation building. Neither could the local courts be solely relied upon to meet this role. The ICC inadvertently got enmeshed in Kenya's ethnic divisions which subsumed justice in cynical politics. The collapse of the cases against Kenyatta, Ruto and Sang preceded by dropping of charges against three of the 'Ocampo six' exposed limitations of a legalistic approach to Kenya's political challenges. The Kenyan cases were a litmus test to the ICC's capacity to try a sitting head of state and the Court came out the worse off. What was required was remedial of Kenya's flawed national character through implementation of reform envisaged under the 2010 Constitutional dispensation to ensure ethnic inclusivity and long-term political stability a challenge that required leadership inspired by the imaginary of Kenya's oneness. Kenya's oligarchy had the capacity to deploy state apparatus to impede justice by canvassing support locally through expedient ethnic alliances, across Africa and internationally against the ICC. The Kenyan governments invoked a spurious form of Pan Africanism that entrenches impunity at the expense of victims of mass atrocities in Africa. Retributive justice might be inimical to Kenya's social cohesion but a deeply entrenched culture of impunity that has reproduced violence throughout the country's post-colonial period could easily result in state collapse.

REFERENCES

Books & Book Chapters

Hoile, D. 2014. *Justice Denied The Reality of the International Criminal Court.* London: The Africa Research Centre.

Nouwen, S. 2013. The International Criminal Court. In *Peacebuilding, Power, and Politics in Africa*, ed. D. Curtis, and G. Dzinesa. Johannesburg: Wits University Press.

Journals

Brown, S., and C. Sriram. 2012. The Big Fish Won't Fry Themselves: Criminal Accountability for Post-election Violence in Kenya. *African Affairs* 111 (443): 244–260.

Deng, F. 2010. From 'Sovereignty as Responsibility' to the 'Responsibility to Protect'. In Special Issue: Africa's Responsibility to Protect. *Global Responsibility to Protect*, vol. 2, no. 4, ed. A. Adebajo, M. Paterson, and J. Sarkin, 388–413.

Kastner, P. 2010. Africa-A Fertile Soil for the International Criminal Court? *Die Friedens-Warte* 85 (1/2): 131–159.

Shilaho, W. 2013. Old Wine in New Skins: Kenya's 2013 Elections and the Triumph of the Ancien Régime. *Journal of African Elections Special Issue: The Evolving Role of Elections in Africa* 12 (3): 89–119.

Shilaho, W. 2016. The Paradox of Kenya's Constitutional Reform Process: What Future for Constitutionalism? *Journal for Contemporary History* 41 (2): 184–207.

Simmons, B., and A. Danner. 2010. Credible Commitments and the International Criminal Court. *International Organization* 64 (2): 225–256.

Reports

Amnesty International 2016. *Africa: Malabo Protocol: Legal and Institutional Implications of the Merged and Expanded African Court.* January 22. Online: https://www.amnesty.org/en/documents/afr01/3063/2016/en/. Accessed August 27 2017.

British Broadcasting Corporation (BBC). 2016. *Western envoys in Uganda walk out on Museveni swearing-in*, May 12. Online: http://www.bbc.com/news/world-africa-36278479. Accessed 17 Dec 2016.

Coalition for the International Criminal Court (CICC). (n.d.). Online http://www.iccnow.org/documents/Africa_and_the_ICC.pdf. Accessed 15 Apr 2015.

Constitutive Act of the African Union. 2000. Online: http://www1.uneca. org/Portals/ngm/Documents/Conventions%20and%20Resolutions/ Constitution.pdf. Accessed 12 Apr 2016.

Human Rights Watch. 2011. 'Turning Pebbles' Evading Accountability for Post-Election Violence in Kenya. Online: http://www.hrw.org/sites/default/files/ reports/kenya1211webwcover_0.pdf. Accessed 1 Jan 2015.

Human Rights Watch. 2014a. Africa Attacks the International Criminal Court. Online: http://www.hrw.org/news/2014/01/14/africa-attacks-interna- tional-criminal-Court. Accessed 14 Mar 2017.

Human Rights Watch. 2014b. ICC: Hopes for Justice Set Back Prosecution with- draws Kenyatta charges. Online: http://www.hrw.org/news/2014/12/05/ icc-hopes-justice-set-back. Accessed 1 Jan 2015.

ICC. 2012a. Situation in the Republic of Kenya in the case of the Prosecutor v. Francis Kirimi Muthaura, Uhuru Muigai Kenyatta and Mohammed Hessein Ali (Decision on the Confirmation of Charges). http://www.icc-cpi.int/icc- docs/doc/doc1314543.pdf. Accessed 28 Jan 2015.

ICC. 2013a. Situation in the Republic of Kenya in the case of the Prosecutor v. Walter Osapiri Barasa Under seal ex parte, only available to the Prosecutor and the Registrar Warrant of arrest for Walter Osapiri Barasa. Online: http:// www.icc-cpi.int/iccdocs/doc/doc1650592.pdf. Accessed 18 Mar 2017.

ICC. 2013b. Situation in the Republic of Kenya in the case of the Prosecutor v. William Samoei Ruto and Joshua arap Sang (Case Information Sheet). Online: http://www.icc-cpi.int/iccdocs/PIDS/publications/RutoKosgeySangEng. pdf. Accessed 18 Mar 2017.

ICC. 2015a. Situation in the Republic of Kenya in the case of the Prosecutor v. Uhuru Muigai Kenyatta (Public Redacted Version of "Second Updated Prosecution Pretrial brief" 26 August 2013. ICC-01/09-02/11-796- cof-AnxA), 19 January. Online: http://www.icc-cpi.int/iccdocs/doc/ doc1904539.pdf. Accessed 18 Feb 2017.

ICC. 2015b. Situation in the Republic of Kenya in the case of the Prosecutor v. Uhuru Muigai Kenyatta (Decision on the withdrawal of charges against Mr Kenyatta), 13 March. Online: http://www.icc-cpi.int/iccdocs/doc/ doc1936247.pdf. Accessed 29 Jan 2017.

ICC. 2015c. Situation in the Republic of Kenya in the case of the Prosecutor v. Paul Gicheru and Philip Kipkoech Bett, 10 September. Online: http://www. icc-cpi.int/iccdocs/doc/doc2056890.pdf. Accessed 28 Jan 2017.

Institute for War & Peace Reporting (IWPR). 2014. Public Confidence in Kenya's Judiciary Plummets Recent dismissals further increase dissatisfaction with national justice system, April 17. Online: https://iwpr.net/global-voices/pub- lic-confidence-kenyas-judiciary-plummets. Accessed 12 Apr 2017.

Kenya Human Rights Commission (KHRC). 2011. Lest We Forget: The Faces of Impunity in Kenya, Nairobi. Online: www.khrc.or.ke.

Kenya Human Rights Commission (KHRC). 1998. *Killing the vote State Sponsored Violence and Flawed Elections in Kenya.* Nairobi: KHRC.

Republic of Kenya. 2008a. *Report of the Independent Review Commission on the General Elections held on 27th December or 'the Kriegler Commission'.* Government Printer: Nairobi.

Republic of Kenya. 2008b. Commission of Inquiry into Post-Election Violence (CIPEV) or 'the Waki Commission'. Nairobi: Government Printer. Online: http://www.dialoguekenya.org/docs/PEV%20Report.pdf. Accessed 10 Nov 2011.

Republic of Kenya. 1999. *Report of the Judicial Commission Appointed to Inquire into Tribal Clashes in Kenya, 'Akiwumi Commission'.* Nairobi: Government Printer.

Republic of Kenya. 1992. *Report of parliamentary Select Committee to Investigate Ethnic Clashes in Western and Other Parts of Kenya, 'Kiliku Commission'.* Nairobi: Government Printer.

Republic of Kenya. 2010. *The Proposed Constitution of Kenya.* Nairobi: Government Printer.

The Final Report of the TJRC of Kenya. 2013. Online: http://digitalcommons. law.seattleu.edu/tjrc/. Accessed 11 Dec2016.

Newspapers

CapitalNews. 2015. Karua sues Moses Kuria for defamation, September 24. Online: http://www.capitalfm.co.ke/news/2015/09/karua-sues-moses-kuria-for-defamation/. Accessed 30 Jan 2016.

CapitalNews. 2013. PNU plotted to 'crucify' Ruto over poll chaos, October 16. Available at: http://www.capitalfm.co.ke/news/2013/10/pnu-plotted-to-crucify-ruto-over-poll-chaos/.

CapitalNews. 2010. Ruto at The Hague to meet Ocampo, November 4. Available at: http://www.capitalfm.co.ke/news/2010/11/ruto-at-the-hague-to-meet-ocampo/.

Daily Nation. 2013. ICC uncertain on action if Uhuru fails to attend trial, October 16. Available: http://mobile.nation.co.ke/News/ICC-expects-Uhuru-to-attend-trial/-/1950946/2035002/-/format/xhtml/-/oyfj52z/-/index.html. Accessed 18 Dec 2016.

Daily Nation. 2013. Ruto defence accuses Kibaki of betrayal, October 31. http://mobile.nation.co.ke/News/Ruto-defence-accuses--Kibaki-of-betrayal-/-/1950946/2055492/-/format/xhtml/-/r5lcv4/-/index.html. Accessed 1 Jan 2017.

Standard Digital. 2012. Ruto in dramatic face-off with Raila over ICC, February 16. Available at: http://www.standardmedia.co.ke/business/article/2000052212/ruto-in-dramatic-face-off-with-raila-over-icc?pageNo=4. Accessed 22 Mar 2017.

The Standard. 2009. Past Offenders on notice as TJRC named, July 23. Available online http://www.standardmedia.co.ke/InsidePage.php?id=1144 019916&catid=4&a=1. Accesses 21 Sep 2010.

The Standard. 2011. Some of the six rejected local tribunal option, April 5. Online: http://standardmedia.co.ke/InsidePage.php?id=2000032682&cid=4&. Accessed 20 Aug 2016.

The Star. 2011. How MPs rejected the proposed Special Tribunal for Kenya Bill, March 12. Available at: http://www.the-star.co.ke/news/article-90352/how-mps-rejected-proposed-special-tribunal-kenya-bill. Accessed 20 Mar 2017.

The Star. 2013. How TJRC Land Chapter was Censored, June 4. Online: http://www.the-star.co.ke/news/article-122777/how-tjrc-land-chapter-was-censored. Accessed 7 June 2013.

The Star. 2013. 'Missing Paragraphs In The TJRC Report On The Land Question' June 3. Online: http://www.the-star.co.ke/news/article-122862/missing-paragraphs-tjrc-report-land-question. Accessed 7 Dec 2017.

CHAPTER 7

Conclusion

Abstract The chapter concludes and synthesizes salient arguments and offers some recommendations. It argues for inclusive politics in Kenya to ensure stability. The sustained exploitation of tribalism by politicians and other influential Kenyans in the media, academe, civil society, religious fraternity could plunge the country into civil strife. Civic citizenship as opposed to ethnic nationalism must be the criterion for inclusion in the state and enjoyment of the attendant benefits. Unlike previously imagined by some modernisation theorists, ethnicity is not an anachronism, a prerogative of the 'unsophisticated' populace, but an integral part of modernity. This chapter also contests the notion that the Kenyan youth are detribalised in comparison to their elderly counterparts. Kenya's viability as a state is predicated on Kenya's renewal in consonance with ideals of the 2010 constitution, implementation of the recommendations contained in the Truth, Justice and Reconciliation Commission Report, and the Ndung'u Report on land injustices to address festering grievances by communities and individuals. The impediment to Kenya's renewal, however, is a self-reproducing old order, in power since 1963 although the opposition parties are also diminished by predatory and tribal politics and so unlikely to devise alternative politics.

Keywords Inclusive politics · Ethnic nationalism · Civic citizenship Tribal politics · Constitution

© The Author(s) 2018
W.K. Shilaho, *Political Power and Tribalism in Kenya*,
https://doi.org/10.1007/978-3-319-65295-5_7

Imagine trying to cover Northern Ireland's troubles without using the words 'Protestant' or 'Catholic'. Or reporting Iraq without referring to 'Shias' and 'Sunnis'. The attempt would be absurd, the result unfathomable. And yet, in Kenya's post-electoral crisis, that is exactly what much of the local media doggedly tried to do. When we read an account in a British newspaper of shack-dwellers being evicted from a Nairobi slum, or see on the BBC gangs attacking inhabitants in the Rift Valley, we are usually told whether these are Kikuyus fleeing Luos, or Kalenjins attacking Kikuyus. But, in Kenya, this particular spade is almost never called a spade. No, it's "a certain metal implement". The "problem of tribalism" may be obsessively debated, the gibe of "tribalist" thrown with reckless abandon at politicians and community leaders, but it is just not done to identify a person's tribe in the media. The results, given a crisis in which the expression of long-running grievances has taken the most explicit ethnic form, can be opaque. When Mr Maina Kiai, chairman of the Kenya National Commission on Human Rights, addressed displaced people in Eldoret earlier this year, he was booed and heckled. Kenyan media reported the incident without explaining why. The answer was that the displaced he met were mostly Kikuyus, and Kiai, a vocal Kikuyu critic of a Kikuyu-led Government, is regarded by many as a traitor to his tribe. Sometimes, the outcome is simply bizarre. When one newspaper ran a vox pop in January, one entry was meant to capture vividly the predicament of a 15-year-old girl of mixed parentage. "My mother is from [one of the tribes that had a Presidential candidate]", Faith was quoted as saying, "but my father is a [member of the other tribe that had a Presidential candidate]." How's that for gritty realism? (New Statesman February 14, 2008).

The excerpt shows how difficult it was for the Kenyan media to openly address the question of tribal identity in its coverage of the 2007 post-election violence. The excerpt captures the tone for a conundrum. Tribalism in Kenya's politics was an issue that both politicians and the citizenry were aware of but not willing to hold a candid dialogue about. Even the 2007 post-election conflagration could not encourage such a conversation yet wishing away the challenge would not result in the challenge resolving itself. Instead it institutionalises amnesia.

This book shows that ethnic politics in Kenya is a phenomenon that provided political and economic advantage to the privileged owing to the fact that there was a close link between tribalism, economic opportunities and state power. This form of politics is relevant to politicians, in control of the state and the economy, the intelligentsia and the populace.

Ethnicity was not an atavistic phenomenon and confined to the poor and the elderly Kenyans. Younger Kenyans were as ethnically conscious owing to socialisation at home and in the education system. The notion that the intelligentsia was 'civilised' and so had been detribalised did not stand the scrutiny. The intelligentsia voted rationally in response to the perceived and real fears, and the opportunities at stake. Paradoxically, the modernisation theories had the intelligentsia as the vanguard of alternative forms of political organisation away from cultural, linguistic, tribal and religious fault lines. The reification of primordial differences by politicians and the intelligentsia feeds into *wananchi's* fears emanating from exclusionary politics. The crosscutting effects of bad governance such as poverty, violence, impunity and corruption disproportionately affected the populace. Civic citizenship, crosscutting socio-economic concerns must be the axes on which politics was conducted. There was need to demobilise politics around vertical ties of kinship, language, clan, tribe, region and even religion so that inclusion in the state and enjoyment of the attendant benefits was meritocratic, inclusive, equitable and just.

The book demonstrates that ethnic groups are social constructs and became vectors of political mobilisation at the interface between the pre-colonial Africa and colonialism. There was no such a thing as a homogenous tribe either in Kenya or elsewhere in Africa because of differentiating aspects such as gender, religion and economic conditions inherent in every community. And these differences were not immutable. The realisation of a sense of national identity was a part of nation building and it required a leadership inspired by the citizens' collective well-being and resistant to sub-national loyalties. Uhuru Kenyatta's ascendancy to power in 2013 highlighted entrenched political dynasties that restrained the democratisation process by making it hard for power to shift based on competing programmes. The seasoned opposition politician, Raila Odinga also exemplified dynastic politics. However, long before the death of his father, Oginga Odinga, the doyen of opposition politics in Kenya, Raila Odinga had established himself as an advocate of political pluralism and a formidable figure in the struggle for human rights and constitutionalism for which Moi detained him thrice without trial for a total of eight years effectively becoming Kenya's longest serving post-colonial political detainee. Upon his father's death in 1994, Odinga outmanoeuvred fellow Luo politicians such as James Orengo, intent on succeeding his father as the Luo ethnic baron. Musalia Mudavadi, a presidential candidate in 2013, was the son of Moses

Mudavadi, at whose prompting, the reluctant Moi joined the Legco in 1955. With the backing of Moi and at 29 years of age, the younger Mudavadi succeeded his deceased father, Moses Mudavadi, unopposed in a by-election in 1989 in which other contestants were prevailed upon to step down and was subsequently appointed to the cabinet in which he served from then until 2002. He holds the record as serving the shortest period (a mere two months) as Kenya's Vice President, position he was appointed to during the 2002 elections at the time when KANU was teetering on the brink of implosion over succession politics. These self-serving dynasties were ethnicity inspired and rendered the state reform circuitous, polarising and destabilising.

The book shows that despite the shift from single-party dictatorship to multiparty politics, ethnicity remained salient in Kenya's politics. Although the book traces the ethnic animosity among Kenya's ethnic groups to instrumentalisation of tribalism during colonialism, it argues that Kenyan politicians continued to mobilise along ethnicity for personal gain. Ethnic politics was not predetermined. Julius Nyerere promoted national cohesion in Tanzania despite with over 120 tribes, Tanzania was more ethnically and religiously diverse. In Kenya, the centralised state, the lack of a regulated political party system or the lack of political will to enforce the law made the appeal to ethnicity almost inevitable. Gatekeepers had taken control of the state, and political parties for rent seeking, corruption and invoked ethnicity to evade accountability and entrench themselves in power. The 2010 constitutional dispensation, strove to institutionalise compromise, reinforce the rule of law through the principle of separation of powers, and promote integrity and accountability in public office. However, the Constitution was as good as the norms and values that undergirded Kenya's society and the calibre of its leaders entrusted with the task of implementing it (Shilaho 2016). The Constitution, in of itself, could not result in Kenya's socio-economic and political renewal.

The book demonstrates that Kenya's political parties were weak, personality driven and tribal. There was a link between the lack of internal democracy within political parties, the winner-takes-all political system on one hand and democratic reversals and the recurrence of ethnic violence at election time on the other. After the turn to multiparty politics, a strong aspect of political party formation was that they were increasingly short-term coalitions whose objectives were not to promote a coherent policy agenda, but rather were formed solely as vehicles for contesting elections. This accounted to the very high turnover of political parties but the leaders of these parties were a constant in Kenya's politics. In the absence of policy-based politics, election campaigns were defined by ethnic profiling, stereotypes, innuendoes, and evocation of primordial differences such as male circumcision to dismiss Luo politicians as unelectable.

Predatory politics encouraged rent seeking as politicians sought to control the state for the opportunities it provided in terms of government contracts, ability to influence recruitment in the civil service, and even divert national resources to one's region. Predatory politics made ethnicity determinant in the country's politics. The exploitation of ethnicity in the post-colonial period and the resultant tribal politics was a rational decision by the successive Kenyan regimes. In Kenya, ethnicity was combustible because it was a prism through which political entrepreneurs—careerists driven by mercenary ethos—interpreted power and defined the state. Enforcement of the rule of law and prosecution of politicians who incited ethnic hatred would accord the government legitimacy. The challenge was that Kenya's successive Presidents since independence were political creatures of politicised ethnicity and so had no incentive to address the ethnic politics in which his power was rooted.

Chapter 3 analyses the autocratic single-party rule. The hallmarks of the *Nyayo* régime such as intolerance to alternative political views, patronage, instrumentalisation of ethnicity, malfeasance, corruption and impunity survived this régime. The chapter highlighted the fact that the absence of the doctrine of the separation of powers resulted in Moi resorting to other structures such as the KANU and the provincial administration to govern. This type of politics continued to undermine and delegitimise the state.

The Moi régime abused the *Harambee* system to distribute state largesse and loot from the public coffers. The noble aim of *Harambee* of mobilising communities to contribute towards self-help projects was lost. *Harambee* became a conduit for perpetrating corruption and reinforcing patronage networks. What ailed Kenya's politics was politicians' refusal to submit their character to the provisions of the Constitution. Regardless of the reform Kenya effected, it would take a selfless and visionary president to confront the entrenched culture of impunity and place the country on a trajectory of progress. Such a president must provide the requisite political will for justice to prevail, must resist centrifugal tribal interests and at all times be guided by Kenyans' collective welfare. The conundrum is that the beneficiaries of impunity-those in charge of the state and their allies-were the very individuals expected to address it. They had no incentive or desire to institutionalise the rule of law. The status quo in which the legitimate instruments of violence such as the police, the army, the paramilitary, tribal militias and the courts were abused for partisan political ends, enhanced the personal gain of the power wielders much as it caused social, economic and political unpheavals to the rest of the citizenry.

Like Kenyatta, Moi schizophrenically condemned and instrumentalised ethnicity at the same time. He banned tribal groups on grounds that they promoted tribalism but he encouraged tribal associations in universities, constantly received tribal delegations and exploited tribalism for his benefit and that of close allies predominantly drawn from the Kalenjin community of which he was affiliated. Moreover, Moi introduced the 'provincial strategy' into Kenya's politics. On the surface, the strategy appeared consistent with affirmative action principles and portrayed him as being sensitive to ethnic sensibilities. However, this strategy institutionalised distribution of party seats along ethno-regional lines without due regard to leadership skills and competence. Although the approach was meant to produce broad ethnic coalitions that were reflective of Kenyans' ethnic diversity, it stifled the emergence of political talent since ethnic balancing and loyalty to the ethnic baron took precedence over credibility, integrity and leadership qualities.

The chapter shows that the unresolved land issue contributed to Kenya's instability during the multiparty system. Jomo Kenyatta sowed seeds of land disputes especially in the Rift Valley and Coast regions through a controversial land redistribution programme that favoured the political elite and Kikuyu tribe and elicited resentment from the communities that opposed further dispossession of their ancestral land by post-colonial politicians. Kenya's successive presidents, Kenyatta, Moi, Kibaki and their allies amassed large tracts of land in a country in which arable land is scarce. In many ways, the Moi régime was a continuation of Kenyatta's in every aspect except for changes in the inner court composition. The politicisation of ethnicity, the use of land as an item of patronage, tribal prioritisation and favouritism in state appointments defined the Jomo Kenyatta, Danie arap Moi, Mwai Kibaki and Uhuru Kenyatta regimes. Kenya's long-term political stability required restitution with regard to the land question and other inequities. Recommendations contained in the Ndung'u Commission as well as Chap. 5 of the Constitution on land and the environment must be implemented to address the question of land dispossession and attendant conflicts. All grabbed land including forests, water towers, road reserves, land meant for public facilities such as schools and agricultural development farms must revert to the government and those responsible for illegally acquiring this land be prosecuted.

The issue of disparities in regional development contributed to the inability of a national identity to emerge and the continued ethnic fragmentation of Kenya. These disparities contributed to ethnic politics precisely because Kenya's successive post-colonial governments used tribalism as the criterion for the allocation of state resources. Thus regional disparities in development and per capita inequalities enhanced ethnic animosity and acrimonious elections, especially at the presidential level because they reinforced the myth of 'collective eating'. There must be equitable resource allocation to all the regions, meritocratic recruitment in the bureaucracy, and application of the rule of law to reduce the passion that ethnicity evoked whenever Kenyans talked about challenges besetting them. The Constitution attempted to address zero-sum politics through the devolution of some power and resources to the 47 counties as well a recommendation that the appointment of personnel in the civil service must be reflective of ethnic diversity. Effective implementation of the Constitution to guarantee institutional independence and the support for the county governments would somewhat reduce the stakes during Presidential elections. However, devolution in itself could not be a panacea to inequalities and inequities. This second tier of government had replicated patronage, corruption, tribalistic and clan politics at the centre (Shilaho 2015). The 2017 elections were as polarising, ethnically charged and disputed as the previous multiparty elections since 1992 except the 2002 ones. The presidency remained the most sought after political prize in Kenya which indicated that devolution had not reduced zero sum politics because the centre still retained a great deal or state resources—85 per cent of state revenue—hence appeal to centrifugal tribal loyalties.

Chapter 4 covers the first and second multiparty elections after Kenya's return to multiparty politics in 1992 and 1997. The chapter argued that in spite of the repeal of Section 2A of the Constitution that had proscribed multiparty politics, there was no transformation in Kenya's politics. Moi shrewdly acceded to the formation of many political parties but retained control of the state. The Moi régime combined state largesse and state-sponsored violence to resist further reform. The two multiparty elections exposed not only the continued salience of ethnicity in Kenya's multiparty politics but also its destructive potential. A second attempt at ideological politics by Safina and the SDP could not dent the tribal factor and so floundered. Ethnicity derailed Kenya's return to multiparty politics although other factors such as opportunism and abuse of state power by the incumbent played a role too. Moi exploited his incumbency and patronage to exacerbate divisions in opposition parties. Insidiously, the Moi régime evoked the autochthonous politics of 'indigene-settler' binary opposites within the distorted *Majimboism* narrative to ignite and stoke ethnic violence.

Chapter 5 covers the period between the 2002 and 2007 elections and argues that the leadership transition from Daniel arap Moi to Mwai Kibaki in 2002 constituted a democratic reversal since they did not mark the beginning of Kenya's social, economic and political renewal despite having been the only credible elections in Kenya's history. A resurgence of Kikuyu dominance of the state drew resistance by the marginalised ethnic groups that snowballed into the divisive 2005 referendum, then the equally divisive 2007 disputed presidential elections, and the subsequent post-election violence. A mix of uneasiness among the local capital, entrenched impunity, ethnicity, historical injustices, especially land related, and weak institutions, particularly the electoral body and the judiciary, almost plunged Kenya into civil war. The chapter debunks the notion that the 2007–2008 post-election violence was atavistic 'tribal' warfare. Although flawed elections were the proximate cause, a legacy of state-related injustices, impunity and institutionalised amnesia were some of the substantive causes. The unresolved issues that precipitated the 2007 electoral violence, spilled over into the 2013 elections and the 2017 ones. Like previous multiparty elections, the 2007, 2013 and 2017 elections were polarising and brought to the fore, once again, the persistence of political dynasties and cynical politicians driven by ephemeral interests.

Governance deficiencies in Kenya's polity militate against access to basic rights the citizens. Crude law enforcement tactics, a carry over of a colonial state and single party rule of use of brute force against defenceless people, antipathy to dissent, and criminalisation of protest, extrajudicial executions, clamp down on public gatherings by the opposition supporters, and torture by security forces undermined democracy. These are the features of electoral authoritarian (EA) systems. These are regimes in which institutions are established as a façade to conceal despotic tendencies. They exhibit the following characteristics,

Electoral contests are subject to state manipulation so severe, widespread, and systematic that the systems do not qualify as democratic. Elites in EA systems tend to devise discriminatory electoral rules to exclude the opposition parties and candidates from entering the electoral arena. They seek to remain in power by infringing on their opponents' political rights and civil liberties, restrict access to mass media and sources of campaign financing. Wholesale electoral fraud is sometimes used (Edozie 2009: 132).

Although elections are not the be-all and end-all of democracy, credible elections are the first step towards building a culture of accountability. Elections whose procedure is certain but results uncertain reinforce procedural accountability that, in the long run, leads to substantive accountability by way of credible institutions. Procedural and substantive accountability are inextricably linked in that, 'The purpose of procedures like elections is to achieve substantive accountability, that is, governments that are responsive to popular wishes' (Fukuyama 2016: 381).

Kenya needs to move away from a culture in which elections are reduced to rituals that occur after every five years and are anxiety inducing events that threaten rather than enhance democratisation, peace and stability through loss of life and property. The subtext to the discourse about secession is alienation from the state and its resources by a section of the Kenyan population who view the state as controlled by the Kikuyu-Kalenjin hegemony. Justice, the rule of law, respect for Kenya's ethnic diversity, and economic growth accompanied by equitable development would neutralise separatist politics.

The peace industry that preceded the 2013 and 2017 elections hinged on the false choice between peace and justice and therefore did not help in mending Kenya's frayed social fabric. Peace is the corollary of justice and the two mutually reinforce each other. To try and dichotomise them was a historical, escapist and mendacious. There was the 'accept and move' on mantra that gained publicity in the wake of the 2013 elections and the 2017 elections in which the triumphant ones urged those who lost to reconcile themselves to the outcome, regardless of the issues of irregularities, entrenched amnesia. Elections need to provide an opportunity for the electorate to participate in politics and shape how they are governed by electing representatives out of their free will without coercion, manipulation or their choice being subverted. In a fragile and tribally divided polity that Kenya was, its was of concern and a threat to stability for elections to demarcate winners and losers.

Chapter 6 focused on the International Criminal Court (ICC) and how it affected Kenya's politics in the wake of the 2007–2008 post-elections. The ICC caused a siege mentality among Kenya's politicians and influenced the results of the 2013 elections. This chapter argues that the indictment of six prominent Kenyans by the ICC for atrocities committed during the post-election violence was the first attempt to break a vicious cycle of impunity deeply entrenched in the country's body politic. However, Uhuru Kenyatta and William Ruto, the foremost among the indictees, astutely exploited the charges against them to exacerbate ethnic fault lines, polarise the country and ensure victory during the 2013 elections. Crucially, the ICC precipitated uncertainty and trepidation among Kenya's plutocrats in power since 1963. Kenyatta's controversial presidential victory in 2013 was both personal, dynastic and oligarchic as it ensured continued stranglehold on Kenya's political and economic spheres by a self-reproducing plutocracy whose power sprang from deft and cynical manipulation of ethnicity. With control over state apparatus, Kenyatta and Ruto successfully fought back against the threat posed by the ICC resulting in the cases collapsing. The pairing between Uhuru Kenyatta and William Ruto was illustrative of paucity of principle in Kenya's politics. Kenya's ethno-regional Big Men changed tribal alliances at every election time for cynical reasons. The ethno-regional Big Men changed ethnic alliances at every election time for cynical reasons.

The intriguing question that merits further research is why the Kenya's poor, irrespective of ethnic background, abhorred the damaging effects of tribalism and were aware of the cynical behaviour of political entrepreneurs yet continually voted along ethnic lines. This was a paradox. Since 1992, election results especially at the presidential level had displayed an ethnic hue. How then, do we explain this paradox? This remains an open question.

REFERENCES

Books & Book Chapters

Shilaho, W. 2015. Third Time Lucky? Devolution and State Restructure under Kenya's 2010 Constitutional Dispensation. In *African State Governance Subnational Politics and National Power*, ed. A.C. LeVan, J.O. Fashagba, and E. McMahon. Basingstoke: Palgrave Macmillan.

Journals

Shilaho, W. 2016. 'The Paradox of Kenya's Constitutional Reform Process: What Future for Constitutionalism? *Journal for Contemporary History* 41 (2): 184–207.

Edozie, R. K. 2009. Electoral Authoritarianisms and Delegative Democrats: Reconstructing African Democratic Consolidation in Africa. In Reconstructing the Third Wave of Democracy: Comparative African Democratic Politics. Rita, R.K. ed. Lanham: University Press of America. 128–154.

Francis Fukuyama. (2016). Reflections on Chinese governance. *Journal of Chinese Governance* 1 (3): 379–391.

News Statesman. 2008. Dont Mention the War. February 14. Online. http://www.newstatesman.com/africa/2008/02/wrong-ethnic-kenya-politicians. Accessed August 29 2017.

BIBLIOGRAPHY

Books & Book Chapters

Barkan, J. 2006. Democracy in Africa: What Future? In *Democratic Reform in Africa Its Impact on Governance & Poverty Alleviation*, ed. M. Ndulo. Oxford: James Currey.

Bayart, J. 1993. *The State in Africa: The Politics of the Belly*. London: Longman.

Hoile, D. 2015. *Justice Denied the Reality of the International Criminal Court*. London: The Africa Research Centre.

Maloba, W. 1996. Decolonisation: A Theoretical Perspective. In *Decolonisation and Independence in Kenya*, ed. B.A. Ogot, and W.R. Ochieng. Nairobi: East African Educational publishers.

Miguna, M. 2012. *Peeling Back the Mask: A Quest for Justice in Kenya*. London: Gilgamesh Africa.

Molomo, M. 2010. Electoral Systems and Conflict in Africa. In *When Elephants Fight: Preventing and Resolving Election-Related Conflicts in Africa*, ed. K. Matlosa, G. Khadiagala, and V. Shale. EISA: Johannesburg.

Mitullah, W. 2005. Civic Elections in Nairobi. In *The Moi Succession Elections 2002*, ed. H. Maupeu, M. Katumanga, and W. Mitullah. Nairobi: TransAfrica Press.

Wrong, M. 2009. *It's Our Turn to Eat: The Story of a Kenya Whistle Blower*. London: Fourth Estate.

© The Editor(s) (if applicable) and The Author(s) 2018
W.K. Shilaho, *Political Power and Tribalism in Kenya*,
https://doi.org/10.1007/978-3-319-65295-5

Journals

Bratton, M., and C. Chango. 2006. State Building and Democratisation in Subsaharan Africa: Forwards, Backwards or Together? In *Comparative Political Studies* 39 (9): 1059. Online: http://cps.sagepub.com/content/39/9/1059.full.pdf+html. Accessed 10 Oct 2016.

Bratton, M., and N. van de Walle. 1992. Popular Protest and Political Reform in Africa. In *Comparative Politics* 24 (4): 419–442. Available Online: www.jstor.org. Retrieved 30 Oct 2016.

Cohen, J. 1995. Ethnicity, Foreign Aid and Economic Growth in Sub-Saharan: The Case of Kenya HIID Development Discussion Paper No. 520. Online: http://www.cid.harvard.edu/hiid/520.pdf. Accessed 12 Jan 2017.

Kagwanja, P. 2003. Facing Mount Kenya or Facing Mecca? The Mungiki, Ethnic Violence and the Politics of the Moi Succession in Kenya, 1987–2002. *African Affairs* 102 (406): 25–49.

Nyinguro, P., and E. Otenyo. 2007. Social Movements and Democratic Transitions in Kenya. In *Journal of Asian and African Studies* 42 (1): 5–24. Available Online: http://jas.sagepub.com/content/42/1/5. Accessed 22 Oct 2016.

Shilaho, W. 2013. Ethnic Mobilisation and Kenya's Foreign Policy in the Face of the International Criminal Court (ICC). *Journal for Contemporary History* 41 (1): 103–125.

Smith, Z.K. 2000. The Impact of Political Liberalisation and Democratisation on Ethnic Conflict in Africa: An Empirical Test of Common Assumptions. *Journal of Modern African Studies* 38 (1): 21–39.

Reports

Africa Centre for Open Governance. 2009. The Maize Scandal. Online: http://www.africog.org/reports/Maize%20Report.pdf. Accessed 11 Nov 2011.

Electoral Institute for Sustainable Democracy in Africa. 2010. Kenya: Interim Independent Boundaries Review Commission Online: http://www.eisa.org.za/WEP/keniibrc.htm. Accessed 22 Dec 2015.

International Criminal Court (ICC). 2009. Prosecutor's Application Pursuant to Chapter 58 as to Francis Karimi Mutahura, Uhuru Muigai Kenyatta and Mohammed Hussein Ali. Online: http://www.icc-cpi.int/iccdocs/doc/doc1050845.pdf. Accessed 11 Nov 2016.

International Criminal Court (ICC). 2009. Prosecutor's Application Pursuant to Chapter 58 as to William Samoei Ruto, Henry Kiprono Kosgey and Joshua arap Sang. Online: http://www.icc-cpi.int/iccdocs/doc/doc1050835.pdf. Accessed 11 Nov 2016.

Kenya Human Rights Commission (KHRC). 2016. Kenya: Termination of Ruto and Sang Case at the ICC: Witness Tampering means Impunity Prevails over justice again April 7. Online: http://www.khrc.or.ke/2015-03-04-10-37-01/press-releases/528-kenya-termination-of-ruto-and-sang-case-at-the-icc-witness-tampering-means-impunityprevkenya-termination-of-ruto-and-sang-case-at-the-icc-witness-tampering-means-impunity-prevails-over-justiceagain.html. Accessed 10 Dec 2016.

Kenya National Commission on Human Rights; Transparency International Kenya. 2006a. Living Large Counting the Cost of Official Extravagance in Kenya: Online www.knchr.org. Accessed 5 Oct 2016.

Kenya National Commission on Human Rights (KNCHR). 2006b. 'Referendum Report'. Available online: http://www.knchr.org. Accessed 28 July 2016.

Kenya National Commission on Human Rights (KNCHR). 2007. Still Behaving Badly Online: www.knchr.org. Accessed 5 Oct 2016.

National Cohesion and Integration Commission (NCIC). Online: http://www.cohesion.or.ke/index.php/about-us/goals-objectives. Accessed 25 July 2016.

Rome Statute of the International Criminal Court. https://www.icc-cpi.int/nr/rdonlyres/ea9aeff7-5752-4f84-be94-0a655eb30e16/0/rome_statute_english.pdf. Accessed 14 July 2015.

The Draft Constitution of Kenya (Bomas Draft) 2004. Available online: http://www.coekenya.go.ke/images/stories/Resources/bomas_draft.pdf. Accessed 22 Dec 2016.

The Hansard. 2008. National Assembly Official Report Thursday 20th March at 2.30 p.m. Online www.parliament.go.ke. Accessed 18 Aug 2016.

Newspapers

Daily Nation. 2002. New President Spells Out His Vision, December 31.

Daily Nation. 2002. Raila's Party to Dissolve and Merge with New Kanu February 15. Kenya National Archives & Documentation section: *Daily Nation* Newspapers-13.2.2002–7.3.2002: Microfilm No. 370.

Daily Nation. 2002. Kanu Plans Sweeping Powers for the Party Boss February 21. Kenya National Archives & Documentation Section: *Daily Nation* Newspapers-8.3. 2002–22.3.2002: Microfilm No. 371).

Daily Nation. 2002. Uhuru's Challenge as He Takes the Baton' November 18. Kenya National Archives & Documentation Section: *Daily Nation* Newspapers-8.11.2002 continuation includes 2003: Microfilm No. 282.

Daily Nation. 2009. 'Return of Kimunya Followed an Emerging Trend in Kenya' 25 January. Online http://www.nation.co.ke/oped/Letters/-/440806/519562/-/ibgqo4/-/index.html. Accessed 4 Oct 2016.

Daily Nation. 2009. 'Ruto and Kiraitu Under Fire over Scandals' January 22. Online: http://www.nation.co.ke/News/-/1056/518438/-/view/printVersion/-/8xscdn/-/index.html. Accessed 4 Oct 2016.

Daily Nation. 2009. 'Kimunya Censure Motion Stands' 26 January. Online: http://www.nation.co.ke/News/-/1056/520398/-/item/0/-/res6ov/-/index.html. Accessed 21 Sep 2016.

Daily Nation 2009. 'Ruto Survives Censure Motion', February, 18. Online http://www.nation.co.ke/News/politics/-/1064/531934/-/ygaxw3z/-/index.html. Accessed 15 Sep 2016.

Daily Nation. 2009. Shs 6 billion School Funds 'Stolen' December, 14. Online: http://www.nation.co.ke/News/-/1056/822668/-/vo33eb/-/index.html. Accessed 21 Sep 2015.

Daily Nation. 2010. 'Nilotes or Bantus? Debate Rages as Basuba Face Identity Threat' October 27. Online: http://allafrica.com/stories/201110280070.html. Accessed 15 Nov 2011.

Daily Nation. 2010. "'No' Camp Concedes Referendum Defeat' August 5. Online: http://www.nation.co.ke/Kenya%20Referendum/-/926046/971494/-/fxedndz/-/index.html. Accessed 13 Aug 2015.

Daily Nation. 2010. 'Kibaki, Raila Clash over Cabinet Purge' February 14. Online: http://www.nation.co.ke/News/politics/-/1064/862086/-/wr7mmdz/-/index.html. Accessed 21 Sep 2016.

Daily Nation. 2010. 'Ruto: I will Not Resign Over Maize Scandal' February 10. Online   http://www.nation.co.ke/News/-/1056/859784/-/vq2l5k/-/index.html. Accessed 15 Sep 2016.

Daily Nation. 2011. 'Kibunja Should Now Find Out Why Certain Tribes Dominate Specific Jobs' April 13. Online: http://www.nation.co.ke/blogs/Kibunjia+should+find+why+certain+tribes+dominate+specific+jobs+/-/446696/1143370/-/view/asBlogPost/-/hgy9tp/-/index.html. Accessed 13 Apr 2016.

Daily Nation. 2012. 'Fresh Doubts Over Election Date' July, 23. Online: http://www.nation.co.ke/News/politics/MPs+float+August+2013+date+for+polls+/-/1064/1461662/-/item/0/-/g0l66tz/-/index.html. Accessed 5 Aug 2016.

Standard on Sunday. 2009. 'Quorum Hitch Halts House Business' 10 November. Online: http://www.nation.co.ke/News/-/1056/684470/-/uon7ds/-/index.html. Accessed 21 Sep 2015.

Standard on Sunday. 2010. 'Public Waits for Answers to Scandals Whose Reports are Still Kept Secret' January 1. Online http://www.nation.co.ke/News/-/1056/509492/-/u0qm58/-/index.html. Accessed 15 Sep 2016.

Daily Nation. 2013. 'Ruto to Pay Sh 5m in Land Case' June 28. Online. http://www.nation.co.ke/News/politics/Ruto-to-pay-Sh5m-in-land-case/-/1064/1898406/-/fl0kl3/-/index.html. Accessed 10 July 2013.

Daily Nation. 2011. 'Truth Commission Complains about Cash' July 19. Online: http://www.nation.co.ke/News/Commission+complains+about+c ash+/-/1056/1204326/-/ui19xhz/-/index.html. Accessed 20 July 2016.

Daily Nation. 2008. 'Uproar over Six Permanent Secretaries Past Retirement Age' July 20. Online: http://allafrica.com/stories/200806200131.html. Accessed 15 Nov 2015.

Daily Nation. 2002. "Wedding' a Purely Kanu Affair' March 19. Kenya National Archives & Documentation Section: *Daily Nation* Newspapers-8.2.2002–22.3.2002: Microfilm No. 371.

Daily Nation. 2010. 'Why Big Two Can't Sack Minister' February 6. Online: http://www.nation.co.ke/News/politics/-/1064/857128/-/wrpoamz/-/index.html. Accessed 21 Sep 2016.

Saturday Nation. 2011. 'Bosire Has Strong Credentials But Past Kanu Ties Could Spoil For Him' April 23. Available online: http://www.nation.co.ke/News/-/1056/1149804/-/item/2/-/1kko90/-/index.html. Accessed 24 Apr 2015.

Saturday Nation. 2002. 'Road to Opposition Unity Will be Rough But Crucial' October 20. Kenya National Archives & Documentation section: *Daily Nation* Newspapers-17.10.2002–8.11.2002: Microfilm No. 381.

Saturday Nation. 2009. No Such Thing as 'Real Power Sharing' in Law May 23. Online: http://www.nation.co.ke/oped/Opinion/-/440808/602274/-/4knkld/-/index.html. Accessed 20 Aug 2015.

Sunday Nation. 2009. Letter to the Cabinet: Are You Playing the Wrong Game?' 18 July.

Sunday Nation. 2002. Uhuru Factor in Moi Succession Strategy February 24. Kenya National Archives & Documentation section: *Daily Nation* Newspapers-13.2.2002–7.3.2002: Microfilm No. 370.

The Weekly Review. 1988. A New Chapter in Kanu Affairs' October, 21.

———. 1988. 'A Strategy for Kenya's Future' October, 21.

———. 1988. Kanu v/s Parliament How Parliamentary Group Meetings Preempt Discussions,' August 12.

———. 1992. 'I Will Contest', July 3.

———. 1997. 'Wooing Kikuyus', April 11.

———. 1998. 'Fruits of Cooperation', May 1.

———. 1988. 'Time to Leave', September 23.

———. 1997. 'Wooing Kikuyus', April 11.

Presidential Speeches

Kenya Presidential Speeches 1963–1988: Kenya National Archives Central Government Library *Jamhuri Day Speeches* Day Kenya became a Republic on 12th December 1964.

Kenyatta day Speeches (Now Mashujaa-Heroes' Day*)* The Day Kenya's Freedom Fighters Were Released from Prison.

Madaraka Day Speeches (Day Kenya Attained Internal Self Rule on 1st June 1963.

INDEX

© The Editor(s) (if applicable) and The Author(s) 2018
W.K. Shilaho, *Political Power and Tribalism in Kenya*,
https://doi.org/10.1007/978-3-319-65295-5

Printed by Printforce, the Netherlands